Evgenii Trubetskoi

Ex Oriente Lux

New Perspectives on Russian
Religious Philosophers

SERIES

VOL. 4

Edited by Artur Mrówczyński-Van Allen, Teresa Obolevitch,
Randall A. Poole, and Paweł Rojek

We believe that Russian religious philosophy of the nineteenth and twentieth centuries has great importance for Christian theology and philosophy. Russian thinkers, rooted in the tradition of the Church Fathers, strove for an integral knowledge of reality, based on the unity of faith and reason. Such philosophers and theologians as Peter Chaadaev, Alexei Khomiakov, Vladimir Soloviev, Evgenii Trubetskoi, Pavel Florensky, Sergei Bulgakov, Nikolai Berdyaev, Semyon Frank, Georges Florovsky, and Aleksei Losev had penetrating insight into the nature of reality and thought deeply about religion and culture, science and philosophy, and history and society. Their legacy deserves a prominent place in contemporary philosophical and theological discussions.

The series *Ex Oriente Lux* aims to meet this need. It serves as a way to bring Eastern Christian intuitions into the current post-secular philosophical and theological context. Each volume focuses on one Russian thinker and includes a selection of essays on the thinker's main ideas in historical and contemporary contexts. The books are prepared by Western and Russian scholars, thus creating a space for intellectual dialogue.

The series comes out of research connected with the annual conferences on Russian religious philosophy held in Krakow, Poland. The "Krakow Meetings" are organized jointly by the Pontifical University of John Paul II in Krakow and the Edith Stein Institute of Philosophy in Granada, Spain.

Previous Volumes

Beyond Modernity: Russian Religious Philosophy and Post-Secularism
Peter Chaadaev: Between the Love of Fatherland and the Love of Truth
Alexei Khomiakov: The Mystery of Sobornost'

Future Volumes

*Paweł Rojek, Theological Philosophy: Theology, Ontology,
and Logic in Russian Religious Philosophy*
Vladimir Soloviev: The Metaphysics of Love
Semyon Frank: The Philosophy of Absolute Realism

Evgenii Trubetskoi

Icon and Philosophy

EDITED BY

Teresa Obolevitch

AND

Randall A. Poole

☙PICKWICK *Publications* · Eugene, Oregon

EVGENII TRUBETSKOI
Icon and Philosophy

Ex Oriente Lux Series 4

Copyright © 2021 Wipf and Stock Publishers. All rights reserved. Except for brief quotations in critical publications or reviews, no part of this book may be reproduced in any manner without prior written permission from the publisher. Write: Permissions, Wipf and Stock Publishers, 199 W. 8th Ave., Suite 3, Eugene, OR 97401.

Pickwick Publications
An Imprint of Wipf and Stock Publishers
199 W. 8th Ave., Suite 3
Eugene, OR 97401

www.wipfandstock.com

PAPERBACK ISBN: 978-1-7252-8840-9
HARDCOVER ISBN: 978-1-7252-8841-6
EBOOK ISBN: 978-1-7252-8842-3

Cataloguing-in-Publication data:

Names: Obolevitch, Teresa, 1974–,editor. | Poole, Randall Allen, 1964–, editor.

Title: Evgenii Trubetskoi : icon and philosophy / edited by Teresa Obolevitch and Randall A. Poole.

Description: Eugene, OR : Pickwick Publications, 2021 | Ex Oriente Lux Series 4 | Includes bibliographical references and index.

Identifiers: ISBN 978-1-7252-8840-9 (paperback) | ISBN 978-1-7252-8841-6 (hardcover) | ISBN 978-1-7252-8842-3 (ebook)

Subjects: LCSH: Trubetskoĭ, E. N. (Evgeniĭ Nikolaevich), kniaz′, 1863–1920. | Philosophy, Russian—Religious aspects. | Philosophical theology.

Classification: B4279.T783 E94 2021 (print) | B4279.T783 E94 (ebook)

03/26/21

Contents

Contributors | vii

Introduction—Evgenii Trubetskoi: Icon of Russian Philosophy
—Randall A. Poole | 1

Part I: Evgenii Trubetskoi and His Religious-Philosophical Worldview

1 *Evgenii Trubetskoi and Russian Liberal Theology*
  —Randall A. Poole | 25

2 *Evgenii Trubetskoi's Search for Peaceful Political Renewal*
  —Eric Lohr | 52

3 *Evgenii Trubetskoi's Idealist Grounding of the Religious Meaning of Life*—Kåre Johan Mjør | 65

4 *Vladimir Soloviev and Evgenii Trubetskoi: A Survey of an Intellectual Relationship about Theocracy, Freedom, and Divine-Humanity*
  —Jeremy Pilch | 79

5 *"I Am Experiencing a Real Image of All-Unity in You!": The Reception of Vladimir Soloviev's Philosophy of Love in the "Loving Friendship" of Margarita Morozova and Evgenii Trubetskoi*
  —Anatolii Chernyaev | 93

CONTENTS

6 *The Role of Antinomies in the Theology of Pavel Florensky and Sergei Bulgakov in Light of Evgenii Trubetskoi's Critique* —Tikhon Vasilyev | 112

Part II: Philosophy of the Icon

7 *The Theology of the Icon: Theological Development in Icon Interpretation in the Twentieth Century*—Irina Yazykova | 127

8 *The Theandric Dimension of Art in the Eastern Christian Tradition* —Teresa Obolevitch | 142

9 *Between Two Worlds: Philosophy of the Icon in Evgenii Trubetskoi and Pavel Florensky*—Ruri Hosokawa | 159

10 *Between Image and Enigma: On the Philosophical Meanings of "Art History" (Evgenii Trubetskoi and Others)*—Natalia Vaganova | 172

11 *Structural-Semiotic Analysis as a Method to Reveal the Invisible World: Fr. Pavel Florensky's "Iconostasis"*—Elena Tverdislova | 181

12 *Finding Meaning: Sergius Bulgakov and a Sophiology of the Icon* —Walter Sisto | 195

Index | 209

Contributors

Anatolii Chernyaev, Leading Research Fellow and Head, Department of the History of Russian Philosophy, Institute of Philosophy, Russian Academy of Sciences, Moscow, Russia.

Ruri Hosokawa, Doctoral student, University of Tokyo, Japan.

Eric Lohr, Professor of History and Susan E. Carmel Chair of Russian History and Culture, American University, Washington, DC, USA.

Kåre Johan Mjør, previously Research Scholar at the Institute for Russian and Eurasian Studies, Uppsala University, now Senior Research Librarian at Western Norway University of Applied Sciences and Associate Professor of Russian at the University of Bergen, Norway.

Teresa Obolevitch, Professor and Chair of Russian and Byzantine Philosophy, Pontifical University of John Paul II in Krakow, Poland.

Jeremy Pilch, Programme Director (Theology, Religion and Ethics), Institute of Theology, St Mary's University, Twickenham, London.

Randall A. Poole, Professor and Chair, Department of History and Politics, College of St. Scholastica, Duluth, Minnesota, USA.

Walter Sisto, Associate Professor of Religious Studies, D'Youville College, Buffalo, New York, USA.

Elena Tverdislova, Independent Researcher, Literature Consultant of Jerusalem Russian Library, Israel.

Natalia Vaganova, Associate Professor, St. Tikhon's Orthodox University and Tchaikovsky Moscow State Conservatory, Moscow, Russia.

Tikhon Vasilyev, Tutor in Patristics and Church History, Online educational platform "Philosophy. Culture. Christianity," Holy Dormition St. Basil Monastery in Nikolskoe, Donetsk Region, Ukraine.

Irina Yazykova, Deputy Rector, St. Andrews Biblical Theological Institute, Moscow, Russia.

INTRODUCTION

Evgenii Trubetskoi

Icon of Russian Philosophy

RANDALL A. POOLE

Evgenii Trubetskoi (1863–1920) exemplified what is best in Russia's religious-philosophical tradition. That tradition began with the Slavophiles Ivan Kireevskii (1806–1856) and Alexei Khomiakov (1804–1860). Trubetskoi embraced their understanding of religious experience, their holistic or integral conception of human nature, and their conviction in the necessity of both faith and reason in the pursuit of truth. His own religious experience inspired his seminal studies of the Russian icon—and they, in turn, inspired the icon studies which form the second part of this book. In the 1880s he was drawn to the Slavophile idealization of Russia, to the "messianic dream of the realization of the kingdom of God on earth through Russia,"[1] but he came to reject it in favor of Christian universalism, while always maintaining his deep personal faith in Orthodoxy.

Trubetskoi's commitment to certain aspects of Slavophilism (its theoretical philosophy) and rejection of others (its social philosophy) helped determine his relation to the two greatest philosophers of nineteenth-century Russia: Boris Chicherin (1828–1904) and Vladimir Soloviev (1853–1900), both metaphysical idealists and pillars of the Russian religious-philosophical tradition. Chicherin is widely regarded as the country's preeminent liberal philosopher, and Soloviev as its most important religious philosopher. Trubetskoi combined elements of their thought in his own philosophical worldview. From Chicherin he took the paramount liberal principles of human freedom and dignity, freedom of conscience,

---

1. Trubetskoi, *Vospominaniia*, 193.

and the rule of law. From Soloviev, to whom he was much closer personally and philosophically, he took the concept of *Bogochelovechestvo* (divine humanity or Godmanhood)—the free human realization of the divine principle in ourselves and in the world (deification)—and found in it the very meaning of life. He used each philosopher to balance the excesses of the other: He accepted Chicherin's view that Soloviev's social ideal of "free theocracy" was dangerously illiberal, while he thought Soloviev's Slavophile-inspired concept of "integral knowledge" offered a much richer account of the full range and depth of human experience than Chicherin's abstract Hegelian rationalism. Integral knowledge became Trubetskoi's lifelong pursuit, the unifying framework for his own powerful, multifarious experience of reality and for his philosophical work—in short, for the synthesis of faith and reason to which he aspired.[2]

From Nihilism to Integral Knowledge

Prince Evgenii Trubetskoi came from one of Russia's most illustrious aristocratic families.[3] One of his brothers, Sergei (1862–1905), was also a major philosopher, disciple of Soloviev, public figure and liberal, and Moscow University professor (serving as the university's first elected rector in the twenty-seven days before his untimely death on September 29).[4] Another brother, Grigorii (1873–1930), was an influential diplomat.[5] The Trubetskoi family was very religious, but in their youth Sergei and Evgenii suffered a loss of faith and experienced a brief "nihilistic period," as Evgenii called it in his fascinating memoirs.[6] The brothers attended gymnasium together, first in Moscow (1874–1877) and then in Kaluga (1877–1881, for their fifth through eighth years of study). As sixth-year gymnasium students (fifteen and sixteen years old, respectively) they were convinced that the natural sciences were the only way to truth (44). Evgenii records that his first doubts about his religious faith arose a year earlier under the influence of Vissarion Belinskii, and then were confirmed by his reading of Henry Thomas Buckle, Auguste Comte, John Stuart Mill, Herbert Spencer, and Charles Darwin

---

2. For an expert exposition of his philosophical and legal views, see Evlampiev, "Filosofskie." See also Osipov, *Filosofiia russkogo liberalizma*, 116–24. For a valuable collection of essays, see Polovinkin and Shchedrina, *Evgenii Nikolaevich Trubetskoi*.

3. For a succinct, valuable study of his life and thought, see Polovinkin, *Kniaz' E. N. Trubetskoi*.

4. Bohachevsky-Chomiak, *Sergei N. Trubetskoi*. Ermishin, *Kniaz' S. N. Trubetskoi*.

5. G. Trubetskoi, *Notes*.

6. Trubetskoi, *Vospominaniia*, 43. Subsequent page references to this source cited parenthetically.

(46, 56). His enthusiasm for "Anglo-French positivism" (which in Spencer took the form of a "purely mechanistic worldview") did not last long (57). In the course of their next (seventh) year of gymnasium study, the Trubetskoi brothers turned to the serious, critical study of philosophy, first through Kuno Fischer's *History of Modern Philosophy* (in Nikolai Strakhov's Russian translation), then through Kant. The immediate result was philosophical skepticism, which freed them of dogmatic thought (in the forms of reductive positivism and scientism) but also shook their confidence in the reliability of reason and even in the very category of truth (56–64).

Trubetskoi recounts that the "resolution of the crisis" took place in their last year at the Kaluga gymnasium. His reading of Arthur Schopenhauer was a turning point. He realized that the problem he faced was not only philosophical but also religious (64–65). From his study of Schopenhauer he concluded that God is the transcendent fullness of being toward which the world strives and in which it alone can find its ultimate fulfillment. The relationship between God and world—more precisely, the idea that the value of the relative depends on how we understand its relationship to the Absolute—would remain one of his central themes. Either God exists or life is not worth it, he declared (66). But skepticism had taught him that abstract thought could not demonstrate the reality of God. He was coming quickly to realize that both faith and reason were necessary to grasp truth, and more generally that inner experience (moral, religious, aesthetic), and not just external sensory experience, offered truthful testimony to the nature of reality. The truthfulness of inner experience of divine reality is the very meaning of faith, or a large part of its meaning. For the Trubetskoi brothers, the final confirmation of this took place through their reading of Dostoevsky's *The Brothers Karamazov* and Soloviev's *Critique of Abstract Principles*, both of which appeared at the time in the journal *Russkii vestnik*,[7] and also through their immersion in Alexei Khomiakov's theological works (66).

Evgenii Trubetskoi makes clear that he was powerfully affected by Khomiakov's theory of the church as the Divine-human (*Bogochelovecheskii*) community that makes possible knowledge of God. He wrote, "God can be known only through living *communion* with Him, to the extent that human nature becomes the embodiment of the Divine principle" (67). Knowledge of God (*Bogopoznanie*) was not an abstract truth but an experiential one, acquired in the loving, faithful community of the church. He said that recognizing this, the truth of Christ, brought him the joy of being healed (*istselenie*) in the literal sense of the word, because it was the restoration of inner wholeness (*tselost'*), the integration of reason and will, feeling and

---

7. 1877–1880 in the case of Soloviev's work, 1879–1880 in the case of Dostoevsky's.

conscience, and all the powers of heart and mind (67). His description of his experience was heavily informed by Ivan Kireevskii's and Khomiakov's account of the disintegrating consequences (for person and society) of abstract rationalism and by their positive concepts of spiritual wholeness, faithful or believing reason, integral personhood, and sobornost.[8]

In his memoirs, Trubetskoi emphasizes that his return to faith, far from resulting in the abandonment of philosophy, caused him to rededicate himself to it: "I came to believe in it like never before, because I felt its vocation was to be an instrument of the knowledge of God" (68). He arrived at this understanding of the task of philosophy under the strong influence of Soloviev's *Critique of Abstract Principles*, with its ideal of "integral knowledge." Trubetskoi thought this ideal should form the program of all future Christian thought, including his own (68). He remained committed to it for the rest of his life.

Moscow University, the Lopatin Circle, and Vladimir Soloviev

In 1881, the Trubetskoi brothers entered the Law Faculty at Moscow University. (Sergei soon transferred to the Historical-Philological Faculty.) Curiously they did not meet Vladimir Soloviev in their undergraduate years, though his works formed the center of their religious-philosophical preoccupations (115). They did have occasion to meet one "very significant person": Boris Chicherin, whose worldview, Evgenii said, was "diametrically opposed" to their own because of Chicherin's opposition to Slavophilism and to Soloviev's mysticism. Nonetheless, what they had in common was more important, namely, their philosophical idealism in the reigning climate of positivism. After their first meeting Chicherin said the young brothers gave him hope for the future of philosophy in Russia. In turn, Trubetskoi wrote that they had deep respect and sympathy for Chicherin until the end of his life (117).

Evgenii Trubetskoi graduated from Moscow University in 1885 as a candidate of law. Following a brief period of military service, he began his academic career at the Demidov Juridical Lycée in Iaroslavl', where he taught philosophy of law from 1886 to 1892. At the same time Sergei began graduate work in philosophy at Moscow University; he was appointed

---

8. Khomiakov's concept of sobornost refers to the qualities of an ideal community (the Church) united by love and faith, through which the community is ever more illuminated by grace, and the human becomes ever more like the divine. See Poole, "Slavophilism," 145–46.

associate professor there in 1890 and full professor in 1900. Evgenii regularly traveled from Iaroslavl' to Moscow, where he took part in the "Lopatin circle" (*Lopatinskii kruzhok*), which formed around Mikhail Nikolaevich Lopatin (1823–1900), a prominent jurist and chairman of a department of the Moscow Judicial Chamber.[9] According to Trubetskoi's warm account of the circle, "in Moscow at the time there was not a home that so brilliantly embodied the spiritual atmosphere of Moscow cultured society as the Lopatin home" (180). Mikhail Nikolaevich hosted dinners every Wednesday that were attended by Moscow's intellectual elite: jurists, Moscow University professors, litterateurs and journal editors, pedagogues, and other scholars. Evgenii thrived in this milieu.[10]

The Lopatin circle also included a group of philosophers: Mikhail Nikolaevich's son Lev Lopatin (1855–1920), Nikolai Ia. Grot (1852–99), Vladimir Soloviev, and Sergei Trubetskoi, among others. As a result of the close friendship between their fathers, Lev Lopatin and Vladimir Soloviev knew each other from early childhood.[11] Lopatin began graduate work in philosophy at Moscow University in 1882 and became a full professor there ten years later. Nikolai Grot was also (from 1886) a Moscow University philosophy professor. By 1888 these four idealist philosophers, led by Grot, took over the direction of the Moscow Psychological Society (founded in 1885) and transformed it into a broad philosophical society, in fact into the first and most important center of the growth of Russian philosophy over the last three decades of the imperial period.[12] Evgenii Trubetskoi was a frequent contributor to the society's journal, *Voprosy filosofii i psikhologii* (*Questions of Philosophy and Psychology*, 1889–1918), and also wrote a chapter for its 1902 symposium, *Problems of Idealism* (as did his brother Sergei). In addition, he served as candidate deputy chair of the society between 1906 and 1909 and gave public lectures for its financial benefit.

It was in the Lopatin circle that Trubetskoi finally met Vladimir Soloviev, in late 1886. From that time on, he later wrote, "all my intellectual life was connected with Soloviev. My whole philosophical and religious *Weltanschauung* was full of Solovievian content and expressed in formulations very close to Soloviev" (191). From the beginning he embraced

---

9. Ognev, *Lev Mikhailovich Lopatin*, 5. The Court Statutes of 1864 created new large judicial regions, "circuits" (*okrugi*). In each circuit were several courts (*okruzhnye sudy*) and one Judicial Chamber (*sudebnaia palata*), which heard appeals and served as first instance for official and state crimes. See Wortman, *Development*, 261.

10. On the Lopatin circle, in addition to Trubetskoi, *Vospominaniia*, 179–83, see Korelina, "Za piat'desiat let."

11. Luk'ianov, *O Vl. S. Solov'eve*, 105–6. Losev, *Vladimir Soloviev*, 11.

12. See Poole, "Philosophy and Politics."

Bogochelovechestvo, but objected to Soloviev's project to achieve it: "free theocracy," the unification of the Christian churches under the spiritual authority of the Pope and the imperial domination of the Russian tsar. For Trubetskoi the issue was not yet the utopianism of Soloviev's vision—he admits that at this stage "we both stood on the ground of the same utopian and essentially *Slavophile* dream of the messianic task of the Russian people and of the Russian state" (193)—but rather the element of Roman supremacy. His debates with Soloviev were a factor in his decision to study the intellectual history of theocracy in medieval Europe, resulting in two volumes on the "Religious-Social Ideal of Western Christianity." For the first volume (1892), on St. Augustine, he earned the *magister*; for the second (1897), on Pope Gregory VII, he earned the doctorate.[13]

Trubetskoi's dissertations receive detailed consideration in chapters 1 and 4 of this book (part I). They helped to convince him that freedom of conscience and separation of church and state were normative liberal principles which invalidated not only theocracy but also its mirror image, the subordination of church to state in "caesaropapism." All along Soloviev, who was a resolute champion of religious freedom in the Russian empire, had hoped that his ideal of "free theocracy" would help call attention to the condition of the Russian church, which Peter the Great had deprived of its patriarch and which the autocratic state had since controlled through the Holy Synod.

Toward the end of his life Trubetskoi could write that Soloviev's "withering and strong critique of our church-state relations, in connection with his courageous exposure of our caesaropapism, convinced me that in the Catholic ideal of independent spiritual power there is a relative truth, which should be recognized" (114–15). By then Trubetskoi had long worked on behalf of church reform in Russia, precisely to end the synodal system and restore the church's spiritual power (see below). But he always remained highly critical of any possible historical form of theocracy, recognizing that it would inevitably violate freedom of conscience and compromise the church's own spiritual autonomy. In 1909 he wrote that he fervently believed in the kingdom of God but theocracy was "only a human falsification," because "God can rule only *from within*, and not externally." External theocracy in the sense of actual divine power cannot exist on earth, he continued, "because it would be an obstacle in the work of salvation; humanity would rely upon it, which would be the end of Christian progress."[14]

---

13. Trubetskoi, *Ideal zapadnogo khristianstva v V veke*; and Trubetskoi, *Ideal zapadnogo khristianstva v XI veke*.

14. "Nasha liubov' nuzhna Rossii," 187.

Trubetskoi's university appointments were in the history and philosophy of law, first at St. Vladimir's University in Kiev (1892–1905) and then at Moscow University (1906–1918), where he in effect succeeded his brother Sergei (although he taught in the Juridical Faculty, not Sergei's Historical-Philological Faculty). His university lecture courses were published and seen as classics in the teaching of jurisprudence.[15] His most original and important philosophical works were published within a five-year period late in his life: *Mirosozertsanie Vl. S. Solovieva* (*Vl. S. Soloviev's Worldview*) (1913), *Metafizicheskie predpolozheniia poznaniia: Opyt preodoleniia Kanta i kantiantstva* (*The Metaphysical Premises of Knowledge: An Essay in Transcending Kant and Kantianism*) (1917), and *Smysl zhizni* (*The Meaning of Life*) (1918). In these works Trubetskoi developed his philosophical idealism and religious philosophy—on which see chapters 1 and 3 of this book (part I).

The Philosophy of the Absolute

Trubetskoi's defense of metaphysical idealism is basic and unassailable. He argued that human reason by its very nature involves consciousness of ideals (e.g., truth, the good, and beauty), that these ideals are a priori and cannot be explained by the empirical data of sensory experience, that as pure ideals they are infinite or absolute, and that we are capable of self-determination according to them (which capacity is the highest sense of free will). For all these reasons, he thought the absolute ideals of reason offered solid grounds for belief in the reality of the Absolute. In short, through our ideals we are conscious of the absolute, and this consciousness all but necessarily involves a conviction—or faith—in the ontological reality of the Absolute. Chicherin and Soloviev also took the general view that consciousness of the absolute was intrinsic to human reason, but Trubetskoi agreed with Soloviev that the reality of the Absolute, though certainly a reasonable conclusion, was nonetheless a matter of faith and not, as Chicherin thought, a strictly logical conclusion of thought itself (see below).

Vl. S. Soloviev's Worldview is perhaps Trubetskoi's best known work. It is a massive critical exposition of Russia's greatest religious philosopher. Because Trubetskoi largely followed Soloviev in metaphysics, epistemology, and ethics, it also provides a valuable account of his own views in these

15. These include Trubetskoi, *Istoriia filosofii prava*; Trubetskoi, *Lektsii po istorii filosofii prava*; and Trubetskoi, *Lektsii po entsiklopedii prava*. He also published several essays on law, including: Trubetskoi, "Filosofiia prava professora L. I. Petrazhitskogo"; Trubetskoi, "Novoe issledovanie o filosofii prava Kanta"; and Trubetskoi, "Uchenie B. N. Chicherina." For an authoritative edition of his works on the history and philosophy of law, see Trubetskoi, *Trudy po filosofii prava*.

areas. Trubetskoi wrote that the "basic principle" of Soloviev's philosophy (and of his own) was the absolute, understood as the All-one (*Vseedinoe*), "for the Absolute is that in which everything and everyone are one."[16] He indicates that Soloviev arrived at this metaphysical principle through analysis of human thought and will, in particular of the ideals of truth, justice, beauty, and the good. Their role in human consciousness convinced Soloviev that the absolute was, in Trubetskoi's words, a "necessary supposition of our thought and life."[17] Both philosophers believed that as bearers of ideals, persons are seekers of the absolute, and that this is the most distinctive aspect of our humanity. Human consciousness of, and aspiration toward, the absolute clearly had metaphysical implications.

Trubetskoi adopted Soloviev's approach of proceeding from analysis of human consciousness to metaphysical conclusions. Five years later, in his own analysis in *The Meaning of Life*, he showed that even at the etymological level *con*-sciousness (*so-znanie*) and *con*-science (*so-vest'*) are relational faculties by which human beings can rise above their immediate experiences, relating them to higher ideals in the search for absolute meaning and truth.[18] "The motive principle of any consciousness," he wrote, "consists in this *conscience*, inherent to man, about the absolute; precisely on account of this conscience does he need to know the *judgment of truth* about all that is experienced and about what ought to be in his own acts. Consciousness and conscience express . . . the theoretical and practical aspect of one and the same thing—*the absolute judgment of thought*."[19] It bears emphasizing that Soloviev's and Trubetskoi's philosophy of the absolute was first a philosophy of consciousness (and more broadly of human nature), then a metaphysics and a religious philosophy. This philosophical approach was integral to their central concept of *Bogochelovechestvo*, as is clear in what Trubetskoi says next, in *The Meaning of Life*, about the human capability for the absolute: "It is not only a capability of the human mind, for in conscience the mind and heart are united. It expresses the spiritual ascent of all of human nature. And it is precisely because of this ascent to the Absolute over sensation, over feeling, and over passion that man can be joined with God not by ties of instinctual attraction but by the ties of conscious *spiritual* solidarity that transfigure the soul's life."[20]

16. Trubetskoi, *Mirosozertsanie Vl. S. Solovieva*, 1:98.
17. Trubetskoi, *Mirosozertsanie Vl. S. Solovieva*, 1:98.
18. Trubetskoi, *Smysl zhizni*, 11–28.
19. Trubetskoi, *Smysl zhizni*, 173.
20. Trubetskoi, *Smysl zhizni*, 173.

For Soloviev and Trubetskoi, the absolute was both the transcendental and ontological premise of reason. Soloviev made this argument in *The Philosophical Principles of Integral Knowledge* (1877) and *A Critique of Abstract Principles* (1880), and Trubetskoi adopted and developed it in *Vl. S. Soloviev's Worldview* and in his subsequent works. In its transcendental aspect, the philosophers argued that the absolute was the condition of the epistemic credibility of logic and rational thought: by their nature, logic and rationality are held to be necessarily and universally valid (that is their defining quality) or *true*. In other words, they are held to be absolute. Truth as an ideal, as the criterion by which we make any judgment, is absolute, and from this the philosophers concluded that the absolute was the transcendental condition of rational thought and knowledge.[21] They also concluded that the absolute was the necessary ontological supposition of reason—"*the real Absolute*."[22] Trubetskoi emphasizes that this is a supposition and not a direct conclusion of reason itself, in the manner of the ontological or cosmological proof of God.[23] The Absolute is the premise or a priori condition of rational thought, of truth, and for that reason it cannot be rationally demonstrated. Its reality is more basic and must be taken on faith by the whole person.

According to Trubetskoi, the ontological reality of the Absolute followed necessarily from the transcendental method, though he recognized that this conclusion will prove to be a "stumbling block" for adherents of the prevailing anti-metaphysical currents in contemporary philosophical thought, neo-Kantianism in particular.[24] He sought to convince them in his next book, *The Metaphysical Premises of Knowledge: An Essay in Transcending Kant and Kantianism*. His qualified defense of the transcendental method exemplified his confidence in human reason. Though he recognized the limits of reason and the need to integrate it with faith, he firmly defended it against its detractors such as Pavel Florensky (see chapter 6 in this book, part I). He was utterly committed to the ideal of truth and believed that human beings could recognize it by their use of reason, orient themselves to it, and ever more closely approximate it. It was the very foundation of his philosophy of the absolute and of his further specification that the Absolute was mind—a perfectly idealist position, of course.

Unsurprisingly, Trubetskoi formulated his fuller understanding of the Absolute in *Vl. S. Soloviev's Worldview*: "To believe in our capability for knowledge is generally possible only on the assumption of the Absolute

21. Trubetskoi, *Mirosozertsanie Vl. S. Solovieva*, 1:98–100.
22. Trubetskoi, *Mirosozertsanie Vl. S. Solovieva*, 1:101–2.
23. Trubetskoi, *Mirosozertsanie Vl. S. Solovieva*, 1:99.
24. Trubetskoi, *Mirosozertsanie Vl. S. Solovieva*, 1:101.

as objective reason and as the meaning of everything," or as "the *logos* of creation."²⁵ In his next two books he developed his thesis: the very ideal of truth meant that the Absolute was mind, an all-one (*vseedinoe*), absolute consciousness. Soloviev had designated the Absolute as all-unity (*vseedinstvo*); Trubetskoi now made it more clear that all-unity was absolute consciousness. To summarize the essential elements of his argument: 1) truth is the ideal and content of our consciousness; 2) by its nature truth is universal and necessary, which means it cannot be merely the content or product of human consciousness in the limited, psychological sense; 3) therefore it must be grounded in a normative, absolute consciousness, which is itself the Absolute as infinite being or the ground of being; 4) absolute consciousness is unmediated, directly intuitive, self-identical, and "concrete," in contrast to our "abstract" consciousness which mediates everything through the forms of space and time;²⁶ 5) through truth and other ideals we relate to, and are drawn ever closer into, this absolute consciousness, which is the highest sense of the relational nature of consciousness and conscience; 6) all-unity designates both the Absolute and the process by which we come into ever closer communion with it.²⁷

Lest this seem too arid and intellectual, it should be noted that Trubetskoi followed Soloviev in recognizing that all-unity could not be exclusively theoretical but had to embrace all spheres of the human spirit, including ethics and aesthetics. Love and beauty were no less integral to it than truth. In the practical sphere of ethics, all-unity was the metaphysical correlate of the ideal of the good (as in the theoretical sphere it was the metaphysical correlate of the ideal of truth). The practical realization of all-unity depended, at least, on the triumph of human solidarity, the highest expression of which, according to Trubetskoi, was the Christian teaching of universal love. "The meaning of life is revealed in love and in it alone," he wrote.²⁸ Interestingly we find these words in one of Trubetskoi's expositions of the ethical context and justification of his legal theory. Everything, including law, relates to all-unity and its realization. In its pure metaphysical reality as the Absolute, Trubetskoi conceived all-unity as absolute consciousness (mind) and infinite love.

It is clear that Soloviev's and Trubetskoi's metaphysical idealism, their philosophy of the absolute, could take the form of a robust religious philosophy, and both philosophers gave it that form. Trubetskoi wrote

---

25. Trubetskoi, *Mirosozertsanie Vl. S. Solovieva*, 1:103–4.
26. Poole, "Neo-Idealist Reception of Kant," 341–42.
27. Trubetskoi, *Metafizicheskie*, 20–30, 306–32; Trubetskoi, *Smysl zhizni*, 11–29.
28. Trubetskoi, *Lektsii po entsiklopedii prava*, 45, 49.

that the Solovievian Absolute was "an essentially religious idea; in it we have a philosophical expression of the idea of God." What Soloviev called the "realization of all-unity" is called in religious language the "realization of the Kingdom of God."[29]

Trubetskoi's great work of religious philosophy is *The Meaning of Life*.[30] It is a profound meditation on the following question, one which was made even more poignant by the terrible suffering of the Great War and Russian Revolution: What is the value and meaning of earthly life in relation to the Absolute? Trubetskoi thought that only Christianity could offer a positive solution to the question, because only it understood the Absolute as all-unity, in which God will be all in all (1 Cor 15:28). This Christian conception preserves and sanctifies the value of the world, even as it becomes one with God. The union does not dissolve the world but transfigures it in a way that, again, preserves and sanctifies its value. Trubetskoi was emphatic about this point: "either the indivisible and unmerged combination of God and world is being accomplished and will be accomplished, or the world process in its entirety is meaningless."[31] Here he invokes Chalcedonian Christology, and he repeats the formula in the next paragraph: What is distinctive to Christianity is its doctrine of "*the indivisible and unmerged unity of the divine and human*," specifically in reference to the two natures of Christ but more generally as well.[32] The human (and through the human the world) retains its distinct identity even in combination with the divine, a clear vindication of its intrinsic worth or dignity. The terms Godman (*Bogochelovek*) and Godmanhood (*Bogochelovechestvo*) are efforts to describe this divine-human unity. Its further fulfillment involves the deification of all humanity and creation, or the divine-human realization of the kingdom of God—which Trubetskoi regarded as the telos of the world process and the source of the meaning of life.[33]

---

29. Trubetskoi, *Mirosozertsanie Vl. S. Solovieva*, 1:107.
30. See Poole, "Religion, War, and Revolution," 224–34.
31. Trubetskoi, *Smysl zhizni*, 63.
32. Trubetskoi, *Smysl zhizni*, 63–64.
33. "God *must* become all in all," he wrote. "That eternal cosmic ideal, personified by the image of Christ the Godman himself, is the ideal of the indivisible and unmerged unity of the *two natures*—God and world (in the person of man)." Trubetskoi, *Smysl zhizni*, 90.

Liberalism and Legal Theory

Trubetskoi's idealist philosophy of the absolute was also the foundation of his liberalism—on which see the first two chapters of this book. The main principles of his liberalism were human dignity (the absolute worth of the person), freedom of conscience, the rule of law, and human perfectibility. His work as a law professor focused on the history and philosophy of law. Idealism in legal theory typically leads to the defense of natural law, and Trubetskoi's defense of it was spirited. In the philosophy of law and of liberalism more generally, he was closer to Chicherin than to Soloviev, though in these areas too he had certain differences with Chicherin.[34] In a commemorative essay, he explained Chicherin's understanding of the "essence and meaning of law [*pravo*]." In the first lines he identifies Chicherin's two underlying (and tightly interconnected) premises: a passionate faith in human dignity and an exceptional respect for the freedom of the human person.[35] These were Trubetskoi's foundations as well.

The basic principles of Chicherin's philosophy of law are straightforward. According to him, the existence of society requires that the external liberty of people be mutually delimited as right (*pravo*) under coercive juridical law (*zakon*). In one of his definitions, "right is a person's external freedom, as determined by a universal law [*obshchii zakon*]."[36] In his understanding of right, Chicherin generally followed (as he acknowledged) Kant's famous definitions in *The Metaphysics of Morals* that right is the coexistence of everyone's freedom in accordance with a universal law and that it authorizes the use of coercion.[37]

Like Kant and Chicherin, Trubetskoi defined right as reciprocally delimited external freedom or negative liberty, but he thought that identifying coercion as the distinctive feature of law (as Chicherin did) was to mistake law for one of its instruments.[38] A wide range of different types of norms, rules, and motives explain why right is observed; the resort to force is a mark of the violation of right and is applied when law fails, not when it

---

34. In his book on Chicherin, Evlampiev labeled Trubetskoi one of Chicherin's "intellectual heirs" and included a chapter on him. See Evlampiev, "Religioznoe opravdanie gosudarstva."

35. Trubetskoi, "Uchenie," 353.

36. Chicherin, *Filosofiia prava*, 84, 86. See also Chicherin, *Liberty, Equality, and the Market*, 363–64.

37. Kant, *Metaphysics of Morals*, 24–25. Chicherin refers to Kant's defintions in his essay, "Kant," in Chicherin, *Istoriia politicheskikh uchenii*, 345–46, 348.

38. As an idealist Chicherin, especially in his mature legal philosophy, recognized the ideal, moral essence of law (human dignity) and he called it natural law or justice. See Poole, "Liberalism," 266–69.

succeeds. When law is upheld, it is because right is respected. In rejecting coercion as the distinctive criterion of law, Trubetskoi's concern was to avoid reducing law to state power and to counter the main thesis of legal positivism that the state is the only source of law.[39] Here is his formal definition of right: "*Right is external liberty, established and delimited by a norm. Or, what is the same, right is the totality of norms that on the one hand establish, and on the other delimit, the external liberty of persons in their mutual relations.*"[40] His definition entirely replaces the concept of right under law (*zakon*), a term he generally avoids, with right under norms. Right, as Kant originally put it in *The Metaphysics of Morals*, authorizes coercion, but for the Russian philosopher it does not, or should not, rest on it. His emphasis on norms rather than coercion enabled him to write: "The primary source of right is always and everywhere our consciousness." We must recognize the legitimacy of positive law for it to have force or validity. This, Trubetskoi says, "irrefutably demonstrates the existence of a moral norm or, what is the same, natural law, which forms the ideal basis and criterion of the whole juridical order." He specifies that the absolute value underlying natural law is, of course, human personhood. Natural law, he says, is the same as justice, and it encompasses all the moral norms that justify, or fail to justify, governmental authority and positive law.[41] His claims on behalf of natural law and justice could hardly have been stronger.

The issue of whether coercion was the distinctive feature of law was not the only difference between Trubetskoi and Chicherin. There was a more significant one, to which I have already referred. In his article, Trubetskoi offered the following statement of his own philosophical position: "Our whole life is affirmed by a dual faith: *in the Absolute*, which serves as our end, and *in ourselves*, that is, in the human being as a free actor, called to realize the Absolute in himself and in the world."[42] Chicherin's great service, according to Trubetskoi, was his recognition and philosophical defense of the metaphysical premises of law: the Absolute (God) and the human person (as a free and immortal spiritual being).[43] But Trubetskoi believed that Chicherin was mistaken in thinking that these metaphysical premises could be rationally deduced through the traditional proofs of the existence of God (or in any other way).[44] Rather they must be taken on

39. Trubetskoi, *Lektsii po entsiklopedii prava*, 3–17.
40. Trubetskoi, *Lektsii po entsiklopedii prava*, 11.
41. Trubetskoi, *Lektsii po entsiklopedii prava*, 58–59.
42. Trubetskoi, "Uchenie," 371.
43. Trubetskoi, "Uchenie," 372.
44. Trubetskoi, "Uchenie," 372–74.

faith.⁴⁵ Though Trubetskoi does not make it explicit here, his point is clear because it was his deepest conviction: Faith alone preserves the Absolute as the supreme *ideal* that makes possible our inner self-determination, which is the ground of human dignity and the condition of our progress in and toward *Bogochelovechestvo*.

Politics and Religion

Evgenii Trubetskoi, the philosopher, was also a public figure who actively worked for a constitutional Russia (see chapter 2 of this book, part I). He was a provincial zemstvo board member from Kaluga and, with his brother Sergei, belonged to the Beseda circle of zemstvo opposition, formed in 1899.⁴⁶ Subsequently he joined the Union of Zemstvo Constitutionalists (established in Moscow, November 1903) and the Union of Liberation (established in St. Petersburg, January 1904). Through these organizations he had a leading role in the Russian Liberation Movement that culminated in the Revolution of 1905. On September 26, 1904 he published an article, "War and Bureaucracy," in the liberal journal *Pravo*. It was a dramatic indictment of the government's handling of the Russo-Japanese War and an unprecedented call in a legal newspaper for the government to reform from above in order to prevent revolution from below. The article gave Trubetskoi a national reputation and launched the constitutionalist campaign in the increasingly free Russian press. According to Evgenii's sister, Olga, "it brilliantly opened an era of new direction in domestic politics."⁴⁷

Trubetskoi took part in the Union of Liberation's national banquet campaign of November–December 1904, speaking at the large banquet which met in Kiev.⁴⁸ More important was his role in the Academic Union, one of the first of the professional and intelligentsia unions to emerge from the banquet campaign. The nascent union sought the corporate organization of the Russian professoriate in the Liberation Movement, both in the common interest of constitutional reform and in the particular interest of defending higher learning during a period of rapid social transformation.⁴⁹ Its principal goal was academic freedom, which it saw as an essential

---

45. Trubetskoi, "Uchenie," 375.
46. See Emmons, "Beseda Circle," 489–90, for the Beseda membership list.
47. Trubetskaia, *Kniaz' S. N. Trubetskoi*, 87.
48. Shatsillo, *Russkii liberalizm*, 299.
49. Kassow, *Students*, 217–18.

condition of true education. The first congress of the Academic Union met in St. Petersburg on March 25, 1905.[50]

Samuel Kassow has described the union's "professorial liberalism," a well-articulated professional ethos that involved not only the professors' desire to see the Russian nation (which they distinguished from the tsarist regime) evolve along liberal, constitutional lines, but also their own self-identity as scholars in Russian society:

> Professors who supported democratic and universal suffrage in national politics argued that in the universities it was essential to preserve the rule that only merit and proven scholarly achievement should be the major determinants of power and position. According to Professor Evgenii Trubetskoi, the "university has always been and will continue to be the sanctum of a spiritual aristocracy: otherwise it will cease to exist." Far from contradicting the idea of democracy, this conception of the university was a *sine qua non* for a successful democratic society. "Only a university based on this principle," he warned, "can serve the interests of the people. . . . The nation and the people need a university that will get its job done."[51]

The Academic Union was among the most moderate of the fourteen unions that confederated into the Union of Unions on May 8, 1905. Unlike most of the unions, which would soon adopt the call for a constituent assembly, the professors did not.[52]

At the Academic Union's second congress (August 25–28, 1905), Trubetskoi proposed the establishment of private, free universities to supplement or replace (if necessary during a crisis) state institutions, to provide greater academic freedom, and to counter the gender, national, and religious discrimination in Russian higher education. The congress approved Trubetskoi's proposal.[53] The Academic Union contributed to important gains for the Russian professoriate during this period. These included the imperial edict of August 27, 1905 that granted autonomy to the universities (which enabled Sergei Trubetskoi immediately thereafter to become the first freely elected rector of Moscow University) and the February 20, 1906 reform of the State Council into an upper house with legislative powers equal to those of the State Duma. The reform provided for six deputies to be corporately elected by the Academy of Sciences and the university faculty

---

50. Kassow, *Students*, 219–23.
51. Kassow, *Students*, 243.
52. Kassow, *Students*, 223.
53. Kassow, *Students*, 228, 234–35.

councils. The Moscow University faculty duly elected Evgenii Trubetskoi to the State Council (February 1907–August 1908).[54] (He served in the State Council again in 1915–1917.)

Trubetskoi participated in the July 9–10, 1905 meeting of the Union of Zemstvo Constitutionalists that took the initiative in forming the Constitutional-Democratic Party.[55] Trubetskoi did become a member of the Kadet party (as it was popularly known), but could not attend (because of the rail strike) the party's first congress, held in Moscow on October 12–18, 1905, and was not elected to its central committee. He was elected to the First State Duma (the new parliament) on the party's ticket. His attendance at the second party congress in St. Petersburg, January 5–11, 1906, convinced him that he already had to part ways with the Kadets, and he promptly resigned. According to Terence Emmons, "This announcement, in the pages of *Russkie vedomosti*, was accompanied by a bill a charges against the party which in several respects foreshadowed the charges brought against the intelligentsia as a whole in the *Vekhi (Signposts)* articles published in 1909."[56] Among these charges was the claim that the party was insincerely monarchist.[57] Trubetskoi also thought that the Kadets were inadequately committed to organic work in the Duma, were inclined to treat it as an instrumental and transitional institution, and were preoccupied with the meaning of the term "constituent assembly," the cherished slogan of the left.[58] Trubetskoi was, no doubt, further provoked by the failure of the party congress to unequivocally condemn the revolutionaries for the December uprising in Moscow (the government was blamed instead). In the middle of November he had published an important newspaper article, "Dve diktatury" ("Two Dictatorships"), in which he counseled work in good faith with the government (for all its shortcomings) in the hope of improving and strengthening it, and warned that an armed uprising might well result in civil war.[59]

It cannot be said that Trubetskoi was very consistent in following the principles underlying his criticism of Kadet political behavior, for he declined possible opportunities to enter the government, where he himself might have been able to work from the inside, "organically," for the consolidation of Russia's new constitutional order. Trubetskoi was one of the

54. Kassow, *Students*, 295, 297.
55. Chermenskii, *Burzhuaziia*, 102.
56. Emmons, *Formation*, 73.
57. Emmons, *Formation*, 56.
58. Emmons, *Formation*, 73.
59. Ascher, *Revolution*, 296–97. The article appeared in *Russkie vedomosti*, November 16, 1905.

first two men (the other was Dmitry Shipov) whom the first Russian prime minister, Count Sergei Iu. Witte, contacted in October 1905 in the hope of including representatives of society (rather than all bureaucrats) in his cabinet. Trubetskoi was to be appointed minister of education, but the negotiations failed.[60] He justified his refusal to enter the government on the grounds that he could not make good on the promises he had publicly made as a leading Kadet.[61]

On July 8, 1906, the government dissolved the Duma. In response the Kadets and their confrères issued an appeal from Vyborg, Finland (where they had convened) to the Russian citizenry to refuse to pay taxes or provide military recruits. Trubetskoi opposed the Vyborg Manifesto, as did a group of Duma deputies (led by Count Petr Geiden and Mikhail Stakhovich from the moderate Union of October 17, the Octobrist Party) who had already taken the initiative in forming a liberal-conservative faction or caucus, Peaceful Renewal, which was legalized as a party in October 1906.[62] At about this time Trubetskoi became a member of the new party.[63] The Party of Peaceful Renewal shared with the right Kadets and left Octobrists a political program of moderate liberalism. This program was advanced in the newspaper that Trubetskoi and his younger brother Grigorii published from March 7, 1906 to August 28, 1910, *Moskovskii ezhenedel'nik (Moscow Weekly)*. Through the newspaper he wished to introduce into Russian political life the concepts of ethics, conscience, and above all human dignity.[64] (On *Moskovskii ezhenedel'nik*, see chapter 2 of this book, part I.)

As a religious philosopher and a person of deep Orthodox faith, Prince Trubetskoi participated in several Moscow religious-philosophical groups. I referred earlier to the Moscow Psychological Society. In addition, he was a member of the "Circle of Seekers of Christian Enlightenment" (*Kruzhok ishchushchikh khristianskogo prosveshcheniia*). As Nikolai Arsen'ev recalls, "It was a circle of people closely united in their Christian faith and rootedness in the life of the Orthodox Church, and of people who lived by

---

60. Startsev, *Russkaia burzhuaziia*, 10–11.

61. Chermenskii, *Burzhuaziia*, 155. Trubetskoi produced the following impression on Witte: "This is a pure man, full of philosophic views, with great knowledge, a splendid professor, as is said, a real Russian man, in the unspoiled (Union of Russian People) sense of the word, but a naive administrator and politician. A perfect Hamlet of the Russian revolution." Quoted by Startsev, *Russkaia burzhuaziia*, 14 and by Polovinkin, *Kniaz' E. N. Trubetskoi*, 36.

62. Emmons, *Formation*, 358.

63. Pipes, *Struve*, 179; Chermenskii, *Burzhuaziia*, 336.

64. Polovinkin, *Kniaz' E. N. Trubetskoi*, 37.

scholarly, theological and religious-philosophical interests."[65] Trubetskoi also took an active part in the Vladimir Soloviev Religious-Philosophical Society (*Religiozno-filosofskoe obshchestvo pamiati Vladimira Solovieva*), founded in 1905–1906. It survived until the middle of 1918.[66] Having in mind the society's exotic and sensationalist moments, Arsen'ev wrote: "It was more gratifying to hear at the meetings of the Soloviev Religious-Philosophical Society—to counterbalance the often dominant morbidly-voluptuous hysterics—the authoritative and sober, spiritually courageous presentations of Prince Evgenii Nikolaevich Trubetskoi, full of an internal sense of measure and religious authenticity."[67]

After the demise of *Moskovskii ezhenedel'nik*, Trubetskoi turned his energies to the religious-philosophical publishing house and editorial society *Put'* (The Way), founded in 1910 by Moscow financier and philanthropist Margarita Morozova.[68] She also provided financial support to the Religious-Philosophical Society and the Moscow Psychological Society, which cooperated with Put'. Trubetskoi was Morozova's closest collaborator and a major factor behind the publishing venture's success (on their relationship see chapter 5 of this book, part I). Under their direction, Put' brought out a whole series of classics in Russian and Western religious philosophy before it closed in 1919. It was one of the main venues within which Trubetskoi developed his liberal conception of Russian national identity.[69]

Trubetskoi's faith and religious experience convinced him that freedom of conscience was the "most precious of all freedoms," because it was their very condition.[70] He was devoted to the Russian Orthodox Church and had long deplored its subordination to the autocratic state through the synodal system. In 1906 he served on the pre-conciliar commission (*predsobornoe prisutstvie*) that met between March 8 and December 15, following the tsar's approval in March 1905 of plans for a national council (*sobor*) of the Russian Orthodox Church.[71] On April 29, 1917 the church declared its intent finally to convene a sobor. A Congress of Clergy and Laity met in Moscow from June 1–14 in preparation for the sobor. Trubetskoi was elected deputy chair. The congress passed resolutions against separation of church and state but for freedom of

---

65. Arsen'ev, "O Moskovskikh religiozno-filosofskikh," 30.
66. Polovinkin, *Kniaz' E. N. Trubetskoi*, 47–56. See also Sobolev, "K istorii," 102–14.
67. Arsen'ev, "O Moskovskikh religiozno-filosofskikh," 36.
68. See the major study by Gollerbakh, *K nezrimomu gradu*.
69. See Poole, "Religion," 195–240.
70. Trubetskoi, *Mirosozertsanie Vl. S. Solov'eva*, 1:177.
71. On church reform and planning for the sobor, see Zernov, *Religious Renaissance*, 63–85; Cunningham, *Vanquished Hope*; and Firsov, *Russkaia Tserkov'*.

religion. Orthodoxy was to have primacy before other religions and enjoy a privileged position as the established church.[72] When the church sobor itself opened on August 15 in Moscow, Trubetskoi was elected lay deputy chair and was instrumental, as was Sergei Bulgakov, in its reestablishment of the patriarchate, which took place on November 21 in a magnificent ceremony in the Uspenskii Cathedral in the Kremlin.[73]

Less than a month before the sobor convened, the Kadet party held its ninth congress. Trubetskoi, who had rejoined the Kadets at the party's seventh congress in March 1917, strongly supported changing the party program to designate the Orthodox Church an "institution of public-legal character." The amendments passed.[74] Trubetskoi's support for Orthodoxy as the established Russian church seems to be at odds with his long standing commitment to freedom of conscience. He may well have hoped that the Russian Orthodox Church, with its patriarch restored, would be a powerful symbol of national unity and that in conditions of growing revolutionary anarchy, it had to be elevated over the normative principle of church-state autonomy.

* * *

In these years of war and revolution, Trubetskoi wrote his three famous icon studies: *Umozrenie v kraskakh: Vopros o smysle zhizni v drevnerusskoi religioznoi zhivopisi* (*Theology in Color: The Question of the Meaning of Life in Old Russian Religious Painting*) (1916), *Dva mira v drevnerusskoi ikonopisi* (*Two Worlds in Old Russian Icon-Painting*) (1916) and *Rossiia v ee ikone* (*Russia in Its Icons*) (1918).[75] For him icons were portals into the moral, religious, and national consciousness of the Russian people. His studies of them were inspired by his own religious experience and drew on all his philosophical and spiritual wisdom. As is clear from even the title of the first essay, the icon studies were meant to go together with *The Meaning of Life*, which Trubetskoi conceived as a philosophical and

72. Gollerbakh, *K nezrimomu gradu*, 269-70; Gollerbakh, *K nezrimomu gradu*, 88-91.

73. Gollerbakh, *K nezrimomu gradu*, 276, 278. Generally on the sobor and restoration of the patriarchate, see the excellent account in Evtuhov, *Cross*, 191-206, 219-29.

74. Rosenberg, *Liberals*, 204.

75. The first was delivered at a public meeting of the Soloviev Religious-Philosophical Society in late November 1915 and published as a brochure (Moscow: Ivan D. Sytin, 1916). The second was delivered as a public lecture during the spring of 1916 and was also published as a brochure (Moscow: Put', 1916). The third appeared in *Russkaia mysl'* 39 (January-February 1918): 21-44. See Gollerbakh, *K nezrimomu gradu*, 260. All three essays are translated in Trubetskoi, *Icons*.

theological explication of the spiritual worldview conveyed by the icon. In short, he wanted his own religious philosophy to be read as iconic. The most important elements of this spiritual worldview were human dignity and, as Trubetskoi put it in his first icon study, universal love and peace and "the transfiguration of the world in the image of the Holy Trinity, that is, the inner union of all beings in God."[76] This was the very ideal, he notes, of St. Sergius of Radonezh (1314–1392), founder of the great Trinity-Sergius monastery in Sergiev Posad, north of Moscow and not far from the Trubetskoi family estate. The monastery's Trinity Cathedral (Sobor) is the site of the family's burial vault.[77] For Evgenii Trubetskoi, the Trinity Sobor must have been a resplendent symbol of his most precious ideals: sobornost, all-unity, and Bogochelovechestvo.[78]

Bibliography

Arsen'ev, Nikolai. "O Moskovskikh religiozno-filosofskikh i literaturnykh kruzhkakh i sobraniiakh nachala XX veka." *Sovremennik: Zhurnal Russkoi Kul'tury i Natsional'noi Mysli* (Toronto) 6 (1962) 30–42.
Ascher, Abraham. *The Revolution of 1905: Russia in Disarray.* Stanford, CA: Stanford University Press, 1988.
Bohachevsky-Chomiak, Martha. *Sergei N. Trubetskoi: An Intellectual Among the Intelligentsia in Prerevolutionary Russia.* Belmont, MA: Nordland, 1976.
Chermenskii, Evgenii D. *Burzhuaziia i tsarizm v pervoi russkoi revoliutsii.* Moscow: Mysl', 1970.
Chicherin, Boris N. *Filosofiia prava.* Moscow: Kushnerov, 1900.
———. *Istoriia politicheskikh uchenii.* Vol. 3. Moscow: Grachev, 1874.
———. *Liberty, Equality, and the Market: Essays by B. N. Chicherin.* Edited and translated by Gary M. Hamburg. New Haven: Yale University Press, 1998.
Cunningham, James W. *A Vanquished Hope: The Movement for Church Renewal in Russia, 1905–1906.* Crestwood, NY: St. Vladimir's Seminary Press, 1981.
Emmons, Terence. "The Beseda Circle, 1899–1905." *Slavic Review* 32.3 (1973) 461–90.
———. *The Formation of Political Parties and the First National Elections in Russia.* Cambridge, MA: Harvard University Press, 1983.
Ermishin, Oleg T. *Kniaz' S. N. Trubetskoi: Zhizn' i filosofiia.* Moscow: Sinaksis, 2011.
Evlampiev, Igor I. "Filosofskie i pravovye vozzreniia Evgeniia Trubetskogo." In *Trudy po filosofii prava*, by E. N. Trubetskoi, edited by Igor I. Evlampiev, 5–38. St. Petersburg: RKhGI, 2001.

---

76. Trubetskoi, *Icons*, 19.

77. Polovinkin, *Kniaz' E. N. Trubetskoi*, 9. Evgenii himself is buried in Novorossiisk, where he died of typhus on January 23, 1920. "Sobor" in Russian means both cathedral and council or assembly. The verb *"sobrat'/sobirat'"* means to gather or assemble.

78. Here I follow the suggestive comments in Polovinkin, *Kniaz' E. N. Trubetskoi*, 9. Sobornost was an important source of Soloviev's concepts of all-unity and Bogochelovechestvo.

———. "Religioznoe opravdanie gosudarstva v filosofii E. N. Trubetskogo." In *Politicheskaia filosofiia B. N. Chicherina*, by Igor I. Evlampiev, 176–97. St. Petersburg: Izdatel'stvo St. Peterburgskogo gosudarstvennogo universiteta, 2013.

Evtuhov, Catherine. *The Cross and the Sickle: Sergei Bulgakov and the Fate of Russian Religious Philosophy, 1890–1920.* Ithaca, NY: Cornell University Press, 1997.

Firsov, Sergei. *Russkaia Tserkov' nakanune peremen (konets 1890-kh – 1918 gg.).* Moscow: Kruglyi stol po religioznomu obrazovaniiu i diakonii, 2002.

Gollerbakh, Evgenii. *K nezrimomu gradu: Religiozno-filosofskaia gruppa "Put'" (1910–1919) v poiskakh novoi russkoi identichnosti.* St. Petersburg: Aleteiia, 2000.

Kant, Immanuel. *The Metaphysics of Morals.* Translated and edited by Mary Gregor. Cambridge University Press, 1996.

Kassow, Samuel D. *Students, Professors, and the State in Tsarist Russia.* Berkeley, CA: University of California Press, 1989.

Korelina, Nadezhda P. "Za piat'desiat let (Vospominaniia o L. M. Lopatine)." *Voprosy filosofii* 11(1993) 115–21.

Losev, Aleksei F. *Vladimir Soloviev i ego vremia.* Moscow: Progress, 1990.

Luk'ianov, Sergei M. *O Vl. S. Solov'eve v ego molodye gody. Materialy k biografii.* Vol. 1. Petrograd: Senatskaia Tipografiia, 1918.

"'Nasha liubov' nuzhna Rossii ...': Perepiska E. N. Trubetskogo i M. K. Morozovoi." Edited by A. A. Nosov. *Novyi mir* 9 (1993) 172–229.

Ognev, Alexander I. *Lev Mikhailovich Lopatin.* Petrograd: Kooperativnoe izdatel'stvo "Kolos," 1922.

Osipov, Igor D. *Filosofiia russkogo liberalizma.* St. Petersburg: Izdatel'stvo Sankt-Peterburgskogo Universiteta, 1996.

Pipes, Richard. *Struve: Liberal on the Right, 1905–1944.* Cambridge, MA: Harvard University Press, 1980.

Polovinkin, Sergei M. *Kniaz' E. N. Trubetskoi: zhiznennyi i tvorcheskii put'.* Moscow: Sinaksis, 2010.

Polovinkin, Sergei M., and Tatiana G. Shchedrina, ed. *Evgenii Nikolaevich Trubetskoi.* Moscow: ROSSPEN, 2014.

Poole, Randall A. "The Liberalism of Russian Religious Idealism." In *The Oxford Handbook of Russian Religious Thought*, edited by Caryl Emerson, et al., 255–76. Oxford: Oxford University Press, 2020.

———. "The Neo-Idealist Reception of Kant in the Moscow Psychological Society." *Journal of the History of Ideas* 60.2 (1999) 319–43.

———. "Philosophy and Politics in the Russian Liberation Movement: The Moscow Psychological Society and Its Symposium, *Problems of Idealism*." In *Problems of Idealism: Essays in Russian Social Philosophy*, edited and translated by Randall A. Poole, 1–78. New Haven, CT: Yale University Press, 2003.

———. "Religion, War, and Revolution: E. N. Trubetskoi's Liberal Construction of Russian National Identity, 1912–1920." *Kritika: Explorations in Russian and Eurasian History* 7.2 (2006) 195–240.

———. "Slavophilism and the Origins of Russian Religious Philosophy." In *The Oxford Handbook of Russian Religious Thought*, edited by Caryl Emerson, et al., 133–51. Oxford: Oxford University Press, 2020.

Rosenberg, William G. *Liberals in the Russian Revolution: The Constitutional Democratic Party, 1917–1921.* Princeton, NJ: Princeton University Press, 1974.

Shatsillo, K. F. *Russkii liberalizm nakanune revoliutsii 1905–1907 gg.* Moscow: Nauka, 1985.

Sobolev, A. V. "K istorii Religiozno-Filosofskogo Obshchestva pamiati Vladimira Solovieva." In *Istoriko-filosofskii ezhegodnik 1992*, edited by Nelli V. Motroshilova, 102–14. Moscow: Nauka, 1993.

Startsev, Vitalii I. *Russkaia burzhuaziia i samoderzhavie v 1905–1917 gg.* Leningrad: Nauka, Leningradskoe otdelenia, 1977.

Trubetskaia, Olga N. *Kniaz' S. N. Trubetskoi (Vospominaniia sestry)*. New York: Chekhov, 1953.

Trubetskoi, Evgenii N. "Filosofiia prava professora L. I. Petrazhitskogo." *Voprosy filosofii i psikhologii* 12.2, kn. 57 (1901) 23–29.

———. *Icons: Theology in Color*. Translated Gertrude Vakar. Crestwood, NY: St. Vladimir's Seminary Press, 1973.

———. *Istoriia filosofii prava, drevnei i novoi*. Kiev: Izdatel'stvo Milevskogo, 1894, 1898.

———. *Iz proshlogo. Vospominaniia. Iz putevykh zametok bezhentsa*. Edited by Sergei M. Polovinkin. Tomsk: Vodolei, 2000.

———. *Lektsii po entsiklopedii prava*. Moscow: Tovarishchestvo Tipografii A. I. Mamontova, 1916.

———. *Lektsii po istorii filosofii prava*. Moscow: Izdanie Obshchestvo Studentov-Iuristov Moskovskogo Universiteta, 1907.

———. *Metafizicheskie predpolozheniia poznaniia: Opyt preodoleniia Kanta i kantiantstva*. Moscow: Put', 1917.

———. *Mirosozertsanie Vl. S. Solovieva*. 2 vols. Moscow: Put', 1913.

———. "Novoe issledovanie o filosofii prava Kanta i Gegelia" [review of P. I. Novgorodtsev, *Kant i Gegel' v ikh ucheniiakh o prave i gosudarstve* (1901)]. *Voprosy filosofii i psikhologii* 13.1, kn. 61 (1902) 581–605.

———. *Religiozno-obshchestvennyi ideal zapadnogo khristianstva v V veke: Mirosozertsanie bl. Avgustina*. Moscow: Tipografiia E. Lissnera i Iu. Romana, 1892.

———. *Religiozno-obshchestvennyi ideal zapadnogo khristianstva v XI veke: Ideia bozheskogo tsarstva v tvoreniiakh Grigoriia VII-go i ego publitsistov—sovremennikov*. Kiev: Tipografiiia S. V. Kul'zhenko, 1897.

———. *Smysl zhizni*. Berlin: Knigoizdatel'stvo "Slovo," 1922. (First edition Moscow: Sytin, 1918.)

———. *Trudy po filosofii prava*. Edited by Igor I. Evlampiev. St. Petersburg: RKhGI, 2001.

———. "Uchenie B. N. Chicherina o sushchnosti i smysle prava." *Voprosy filosofii i psikhologii* 16.5, kn. 80 (1905) 353–81.

———. *Vospominaniia*. In *Iz proshlogo. Vospominaniia. Iz putevykh zametok bezhentsa. Umozrenie v kraskakh*. Introduction by Martha Bohachevsky-Chomiak. Newtonville, MA: Oriental Research Partners, 1976.

Trubetskoi, Grigorii N. *Notes of a Plenipotentiary: Russian Diplomacy and War in the Balkans, 1914–1917*. Translated by Elizabeth Saika-Voivod. Edited by Borislav Chernev. Introduction by Eric Lohr. DeKalb, IL: Northern Illinois University Press, 2015.

Wortman, Richard S. *The Development of a Russian Legal Consciousness*. Chicago: University of Chicago Press, 1976.

Zernov, Nicolas. *The Russian Religious Renaissance of the Twentieth Century*. New York: Harper & Row, 1963.

PART I

Evgenii Trubetskoi and His Religious-Philosophical Worldview

1

Evgenii Trubetskoi and Russian Liberal Theology

RANDALL A. POOLE

Evgenii Trubetskoi was a Russian Orthodox liberal whose worldview was consistently and at once theological and liberal. The essential liberal principle is respect for human dignity, the idea that human beings are persons or ends-in-themselves, each having an intrinsic and insuperable worth. Trubetskoi embraced and defended this principle throughout his life and work. It connected his theology and liberal political philosophy into one coherent whole, in two basic ways.

First, it made *his theology liberal*, because he thought that even God was bound to respect human dignity and that salvation could not be a matter of external divine determination alone (which would violate human dignity) but had to be a process involving human self-determination. In this he closely followed Vladimir Soloviev, who conceived salvation as deification (*theosis*) through the divine-human project of building the kingdom of God. Soloviev thought that the kingdom of God would come through what Kant called the kingdom of ends:

> In man's consciousness and in his freedom lies the inner possibility for each human being to stand in an independent relation to God, and therefore to be His direct end [*tsel'*], to be a citizen possessed of full rights in the kingdom of ends. Universal history is the realisation of this possibility for everyone. Man who takes part in it attains to actual perfection through his own experience. . . . This perfection attained by himself, this full,

conscious, and free union with the Godhead, is that which God definitely desires—the unconditional good.[1]

Soloviev's term for this process of deification through free human perfectibility was *Bogochelovechestvo* (divine humanity, also translated as Godmanhood, theanthropy, or the humanity of God). Trubetskoi regarded it as the highest possible expression of religious consciousness in general, precisely because it was premised on human dignity.[2] This, again, is what made his theology liberal.

Second, the principle of human dignity made *his liberalism theological*, because Trubetskoi believed that it entailed a theistic metaphysics. His view was not merely that the principle required a religious-philosophical worldview, but that human dignity *itself provided* a rational foundation for theism because it is a striking example of human consciousness of the absolute (as value, concept, or category). Since nothing in nature suggests the idea of the absolute, the very idea defeats naturalism and substantiates theism. (This argument, which is similar to Descartes's version of the ontological proof, was advanced by Boris Chicherin, in whose works Trubetskoi encountered it.[3]) But for Evgenii Trubetskoi (as for his brother Sergei) the theistic implications of human dignity followed from it not only as an idea (though the argument from consciousness was very important for them), but also from it as life and being—*being a person*.[4] Evgenii Trubetskoi was a man of deep Orthodox faith, but he held that theism was a reasonable, indeed a highly compelling philosophical worldview. His "theological liberalism," in both senses of the term indicated here, is perhaps the most notable feature of his work, including the

---

1. Solovyov, *Justification*, 150. I have modified the translation in accordance with the Russian text: *Opravdanie dobra: nravstvennaia filosofiia*. Kant himself explicitly affirmed that in the kingdom of ends "the human being (and with him every rational being) is an end in itself, that is, can never be used a means by anyone (not even by God) without being at the same time himself an end." See Kant, *Critique*, 245. For further development, see Poole, "Kant."

2. For his explicit statement of this, see the first extended quote in the section below, "Trubetskoi on Soloviev's Worldview."

3. In contrast to Chicherin, Tubetskoi did not think that the reality of the Absolute could be deduced by reason alone, as in the traditional proofs of the existence of God. Rather, it was a matter of both faith and reason. See Trubetskoi, "Uchenie," 373–75. For Chicherin's approach, see Poole, "Liberalism," 260.

4. Sergei Trubetskoi made this essential argument in his famous essay on immortality. He wrote, "The deeper we know the higher spiritual possibilities of man, the more intimately and deeply we love and know the human person, the more we enter into consciousness of its absolute divine value. . . . Faith in immortality depends on the depth and intensity of this consciousness. One who sees the 'image of God' in the human person does not believe in its annihilation." See S. Trubetskoi, "Vera v bessmertie," 415–16.

two major treatises that are the focus of this chapter: *St. Augustine's Worldview* (1892) and *V. S. Soloviev's Worldview* (1913).

The foundation of Trubetskoi's liberalism, in both his theology and political philosophy, was his idealist conception of human nature, which he shared with other prominent Russian philosophers such as Boris Chicherin, Vladimir Soloviev, Sergei Trubetskoi, and Pavel Novgorodtsev.[5] It was idealist in the basic meaning of the term: human beings are bearers of ideals and can act freely on them.[6] In their philosophical anthropology (or this central aspect of it), the Russian philosophers closely followed Kant, who located the inner source of human dignity in the dual capacity of reason to 1) recognize or posit ideals such as the moral law and 2) determine the will according to such ideals. Kant called this astonishing power "autonomy," "self-determination," or "practical reason."[7] Sergei Trubetskoi called it "ideal self-determination."[8] Russian neo-idealists regarded it as the quintessential human capacity. As we shall see, Kant's conception of human autonomy and dignity was central to Evgenii's liberal theology. It should be emphasized that, for both Kant and his Russian followers, autonomy did not mean anything like radical human freedom from higher ideals. To the contrary, they recognized that freedom itself (free will in its higher, positive sense) consisted precisely in "ideal self-determination." The Russian philosophers, even more emphatically than Kant, thought this capacity refuted naturalism, had metaphysical implications, and substantiated theism. Hence their "religious idealism," as it might be called.

---

5. See Poole, "Liberalism."

6. For two statements of this basic idealist position, see Trubetskoi, "Toward Characterization of the Theory of Marx and Engels"; and Trubetskoi, *Lektsii po entsiklopedii prava*, 36–52.

7. Kant's most influential account of human autonomy and dignity is the *Groundwork of the Metaphysics of Morals* (1785). His moral theory fundamentally shaped the development of Russian neo-idealism, beginning with Boris Chicherin and Vladimir Soloviev. On this development, see my essays: "Vladimir Solovëv's Philosophical Anthropology: Autonomy, Dignity, Perfectibility"; "The Defense of Human Dignity in Nineteenth-Century Russian Thought"; and "The Liberalism of Russian Religious Idealism." Trubetskoi gives a good, succinct account of Kant's moral philosophy in his essay on the German philosopher in *Lektsii po istorii filosofii prava*. See Trubetskoi, *Trudy po filosofii prava*, 237–54.

8. S. Trubetskoi, "O prirode chelovecheskogo soznaniia," 108; S. Trubetskoi, "Psikhologicheskii determinism," 121.

Five Principles of Trubetskoi's Liberalism

Trubetskoi's fundamental liberal principles followed directly from his idealist conception of human nature. First and foremost was human dignity, which was the source, in turn, of human equality and of natural or human rights. In March 1906 Trubetskoi wrote that liberal democracy had to rest on certain unshakable moral principles, "first of all the recognition of human dignity, the absolute value of the human person as such." Only this "excludes the possibility of reducing the person to the level of a means and guarantees its freedom independent of whether it represents the majority or minority in society." A human being is sacred, Trubetskoi continued, but this recognition demands a definite philosophical and religious worldview. "If man is only a temporary, fleeting combination of atoms of matter, then preaching respect for the human person, for its dignity and freedom, is sheer nonsense: it is possible to speak of respect for man only on the supposition that man is a vessel of the absolute, a bearer of the eternal, abiding meaning of life." This supposition, he adds, is expressed in the biblical idea that humanity is created in the image and likeness of God.[9] Trubetskoi thought that human dignity, "the absolute value of the human person as such," led directly to a metaphysical conception of personhood (personalism).

The second principle of Trubetskoi's liberalism was freedom of conscience, which he called "the most precious of all freedoms."[10] For him and the other Russian neo-idealists, the concept had a dual meaning. First, as inner freedom, it was a synonym for ideal self-determination, which is the core of personhood. Second, as external freedom, it named the human right to seek, express, and live according to one's ideals or beliefs. Clearly freedom of conscience as inner freedom was another way of specifying Kantian autonomy or self-determination as the ground of human dignity. Boris Chicherin regarded this as its "supreme meaning," which is why he thought freedom of conscience was also (as external freedom) "the first and most sacred right of a citizen."[11] Prince Trubetskoi followed this logic. Throughout his main philosophical works (including the studies of St. Augustine and Soloviev considered below), he argued that the ideals that make self-determination possible must, by their very nature, be freely recognized from within; otherwise there is no power of self-determination, only external determination (or coercion). He thought that such ideals were objective, but that their truth needed to be inwardly and freely recognized. Thus for

---

9. Trubetskoi, "Vseobshchee," 302–3.
10. Trubetskoi, *Mirosozertsanie Vl. S. Solovieva*, 1:177.
11. Chicherin, *Mistitsizm v nauke*, 62; Chicherin, "Contemporary Tasks," 135.

him freedom of conscience was a very powerful concept: it had both epistemological significance (it specified the condition for the recognition of truth) and metaphysical implications (since ideal self-determination or free will refuted naturalistic determinism).[12]

The third principle of Trubetskoi's liberalism was a corollary of the second. Freedom of conscience entailed respect for the relative autonomy of the various distinct spheres of human experience, inquiry, and aspiration: not only church and state, or religion and politics, but also philosophy, science, economy, and art. This principle held that the free and autonomous development of each sphere enabled the balanced and integrated development of the whole (whether self or society).[13] The spheres are legitimate in their own domain; one cannot substitute for any of the others; they are relatively autonomous parts of a whole in which each has its own place. This liberal principle deeply informed (and was informed by) Trubetskoi's understanding of church-state relations, as we will see.

Trubetskoi's fourth liberal principle was the rule of law, conceived ultimately as the guarantee and protection of human rights. Together with Pavel Novgorodtsev, he was one of the main figures in the Russian revival of natural law. He defined natural law as the higher moral norms that form "the ideal basis and criterion of the whole juridical order."[14] In his view the rule of law ultimately depended not on the threat of coercion but on a highly developed legal consciousness, one permeated with a deep respect for human dignity, a conviction in the inviolability of natural rights, and a keen sense of justice. This position was perfectly consistent with his idealism and directly countered the main thesis of legal positivism that state power is the source of law.

Trubetskoi's fifth and most general liberal principle was human progress or perfectibility, the transcendent culmination of which he imagined to be the kingdom of God.

Christian Humanism

Trubetskoi's liberal theology can be seen as a highly developed philosophical form of Christian humanism. What is distinctive to Christian humanism

---

12. In *Smysl zhizni* (1918), his profound meditation on Orthodox religious consciousness, Trubetskoi argued forcefully that recognition of the truths of faith (including those conveyed by miracles, revelation, the church, and the very person of Christ) depended on freedom of conscience. See Poole, "Religion," 230–31.

13. For an exposition of this important point, see Valliere, "Theological Liberalism."

14. Trubetskoi, *Lektsii po entsiklopedii prava*, 58–59.

is its emphasis on human capabilities—on human dignity rather than human depravity. Part of its meaning is that the human itself entails the divine, since (as I have suggested) certain core human capabilities refute naturalism and hold theistic implications. (Anti-humanistic forms of Christian thought such as fundamentalism thus deny themselves perhaps our best grounds—certainly our most immediate ones—for theistic belief.) First is reason or consciousness of higher ideals (e.g., truth, the good, beauty), which by their nature are absolute or infinite; such consciousness invalidates positivism, since the positive data of ordinary sensory experience are finite and suggest nothing of the absolute. The very concept of human dignity rests on the notion of absolute value, so it too, or rather it especially, implies the reality of the Absolute. Second is free will, the highest form of which is the capacity for "ideal self-determination." This power overrides external causal determination and again makes naturalism untenable. As Trubetskoi argued eloquently in "Freedom and Immortality," his inaugural lecture at Moscow University: A true appreciation of human dignity, consisting in the combination of reason and freedom which "always is the possibility of self-determination," leads unfailing to the conviction that man is "a vessel of the Absolute." Either freedom, universal reason, and human dignity are delusional defense mechanisms that we use to cope with the certain death that awaits everyone and eventually everything (as naturalism maintains) or, Trubetskoi says, they are real and man is immortal.[15]

On the basis of its conception of human nature, Christian humanism maintains that human beings are capable of recognizing the absolute divine ideal within themselves and of striving to become ever more worthy of it, to approximate it ever more closely, and to realize it ever more fully in themselves and in the world. In biblical language, we are graciously created in the divine "image" but are endowed with capabilities—reason, conscience, free will—that enable us to assimilate progressively to the divine "likeness" by our own efforts. This dynamic, synergetic interpretation of Genesis 1:26 was central to the development of Renaissance humanism, but its roots go back to Greek patristic theology.[16] In sum, the essential position of Christian humanism is the possibility of human progress (or perfectibility) toward the divine.

In contrast to the Christian humanist (or liberal theological) conception is the conservative view that human beings are so corrupted by sin

---

15. Trubetskoi, "Svoboda i bessmertie," 372, 377. Trubetskoi dedicated this essay to his brother Sergei, to signal their common understanding of freedom, human dignity, and immortality.

16. See Trinkaus, *In Our Image and Likeness*; Jaeger, *Early Christianity*, 100–101; and Poole, "True Meaning of Humanism."

that any capacity for ideal self-determination is radically impaired. This view largely rejects the possibility of human progress, or the possibility that human beings can contribute to or participate in their own salvation. The conservative theological position can be traced to St. Augustine, whose ideas Trubetskoi criticized from his own theological perspective, as we will see. A striking expression of Trubetskoi's Christian humanism can be found in one of his Christological-soteriological formulations: "Christ's complete sacrifice saves man not as sorcery from outside, but as spiritual influence *liberating him from inside* and transforming his nature only on the condition of the *autonomous* self-determination of his will."[17]

Vladimir Soloviev and *Bogochelovechestvo*

The greatest Russian Christian humanist was Vladimir Soloviev, whose influence on Trubetskoi was immense. The central concept of Soloviev's religious philosophy is *Bogochelovechestvo*. It was the vehicle, Paul Valliere has written, "for a principled and profound Orthodox Christian humanism."[18] Bogochelovechestvo refers to the free human realization of the divine principle in ourselves and in the world, to the realization of humanity's intrinsic divine potential—deification or, to use the patristic term, *theosis*. It is the divine-human project of building the kingdom of God and of cosmic transformation in the unity of all (*vseedinstvo*), in which God will be all in all (1 Cor 15:28). In developing the concept, one of Soloviev's main theological sources was Chalcedonian Christology, which confirms that the two natures of Christ, divine and human, are united in his person in perfect harmony, without "division or confusion"—Christ being the integral "Godman." Another patristic source was the doctrine of salvation as deification or theosis, effectively conveyed by St. Athanasius's teaching that "God became man so that man might become God."[19] For Trubetskoi, Bogochelovechestvo was the very "meaning of life," the title of his last book. His religious philosophy, especially in that work, was deeply informed by both Chalcedonian Christology and the idea of deification.

---

17. Trubetskoi, *Smysl zhizni*, 204.

18. Valliere, *Modern Russian Theology*, 12. This important study is largely devoted to the development of the concept of Bogochelovechestvo in modern Russian theology.

19. As Richard Gustafson wrote in a seminal essay, Soloviev made theosis "the cornerstone of his theology of Godmanhood." See Gustafson, "Soloviev's Doctrine of Salvation," 39. More recently see Pilch, *'Breathing the Spirit with Both Lungs'* and Coates, *Deification*.

Soloviev gave the patristic sources a modern philosophical development, specifically a Kantian one (I argue) that emphasized human agency and autonomy in the salvific process. He also shifted the emphasis from mysticism and monasticism to full, multi-faceted engagement with the world—a truly modern path to deification, but one which preserves the essential theological anthropology. In Soloviev's conception of Bogochelovechestvo, salvation comes not through divine agency alone but also through human autonomy and perfectibility according to the freely recognized inner divine ideal. It is a divine-human process. In his magnum opus, *Justification of the Good* (1897), Soloviev said that the kingdom of God cannot be expected by the immediate action of God, for "God has never acted immediately"—a striking statement of the need for free human cooperation with divine purposes. "Man is dear to God," he wrote, "not as a passive instrument of His will . . . but as a voluntary ally and coparticipant in His work in the universe."[20]

For Soloviev, Bogochelovechestvo was necessarily a social and cultural project, since human perfectibility, the ever fuller realization and development of human potential, is inconceivable apart from society and history. In his doctoral dissertation, *Critique of Abstract Principles* (1880), he called his social ideal "free theocracy"—"free" precisely because it purported to respect human autonomy, not only in the form of freedom of conscience but also as the rule of law.[21] Elsewhere I have argued that Soloviev's theocratic ideal was modeled on Kant's great vision of the kingdom of ends.[22] For both philosophers, the foundation of society was external right in the *political* community of the lawful state. The rule of law made possible progress to the higher, *ethical* community of the kingdom of ends, which Kant no less than Soloviev thought of as the church. Kant called it the ethical community of "a people of God."[23] The Russian philosopher may have wanted to suggest that the kingdom of God would not be possible until, at least, "free theocracy" was; or, in other words, that the kingdom of God will come only through the kingdom of ends. While "free theocracy" was not necessarily illiberal (or no more illiberal than the kingdom of ends), generally Soloviev's fellow Russian idealist philosophers were confounded by his combination of autonomy, dignity, and theocracy. Chicherin in particular was a harsh critic. He wrote a small book against *Critique of Abstract Principles* and a long

---

20. Solovyov, *Justification*, 150.
21. See Soloviev, *Kritika otvlechennykh nachal*, viii–ix.
22. Poole, "Kant."
23. Kant, *Religion*, 134.

essay against *Justification of the Good* (1897).[24] He thought the idea of free theocracy was a flagrant violation of freedom of conscience, at one point comparing Soloviev to Torquemada.[25]

Trubetskoi embraced Bogochelovechestvo as his own religious-philosophical framework and made it the foundation of his liberal theology. Like Soloviev, he emphasized that Bogochelovechestvo cannot be achieved without human autonomy or self-determination, and that working toward it is the supreme manifestation of human dignity. Echoing him, he wrote, "The justification of freedom consists precisely in the fact that without it *partnership* [*druzhestvo*] between God and creation would be impossible. A being deprived of freedom, i.e., the possibility of self-determination, could not be a free collaborator [*sotrudnik*] with God, a co-participant in His creative work. And this is precisely what God wants from His partner."[26] Though Trubetskoi largely followed Soloviev in matters of philosophical anthropology and metaphysics, he was sharply critical of him in social philosophy. Like Chicherin, he rejected "free theocracy" as a violation of human autonomy and freedom of conscience. However, Trubetskoi criticized Soloviev on his own terms (i.e., from the philosophical perspective of the idea of Bogochelovechestvo), which made him a more interesting critic.

Trubetskoi on St. Augustine's Worldview

Trubetskoi's first major book was his *magister* dissertation: *The Religious-Social Ideal of Western Christianity in the Fifth Century: St. Augustine's Worldview* (1892).[27] In it his liberal theology and Christian humanism are already clearly evident. Trubetskoi's study of the great father of the Western church and of the founder of medieval theocracy is a penetrating and powerful analysis, especially for its time. Though it stands on its own as a work in medieval intellectual history, in certain respects it was a response to Soloviev, both (negatively) as a critique of any attempt to forcibly realize the kingdom of God and (positively) as an affirmation of the theological anthropology of Bogochelovechestvo, which could not be more different than Augustine's conception of human nature. The book can also be read as an implicit critique of church-state relations in the Russian empire, where

24. Chicherin, *Mistitsizm v nauke*; and Chicherin, "O nachalakh etiki."
25. Chicherin, "O nachalakh etiki," 644–45.
26. Trubetskoi, *Smysl zhizni*, 104–5.
27. Trubetskoi, *Ideal zapadnogo khristianstva v V veke*. Five years later he published a second volume on the theocratic idea in Western Christianity, specifically on Pope Gregory VII and his era: *Ideal zapadnogo khristianstva v XI veke*.

autocratic subordination of church to state was the mirror-image of theocracy. In short, Trubetskoi's burden in *St. Augustine's Worldview* is to defend the liberal theological principles of human autonomy and dignity, freedom of conscience, and the relative independence of the various spheres of human life—church and state first of all.[28]

It would be difficult to find a more determined opponent of freedom of conscience than Augustine, who held that state power should be used against heretics and enemies of the church. Trubetskoi's account of Augustine is fair, sophisticated, and on the whole very critical. He believed that Augustine laid the intellectual foundations of Western theocracy in the Middle Ages and that the medieval Catholic Church cannot be understood apart from him. In the introduction to his study he compares the overall character of church-state relations in the eastern and western halves of the Roman empire, beginning with Constantine. In both the West and East the two spheres of church and state were intermingled and conflated, but in opposite ways. It is significant that Trubetskoi characterizes the two spheres as intermingled, as though they ought not to be, which was precisely his view. In Byzantium the conflation took the form of caesaropapism, state dominance over the church. In the Latin West, it took the form of theocracy proper, the supremacy of church over state. The Roman church enjoyed independent spiritual power compared to its Orthodox counterpart and indeed came to exercise secular powers, compensating for the weak state. Although the church's relative independence contributed over the long run to the dualism of church and state that many historians have seen as an important element of Western liberalism, the church's very power involved its own type of dangers to autonomy, as Trubetskoi will show at some length. At this point, in his introductory remarks, he writes, "The conflation of church and state, having taken the form of worldly despotism in the East, of the dominance of secular power over the church, in the West leads by contrast to the state gradually yielding to the church and to the church taking the form of the state."[29]

The barbarian invasions of Rome had a profound effect on Augustine's worldview, including his ideas of the church's worldly role. Trubetskoi, in reconstructing and analyzing his thought, begins at the more basic level of Augustine's conception of human nature, before proceeding to his social philosophy and teaching on the church. Already at this level the Russian

---

28. Trubetskoi's treatment of the problem of the correlation of the absolute and relative, supernatural and natural, transcendent and immanent, God and world has occupied Igor I. Evlampiev in a series of articles, including Evlampiev, "Problema."

29. Trubetskoi, *Ideal zapadnogo khristianstva v V veke*, 11. Subsequent page references cited parenthetically.

religious philosopher fundamentally differs with the Western church father. Trubetskoi emphasizes Augustine's extremely pessimistic view of human nature. St. Augustine thought that human nature, in the case both of the individual person and of humanity as a whole, was wracked by sin and could not save itself or even make progress toward salvation. According to him, freedom cannot overcome human weakness and depravity. Left to our own devices, we are doomed. Salvation is possible only externally, by the action of divine grace. Between the overwhelming force of evil and the invincible force of grace, as Trubetskoi characterizes Augustine's outlook, "man is nothing: his freedom is entirely nullified from below or from above" (24). Within this conception of human nature, it is clear that freedom of conscience could have no role.

Trubetskoi, much more sanguine about human possibilities, is highly critical of Augustine's annihilation of human freedom. He refers to it as the "great imperfection" of his teaching and as a fundamental departure from Christianity itself (205, 208). In Augustine's fatalistic theory, salvation is predestined for the elect and is a consequence of the unilateral action of grace, without active human involvement or cooperation. Trubetskoi objects that this is contrary to the "basic Christian principle" that "salvation can be the work [*delo*] of neither God alone nor man alone." Clearly writing under Soloviev's influence, he continues, "the Christian idea of Bogochelovechestvo requires, besides grace's action from above, also the *co-action* [*sodeistvie*] of human freedom in the work of salvation" (202).[30] Bogochelovechestvo, as we have seen, refers to humanity's divine origin, potential and destiny, which it is our task to (co-) realize. It is a powerful affirmation of human dignity and personhood. Both Soloviev and Trubetskoi believed Bogochelovechestvo to be the core meaning of the incarnation. "The Christian ideal," Trubetskoi writes, "requires the perfect reconciliation of human freedom with Divine grace in Christ—the organic unity and interaction of free Divinity and free humanity" (208). With this he levels perhaps his sharpest criticism of Augustine: the church father, in denying human freedom and thinking that the good is wholly a supernatural principle, not an intrinsic human potential to be freely chosen and realized, devalues the human nature of Christ and thus misses the very meaning of the incarnation (89–92, 206–8).

Augustine developed his theory of grace in opposition to Pelagius, who held that the main factor in salvation was free will, the individual

---

30. In general Orthodox theology has not drawn the sharp opposition between (human) nature and grace that has characterized much of Western Christian thought. See Valliere, "Introduction," 508, and Valliere, "Vladimir Soloviev," 554. Soloviev's view was that grace comes as human beings freely perfect themselves and is a result of that process. See Soloviev, *Istoriia*, 337–42.

effort of the human person. Trubetskoi criticizes Pelagius for his excessive individualism and naïve faith in natural human goodness and rational perfectibility, but writes with sympathy about his overall view of human nature (179–83). Pelagius, in sharp contrast to Augustine, extolled human dignity and the absolute value of the human person (173). Free will and conscience are essential to his idea of man. Paraphrasing him, Trubetskoi says "conscience, in condemning evil as something foreign to us and in recognizing good as *our own*, thus proves the goodness of our nature, a certain holiness inherent to our soul. This is the moral law, written in the hearts of people, of which the apostle Paul speaks" (174). Despite his various criticisms of Pelagius (including aspects of his Christology), Trubetskoi clearly believed (although he could not explicitly say) that Pelagius was closer to the "basic Christian principle" of Bogochelovechestvo than was Augustine's "anti-human" theology, as he often refers to it. While Bogochelovechestvo—the deification of humanity in God (*theosis*)—may not be entirely a *self*-realization of human potential, it rests on conscious human aspiration and self-determination, for an achieved perfection is higher than one by grace alone. It rests, in other words, on freedom of conscience. This is Trubetskoi's underlying criticism of Augustine.

Augustine's view of human nature is the basis for his social philosophy and understanding of the church. He held that since salvation cannot be achieved by human effort but only by grace, our main social and political task is not to strive for progress (which is impossible given human depravity) but rather to establish and maintain order while we await our predestined fate. Order is not a framework for internal development and progress, but rather one for stasis pending external salvation through grace. Augustine's ideal is a timeless universe, in which everything is one and whole, in a perpetual state of peace, rest, and equilibrium (30–31). This is a transcendent ideal, but it is also his model for social and historical reality, one that is antithetical to the very idea of progress. In our fallen state, the best that we can do is to maintain order and prevent further degeneration. Order is not only the framework for salvation through grace, it is already the working of grace, to be further fulfilled in a higher transcendent perfect order.

Together with order, Trubetskoi identifies two other main principles of Augustine's worldview: law and unity. These too are aspects of divine grace and providence. All three metaphysical principles are normative for intramundane reality. The church is their truest historical embodiment. It is to rule as a theocracy over human society, preventing further decay until the end of time.[31] The church, as the earthly embodiment of divine

---

31. Trubetskoi suggests that Augustine's idea of theocracy was inspired by Ambrose:

order, commands absolute authority. Augustine understood it as "the earthly manifestation of God's power [*Bogovlastie*] in the social order," as Trubetskoi phrases it (106).

Such a conception of the church was obviously incompatible with freedom of conscience. Against enemies of order and unity such as the Donatists and other heretics, the church was to wield the full force of the secular sword (155). More generally, in view of the depravity of corrupted human nature, Augustine maintained that most people can be brought to the good only by force; for the large majority the unity of Christ is inevitably an external, forcible one (155). "The unity of a universal divine organization was his ideal," Trubetskoi remarks, "and it was to be realized through coercion and violence" (156). The necessity of violence followed from his view that human beings do not have free will in relation to the divine. Thus for Augustine coercion, as Trubetskoi puts it, "is the universal and necessary mode of the action of grace. The whole theory is no more and no less than the result of the most complete conflation of the order of grace with the juridical, coercive order" (157).

Augustine's theocratic idea rested on a metaphysical foundation that Trubetskoi calls the "divine unity of all" (66 ff.). Certainly this suggests Soloviev's system of the same name (*vseedinstvo*), but for Soloviev the unity of all specified a cosmic transformation that was to be achieved through human freedom, self-realization, and progress; for Augustine it was an all-encompassing divine order that excluded progress. Indeed he thinks divine all-unity has already been realized. For him unity, order, and law are in themselves an absolute good. He takes their presence in the structure of the natural universe as not only the form of "what is" but also the absolute ideal, the norm of all that "ought to be" (70). This identification of order or unity with the absolute good is, for Trubetskoi, one of Augustine's fundamental errors (72). It conflates the natural and supernatural worlds. Trubetskoi describes the curious results: on the one hand Augustine proclaims that the transcendent divine principle is the antithesis of earthly reality and corrupt human nature, but on the other hand he deifies the natural order. Without a clear border between the natural and the divine, extreme asceticism, which rejects everything temporal because it is not eternal, merges with its polar opposite, the deification of the temporal as eternal. Trubetskoi remarks that this merging of two extremes—ascetic contempt for everything worldly and conflation of the spiritual with the

---

"In the person of Ambrose the Christian ideal appeared to Augustine as the total dominance of Divine order over life, as an omnipotent church ruling over individual and society, as a *theocracy* in which the worldly principle is subordinate to the spiritual" (44).

worldly—was not peculiar to Augustine but characteristic of the whole structure of medieval Western theocracy (73).

Augustine's treatment of the natural order of the universe as an ideal moral order and embodiment of divine all-unity had perverse consequences. Natural necessity, "what is," is given ethical significance and conflated with "what ought to be." In Trubetskoi's words, "everything in the world is put together excellently and purposefully, *what is coincides with what ought to be*" (74). The Russian philosopher describes this as "false supernaturalism." But it also easily turns into "false naturalism": the moral ideal is reduced to a type of natural necessity, "annihilating any moral freedom" (74). This is the most radical denial of freedom of conscience and the philosophical basis for theocracy and for other types of ideological absolutism (such as communism), as has often been pointed out since Trubetskoi's time. Interestingly he says that Augustine's reasoning anticipates Hegel's idea that "all that is real is rational," and suggests that Augustine's cosmology might be called a system of Christian panlogism (75). In it the individual person is not an end in itself but only a means for the realization of the divine objective order. Hence the "anti-human character" of Augustine's system, in which the divine law triumphs over the individual as natural necessity (78–79).

The culmination of Augustine's system is his teaching about the City of God. Although the City of God is an absolute transcendent ideal, it is also being realized in history, most completely in the church. Despite the imperfection of the historical realm, Augustine thought that, "even now the church is the kingdom of Christ and the heavenly kingdom" (234). The implications of this view are striking, as Trubetskoi makes clear: "Once the kingdom of Christ exists on earth, any other kingdom must disappear from the face of earth" (237). The state has no legitimate existence outside the church. Augustine rejects the idea of an autonomous earthly kingdom (the state) alongside but separate from the church (241). There can be no autonomous sphere whatsoever outside the church as the historical form of the City of God. In a key summary of Augustine's whole approach, Trubetskoi writes that grace and freedom oppose each other "as two mutually hostile social principles, which in their mutual antagonism determine the course of world history. Grace is embodied in the collective organization of the City of God, while freedom appears as an evil, satanic principle, giving rise to the sinful organization of the earthly kingdom" (244).

Trubetskoi's study can be appraised as a penetrating liberal critique of Augustine. At the most fundamental level, the Russian philosopher rejects Augustine's view of human nature as incompatible with human dignity, personhood, and the "basic Christian principle" of Bogochelovechestvo. Augustine's debased conception of human nature excludes freedom of conscience and thus also the very possibility of authentic human development and self-realization. At another level, Trubetskoi criticizes the church father's cosmology and philosophy of history, which depict the natural and historical worlds as reflections or embodiments of divine all-unity and order. The church is the highest historical embodiment of the City of God and thus ought to rule humanity as a theocracy.

Trubetskoi emphasizes four main consequences of Augustine's conflation of the natural and historical realms with the supernatural and divine ones, or of the relative and temporal with the absolute and eternal. First, it obliterates moral freedom, since the absolute ideal of "what ought to be" already "is" (or will be); the good is realized in the world with the force of natural necessity, without a role for human moral choice and aspiration. Theocracy (or another ideological absolutism) presents itself as the instrument of this necessary realization of the good. Second, making part of the world (such as the church) absolute denies the rest of it autonomy and independent value. Once one part is deified, the rest is rejected. This accounts for the peculiar medieval attitude of simultaneous ascetic contempt for, and deification of, the world. There was no middle ground between these two extremes. Third, without a middle ground, without recognizing the autonomy and value of the world as relative (instead of mistaking it as worthless or absolute), there is no possibility of progress. (This is also the result of collapsing "ought" into "is," since progress requires an ideal.) Fourth, bringing the absolute into the world (again, in the form of theocracy or any ideocracy) necessarily excludes freedom of conscience. And without it the only absolute on earth—the human person—cannot realize its fullest, truly divine potential.

Trubetskoi on Soloviev's Worldview

More than twenty years after his study of St. Augustine, Trubetskoi published his massive two-volume study, *Vladimir S. Soloviev's Worldview* (1913). It is the classic work on Russia's greatest religious philosopher and probably Trubetskoi's best known work. Written after the 1905 revolution and relatively late in Trubetskoi's short life, it is informed by (and further develops) the liberal theological principles that Trubetskoi had defended since the 1890s. The most encompassing of those principles was Bogochelovechestvo, which Trubetskoi identifies as the "immortal soul" and "center" of Soloviev's philosophy.[32] At the same time, he was highly critical of "free theocracy," which he thought was plainly incompatible with Bogochelovechestvo.

32. Trubetskoi, *Mirosozertsanie Vl. S. Solovieva*, 1:x, 325. Subsequent references

In *Vladimir Soloviev's Worldview*, Trubetskoi's account of Bogochelovechestvo contains the following striking passage, one highly revealing of his own approach to the problem:

> Religious consciousness includes two necessary elements—faith in God and faith in man. The basic content of any religion is faith in the meaning of life. It is clear that this faith cannot have as its object *only* God: in order for life to have meaning *for man*, he must also believe in his own absolute dignity, in himself as a possible participant in eternal Divine life. Faith in God can have absolute value for man only if God can unite with man, without suppressing or absorbing him. This is the same as what is expressed in the idea of Bogochelovechestvo. This idea, as is thus obvious, is not just one of the possible forms of religious consciousness: it is the most perfected, supreme expression of religious consciousness in general—that which all religions have sought and seek with greater or less success [332].

Bogochelovechestvo, Trubetskoi writes, "is the universal principle that unites the positive content of all religions in an organic synthesis" (333). In these pages he draws attention to some of Soloviev's most distinctive formulations of the idea of Bogochelovechestvo—for example, that our likeness to God consists in our capacity for self-determination;[33] that perfectibility or the capacity "to become" is the essentially human attribute;[34] and that it is necessary to distinguish between two absolutes, or two poles of the absolute, where the first is self-subsistent being (God), the second is in the process of becoming (man), "and the full truth can be expressed by the word 'Bogochelovechestvo'" (329–30).[35]

Following Soloviev, Trubetskoi declares that Bogochelovechestvo is the mystery of the universe, its meaning and reason. It is the ultimate end or *telos* of the cosmic process. In a remarkable section of *Vladimir Soloviev's Worldview* called "Bogochelovechestvo and Anthropocentrism," Trubetskoi argues that Bogochelovechestvo is not really anthropocentric: it would be the goal of rational, self-determining consciousness anywhere in the universe, except that "human" in "Bogochelovechestvo" would have to refer to any such consciousness, human or not. In a theistic universe, according to Trubetskoi, extraterrestrial self-conscious and moral beings

---

cited parenthetically, all to the first volume.

33. See Solovyov, *Justification*, 145, 152, 176.

34. Solovyov, *Justification*, lv. See also Soloviev, "Meaning of Love," esp. 92, and Soloviev, "Idea of a Superman."

35. The quoted phrase is Soloviev's: *Kritika otvlechennykh nachal*, 323.

are also created in the image of God and strive to realize the divine likeness in themselves and in their worlds. "If God is really *Absolute*," Trubetskoi writes, "then no planet, no heavenly body or constellation in the cosmos, can have any other goal except the incarnation of this Absolute. The entire goal and task of the evolution of these solar systems comes down to preparing a venue for the incarnation of God, to generating a being worthy of receiving God, one capable of uniting with Him without division or confusion" (341). With this last phrase Trubetskoi uses the Chalcedonian formula to describe the emergence of Christ, or Christs, among non-human but self-determining species elsewhere in the universe. This was a startling line of theological inquiry for Russia in 1913. Trubetskoi practiced a type of philosophical theology that, like Soloviev's own approach, was universalistic and opposed to revelation in any arbitrary, brute sense, which is always inimical to freedom of conscience.

It is clear that Trubetskoi made Bogochelovechestvo the central concept of his own religious philosophy, and that in this he was deeply indebted to his friend and mentor. We know that Soloviev thought that the path to Bogochelovechestvo was "free theocracy." Trubetskoi could hardly have been more critical of this element of Soloviev's system. Even in 1913, more than a decade after Soloviev's death and despite Trubetskoi's view that the great philosopher had abandoned his theocratic project in the last several years of his life, Trubetskoi felt obliged to devote many pages of *Vladimir Soloviev's Worldview* to criticizing the idea. Indeed the book's overall framework is the critique of what Trubetskoi takes to be Soloviev's utopianism, in its theocratic and other aspects.

Part three of the first volume covers what Trubetskoi calls Soloviev's "utopian period" (1882–1894). Here Trubetskoi analyzes "free theocracy" at length, but he also discusses it in an earlier chapter, on Soloviev's objective ethics in *Critique of Abstract Principles*. In the earlier chapter, Trubetskoi reconstructs the philosopher's argument that absolute human value entails the metaphysics of the unity of all, that love is ultimately the expression of and longing for such unity, that this conception of absolute morality implies a higher divine order and the divine principle in man, and that all this is the anthropological basis for Soloviev's mystical social ideal of free theocracy. Trubetskoi appreciates, of course, that the very meaning of this ideal is the free, autonomous, human realization of the divine principle. In his close paraphrase,

> The rational [or human] principle serves as the necessary *formal* means for the realization of the divine idea: this means that the divine idea, forming the eternal essence of man, must at the

same time be freely appropriated by him and rationally realized in external phenomena. It cannot be for him an external necessity; man must, by his own activity, own this idea and *become conscious* of it. The divine principle is not confined to the dark sphere of immediate feeling and naïve, half-conscious faith: that would be contrary to human dignity. The mystical principle must be brought into the form of reason and become an object of free *assimilation* [182].

Trubetskoi remarks that in these reflections on the "true religious principle in normal society" (a section of *Critique of Abstract Principles*), Soloviev's deepest religious experiences are expressed and "perfection of form is in full accordance with depth of content" (183). Nonetheless he is convinced that "free theocracy" can only be a transcendent ideal—Bogochelovechestvo or the kingdom of God—not an earthly order, since once the state is included in theocracy (which is theocracy's typical meaning) then it is no longer free but coercive (178). It is obvious to Trubetskoi that the state cannot be a constituent part of the kingdom of God. His fundamental criticism, which he develops throughout his book, is that "free theocracy" is an immanentization or utopianization of the transcendent ideal of Bogochelovechestvo or the kingdom of God. Since the term "free theocracy" can properly describe only Bogochelovechestvo, there is no good reason to use it (as Trubetskoi might have put the point). But Soloviev did use it—thus confusing the essential differences between transcendent and intramundane possibilities and obscuring the very nature of Bogochelovechestvo, namely, that it can only be freely achieved.

Trubetskoi appreciates that Soloviev wanted to contrast his ideal of "free theocracy" to "abstract clericalism" or false theocracy. Both philosophers emphasized the stark defects of these historical forms: violation of freedom of conscience, displacement of reason by church authority, suppression of civil society and the autonomy of its constituent spheres. But Trubetskoi thinks that any theocracy will reproduce, to greater or lesser extent, these defects. His abiding concern is autonomy not only as self-determination or freedom of conscience, but also as the relative independence of the various spheres of human life. Notwithstanding Soloviev's assurances in *Critique of Abstract Principles* about the "inner relation of social spheres in free theocracy," Trubetskoi does not see how the autonomy of these spheres can be preserved. Soloviev's social ideal is not Cavour's "free church in a free state," but rather, Trubetskoi says, a great theocratic synthesis that "must encompass all spheres of human life—church, state, and economy" (176). In Soloviev's own words, "The

Church as the Kingdom of God must embrace absolutely everything." To Trubetskoi, this sounds like a dire threat to autonomy.

In his preliminary consideration of free theocracy, Trubetskoi points to "one striking utopian trait of this project of the earthly transformation of humanity": it rests on the free subordination of state and economy to the church, which subordination, as Soloviev himself recognized, "presupposes that all members of the given society belong equally to both church and state." This condition cannot, however, be freely met, and therefore, Trubetskoi declares, it violates "the most precious of all freedoms—freedom of conscience" (177). Moreover, the fact that this condition is the premise of free theocracy and yet cannot be freely met reveals the utopian character of the whole project. More generally, "the utopia is expressed in the attempt to fit the Kingdom of God within the framework of the church-state organization, in the dream of making the state into a church, of achieving in it the likemindedness that is possible only in a society of believers." In short, "the utopia consists... in the attempt to bring the state with its external coercive mechanism into the Kingdom of God." But if Soloviev's great synthesis cannot be realized within the bounds of state and economic life, Trubetskoi remarks, this does not mean that it is false; we must rather seek its realization in a higher, transcendent sphere of being (178).

Soloviev believed that free theocracy was to be prepared by the reunification of the Christian churches. Trubetskoi was also very critical of this aspect of Soloviev's project. His criticisms are interesting and are part of his fuller discussion of theocracy, to which he turns in part three of his book. Trubetskoi's objection is that reunification of the churches, especially under Rome's direction, would come at the expense of their individual distinctiveness and particularities, spiritual differences that he believes are valuable and ought to be preserved.[36] For this reason, he contends that the division of the churches serves universal Christian purposes better than would one universal church, which, contrary to Soloviev's ecumenical vision, would likely be subject to Romanization. He criticizes Soloviev for equating the Catholic Church with his ideal universal one.

Trubetskoi is specifically concerned that Soloviev's project diminishes the mystical distinctiveness of Orthodoxy. In his 1883 essay "The Great Schism and Christian Politics," Soloviev suggested that the Orthodox Church takes a passive, merely contemplative approach to the divine principle, while the Catholic Church strives to actively realize it in building the kingdom

---

36. This was also Boris Chicherin's point of view. See Chicherin, *Filosofiia prava*, 111.

of God on earth.[37] Trubetskoi regards this as a crude misrepresentation of Orthodoxy. According to him, "The Eastern church, despite Soloviev, not only does not reject the *effectualness* of the divine principle in man, but, to the contrary, this effectualness—the materialization of the divine and the *deification* of man in consequence of the incarnation of God—is for it the center of all religious life" (482). The difference between the two churches is in their respective approaches to the effectualness of the divine principle: Orthodoxy understands it mystically while Catholicism understands it practically, externally, and institutionally. For Catholicism the divine is a matter of power, as Trubetskoi puts it bluntly. For Orthodoxy it is "the metaphysical source of an inner spiritual-physiological process taking place in man" (483). In another version of the contrast, for the West the church is spiritual power over this world, while for the East it is the mysterious house of God, the place where the divine-human mystery happens (483). In the church Orthodoxy sees a kingdom not of this world (486).

Trubetskoi appreciates that Orthodox mysticism does not exhaust the fullness of the Christian ideal, and that an exclusive mysticism can lead to indifference and enslavement to the world. This is just what happened, he observes, in the case of Byzantine caesaropapism, "which distorts the religious idea of the Christian East" (487). The West, by contrast, preserved the independence of spiritual power from the state's yoke, and this, Trubetskoi remarks, is without doubt the "relative truth of Roman Catholicism." Indeed in this "Roman Catholicism contains an element that is valuable and necessary for universal Christianity" (488). However, Trubetskoi thinks that the exclusive assertion of this practical element, what Soloviev criticized as papism, is more dangerous than the exclusive mysticism of the Orthodox East, because it mistakes the relative for the absolute. "Precisely because the Roman Catholic Church affirms its center *in the world*, and the Orthodox Church—*outside the world*, the world poses a much greater danger for the first," Trubetskoi writes (490). This man of deep Orthodox faith sides with his church, judging that its mysticism is a truer path to the realization of the divine principle in man than the practical Christianity of Rome. But he fully acknowledges that both paths are needed, "and from this point of view," he says, "the separation of the churches has had its good side."

There is a broader point in these reflections. In this world, Trubetskoi writes, the Christian ideal can only be grasped in pieces and only partially realized.

> The *fullness* of the universal truth does not fit within the bounds of mundane, *limited* existence. Coming into our dim earthly

---

37. See Solovyov, "Great Dispute."

> sphere, the single beam of divine light is inevitably refracted: separate parts of humanity see it differently. And, so long as people remain in their state of sin, imperfection and finitude, any attempt to collect these multicolored rays into one undivided and perfectly white beam of divine light will inevitably fail.

Soloviev's project of church unification is such an attempt, in Trubetskoi's estimation. It shares the fate of his overall vision of the unity of all and absolute synthesis: for Trubetskoi these are transcendent ideals, and attempting to make them immanent realities "inevitably leads to the replacement of the unity of all with something partial, limited, earthly" (492). Here Trubetskoi applies the logic of Soloviev's *Critique of Abstract Principles* to the philosopher himself, or the philosopher as Trubetskoi understands him.

Trubetskoi's view that Orthodox religious consciousness emphasizes the mystical and transcendent informs his final assessment of "free theocracy." This approach is perfectly consistent with his adoption throughout of Bogochelovechestvo as the critical perspective from which he analyzes "free theocracy," since human autonomy, self-determination, and freedom of conscience ultimately depend on ideals that are, by their nature as ideals, transcendent. The immanentization of these ideals in "free theocracy" and other forms of utopianism closes off the possibility of self-determination and so also of human progress toward Bogochelovechestvo. This is Trubetskoi's basic criticism: "free theocracy" defeats Bogochelovechestvo. Much to his consternation, Soloviev uses the term "free theocracy" to mean both Bogochelovechestvo or the kingdom of God—"the free unification of God and man"—and a temporal church-state order (565). If it means the kingdom of God, then it cannot include the state, which is coercive and thus incompatible with the freedom that is the condition of Bogochelovechestvo. Yet Soloviev does include the state as a constituent part of the church in "free theocracy" (536, 565–66). The result is the first of two main contradictions that Trubetskoi identifies: once the state enters into its composition, "free theocracy ceases to be a *free* union between God and man and becomes instead a coercive order" (567). The second contradiction is, of course, that "free theocracy" violates freedom of conscience (569). These contradictions lead Trubetskoi to declare, "'Free theocracy' is just as absurd as 'round square' or 'wood iron.'" In short, "free theocracy" is not free and therefore can describe neither Bogochelovechestvo nor the path to it (576).

The transcendence or other-worldliness of the kingdom of God is a principle of paramount importance for Trubetskoi. "The worst enemy of Christian religious thought," he writes,

> is immanentism, the essence of which consists in the affirmation of the earthly present as ultimate and absolute. In its pure aspect it is expressed in the complete and total denial of the transcendent. For religious thought this open paganism is of comparatively little danger. . . . Much more dangerous for Christian philosophy in general and for Soloviev's philosophy in particular are those mixed, compromised forms of immanentism . . . where the transcendent and Divine are imperceptibly . . . overshadowed by one or another earthly value [88].

"Free theocracy" is the perfect example of such "mixed forms of immanentism" in Soloviev's thought. It typifies how "he settles the problem of the realization of the Kingdom of God on earth by, in essence, constantly neglecting the border between the two worlds" (573). The "earth" on which the kingdom of God is realized is a new and utterly transformed one, where the state, obviously, has been left behind. This new earth is thus not theocratic but anarchic (576). Until its advent, "the state presupposes just that condition of humanity when social life has not yet become the embodiment of the Divine, and when accordingly there has not been an *internal* victory of good over evil . . . as must happen with the organic unification of God and man. . . . This is the whole meaning of the coercive organization of the state, and it is also why the state cannot be transformed into the Kingdom of God or enter as a link into its composition" (578).

Trubetskoi argues that Soloviev's failure to firmly distinguish between the transcendent and immanent realms accounts for his conflation of church and state, the same type of conflation that characterized medieval theocracy (578). The essential principle that Trubetskoi defends here is respect for the relative autonomy of the secular and spiritual spheres, each of which is legitimate in its own domain, has its own tasks, and cannot take the place of the other. The fact that the state belongs to this world and not the next one does not justify a negative attitude toward it. The state has essential positive tasks in its own domain. As Trubetskoi writes, "rejecting Soloviev's theocratic understanding of the state, we are not at all obliged to fall into the opposite extreme of earthly anarchism" (583).

Soloviev himself understood perfectly well the positive tasks of the state, and more generally of law, and he gave them powerful formulation in a number of places, though Trubetskoi's view is that he also completely obscured them in "free theocracy." For Soloviev the virtue of state and law is that they make possible the realization of all higher potentials of human nature, for they are the very conditions of civilized life and peaceful society. By equalizing human relations, law enables people to develop as persons. It is thus an essential spiritualizing force. In *Justification of the Good*, Soloviev says that society is necessary for people to "freely perfect themselves." But society cannot exist if anyone who wishes can rob, maim, and murder. Law forcibly prevents this and so, according to Soloviev, "is a necessary condition of moral perfection."[38] Or, as Trubetskoi writes, "Anyone who wants human life at some point, though beyond earth's limits, to become heaven, must bless the force that, albeit externally, meanwhile prevents the world from becoming hell" (583). The last phrase is Soloviev's, also from *Justification of the Good*, the very concept of which is progress, or the valuation of the relative as the necessary means to the absolute. Trubetskoi does not refer to *Justification of the Good* in this context, but he does capture its meaning with a famous biblical metaphor: "The path to the Kingdom of God once appeared in a dream to Jacob: it is a ladder whose top is in heaven and whose base is on earth" (582).

Justification of the Good was written during that last several years of Soloviev's life, during what Trubetskoi calls his "positive" period—positive because, in Trubetskoi's view, it was marked by the collapse of Soloviev's theocratic utopianism. He devotes the second volume of his study to this period and to close analysis of *Justification of the Good*. Trubetskoi's belief that Soloviev had abandoned "free theocracy" in his final period makes it all the more remarkable, as noted above, that he devoted so much of his study to critiquing the project. Clearly he thought that freedom of conscience, the autonomy of church and state, and the transcendence of the kingdom of God were principles that still needed to be defended—against the autocracy, which had not fulfilled the promise of freedom of conscience that it had made in the October Manifesto of 1905; against what Trubetskoi disparaged as the Russian "state church," which paid for its privileged status with lost spiritual independence; and against the radical intelligentsia, which sought the forcible realization of its own versions of the kingdom of God on earth.

Trubetskoi's interpretation of Soloviev is on balance a liberal one, both in its embrace of Bogochelovechestvo as the inner, autonomous, human realization of the divine principle and in its criticism of free theocracy. It is likely that Trubetskoi's sharp criticism of free theocracy as a utopianization of the transcendent ideal of Bogochelovechestvo was partly a reaction to contemporary utopian appropriations of Soloviev, though no doubt Trubetskoi thought that free theocracy was itself utopian and that it invited the appropriations it received. He seems to have missed the extent to which Soloviev's social ideal was modeled after Kant's kingdom of ends. It is ironic, given the utopianism of his times, that Trubetskoi thought (writing in 1913)

---

38. Solovyov, *Justification*, 320, 322, translation slightly modified and without italics in original. See also Soloviev, "Law and Morality," 148–50.

that the new century was marked by a collapse of the utopianism typical of nineteenth-century Russian intellectual life. He believed that the new, sober sense of reality permitted sound assessment of Soloviev's legacy. "Namely in our critical epoch," he writes, "when the catastrophes descending upon us have brought the crushing blow to romantic utopianism in all its aspects and forms, the time has come to understand Soloviev's thought and to give it objective evaluation" (viii). In this Trubetskoi may have hoped to make utopianism a thing of the past by asserting that it already was one. He presented Soloviev as a microcosm of his historical epoch (as Trubetskoi imagined it), arguing that the great philosopher, in the last decade of his life, had triumphed over his former utopianism, repudiating his belief in the kingdom of God on earth.[39] He explained this change by emphasizing Soloviev's new awareness of the power of evil, dramatized in his last work, *Three Conversations on War, Progress and the End of World History, with a Brief Tale of the Anti-Christ*. This particular emphasis (the displacement of Soloviev's humanist optimism by eschatological premonitions) was itself a characteristic reading of the times.[40]

Conclusion

Within five years of Trubetskoi's book on Soloviev, the tsarist regime had collapsed and the Bolsheviks had come to power. Trubetskoi believed that the Russian Revolution had, ironically, brought the Russian Orthodox Church benefit. As he put it in one of his 1919 essays: "In the days of secular prosperity under tsarism, the Church found itself in a condition of deep humiliation and decline. By contrast, the catastrophe of the secular order has been for it a source of creative work and ascent."[41] The process of church renewal began with the national council (*sobor*) that opened in August 1917. Trubetskoi believed that the restoration of the patriarchate

---

39. Trubetskoi, *Mirosozertsanie Vl. S. Solovieva*, 1:89–91; 2:17–24.

40. By contrast, recent scholarship has tended to emphasize the overall continuity in Soloviev's thought. At the end of his life Soloviev might well have acquired a heightened sense of evil threatening the world, though his response was not passive resignation, but a redoubled commitment to struggling against it (contrary to the Tolstoyan doctrine of non-resistance). This suggests that he continued to believe that historical progress was the necessary preparation for the kingdom of God. As Judith Deutsch Kornblatt put it in her path-breaking article on *Three Conversations*, "salvation comes, even in this most apocalyptic of works, only because of, and by means of, human participation." See Kornblatt, "Soloviev," 70.

41. Trubetskoi, *Velikaia revoliutsiia*, 24. He made this same argument in *Smysl zhizni*, 261–64.

marked a decisive break with two centuries of the church's spiritual slavery, a condition that he diagnosed as one of the underlying causes of the Russian Revolution. One of his last articles was published abroad in English under the title, "The Bolshevist Utopia and the Religious Movement in Russia."[42] In it he pinned his hopes for Russia's national recovery on the popular religious movement that he thought was developing across the country in the wake of the church sobor.

In the last several years of his life Trubetskoi witnessed human beings at their worst, amidst total war, the militarization of life, revolutionary anarchy, and the collapse of the rule of law. He referred to the human capacity for evil as *zverchelovechestvo* (beastmanhood) and had no doubt about the abundance of its historical manifestations.[43] Yet to the end Trubetskoi's theological liberalism sustained his faith in the ultimate triumph of the good and in Bogochelovechestvo as the meaning of life.

Bibliography

Chicherin, Boris N. "Contemporary Tasks of Russian Life." In *Liberty, Equality, and the Market: Essays by B. N. Chicherin*, edited and translated by Gary M. Hamburg, 110–40. New Haven, CT: Yale University Press, 1998.

———. *Filosofiia prava*. Moscow: Kushnerev, 1900.

———. *Mistitsizm v nauke*. Moscow: Tipografiia Martynova, 1880.

———. "O nachalakh etiki." *Voprosy filosofii i psikhologii* 8.4, kn. 39 (1897) 586–701.

Coates, Ruth. *Deification in Russian Religious Thought: Between the Revolutions, 1905–1917*. Oxford: Oxford University Press, 2019.

Evlampiev, Igor I. "Problema soedineniia zemnogo i bozhestvennogo v filosofskom tvorchestve E. N. Trubetskogo." In *Evgenii Nikolaevich Trubetskoi*, edited by Sergei M. Polovinkin and Tat'iana G. Shchedrina, 10–57. Moscow: ROSSPEN, 2014.

Gustafson, Richard. "Soloviev's Doctrine of Salvation." In *Russian Religious Thought*, edited by Judith Deutsch Kornblatt and Richard F. Gustafson, 31–48. Madison, WI: University of Wisconsin Press, 1996.

Jaeger, Werner. *Early Christianity and Greek Paideia*. Cambridge: Harvard University Press, 1961.

Kant, Immanuel. *Critique of Practical Reason*. In Kant, *Practical Philosophy*, translated and edited by Mary J. Gregor, 133–272. Introduction by Allen Wood. Cambridge: Cambridge University Press, 1996.

———. *Religion within the Boundaries of Mere Religion*. In Kant, *Religion and Rational Theology*, translated and edited by Allen W. Wood and George di Giovanni, 39–216. Cambridge: Cambridge University Press, 1996.

Kornblatt, Judith Deutsch. "Soloviev on Salvation: The Story of the 'Short Story of the Antichrist.'" In *Russian Religious Thought*, edited by Judith Deutsch Kornblatt and Richard F. Gustafson, 68–87. Madison, WI: University of Wisconsin Press, 1996.

---

42. See Trubetskoi, "Bolshevist Utopia."

43. Poole, "Religion," 233–37.

Pilch, Jeremy. *'Breathing the Spirit with Both Lungs': Deification in the Work of Vladimir Solov'ev*. Leuven: Peeters, 2018.

Poole, Randall A. "The Defense of Human Dignity in Nineteenth-Century Russian Thought." In *Iosif Volotskii and Eastern Christianity: Essays across Seventeen Centuries*, edited by David Goldfrank, et al., 271–305. Washington, DC: New Academia, 2017.

———. "Kant and the Kingdom of Ends in Russian Religious Thought (Vladimir Solov'ev)." In *Thinking Orthodox in Modern Russia: Culture, History, Context*, edited by Patrick Lally Michelson and Judith Deutsch Kornblatt, 215–34. Madison, WI: University of Wisconsin Press, 2014.

———. "The Liberalism of Russian Religious Idealism." In *The Oxford Handbook of Russian Religious Thought*, edited by Caryl Emerson, et al., 255–76. Oxford: Oxford University Press, 2020.

———. "Religion, War, and Revolution: E. N. Trubetskoi's Liberal Construction of Russian National Identity, 1912–1920." *Kritika: Explorations in Russian and Eurasian History* 7.2 (2006) 195–240.

———. "The True Meaning of Humanism: Religion and Human Values." *Filosofskii zhurnal (The Philosophical Journal)* (Institute of Philosophy, Russian Academy of Sciences, Moscow) 12.1 (2019) 17–33.

———. "Vladimir Solov'ev's Philosophical Anthropology: Autonomy, Dignity, Perfectibility." In *A History of Russian Philosophy, 1830–1930: Faith, Reason, and the Defense of Human Dignity*, edited by G. M. Hamburg and Randall A. Poole, 131–49. Cambridge: Cambridge University Press, 2010.

Soloviev, Vladimir. "The Idea of a Superman." In *Politics, Law, and Morality: Essays by V. S. Soloviev*, edited and translated by Vladimir Wozniuk, 255–63. New Haven: Yale University Press, 2000.

———. *Istoriia i budushchnost' teokratii*. In *Sobranie sochinenii Vladimira Sergeevicha Solovieva*, edited by Sergei M. Soloviev and Ernest L. Radlov, 2nd ed. Vol. 4, 243–633. St. Petersburg: Prosveshchenie, 1911–14.

———. *Kritika otvlechennykh nachal*. In *Sobranie sochinenii Vladimira Sergeevicha Solovieva*, edited by Sergei M. Soloviev and Ernest L. Radlov, 2nd ed. Vol. 2, v–397. St. Petersburg: Prosveshchenie, 1911–14.

———. "Law and Morality: Essays in Applied Ethics." In *Politics, Law, and Morality: Essays by V. S. Soloviev*, edited and translated by Vladimir Wozniuk, 131–212. New Haven: Yale University Press, 2000.

———. "The Meaning of Love." In *The Heart of Reality: Essays on Beauty, Love, and Ethics by V. S. Soloviev*, edited and translated by Vladimir Wozniuk, 83–133. Notre Dame: University of Notre Dame Press, 2003.

———. *Opravdanie dobra: nravstvennaia filosofiia*. In *Sobranie sochinenii Vladimira Sergeevicha Solovieva*, edited by Sergei M. Soloviev and Ernest L. Radlov, 2nd ed. Vol. 8, 3–516. St. Petersburg: Prosveshchenie, 1911–14.

Solovyov, Vladimir. "The Great Dispute and Christian Politics." In *A Solovyov Anthology*, edited by Semen L. Frank, translated by Natalie Duddington, 75–101. 1950. Reprint, London: The Saint Austin Press, 2001.

———. *The Justification of the Good: An Essay on Moral Philosophy*. Translated by Natalie A. Duddington, edited and annotated by Boris Jakim. Grand Rapids: Eerdmans, 2005.

Trinkaus, Charles. *In Our Image and Likeness: Humanity and Divinity in Italian Humanist Thought*. 2 vols. 1970. Reprint, Notre Dame: University of Notre Dame Press, 1995.

Trubetskoi, Evgenii N. "The Bolshevist Utopia and the Religious Movement in Russia." *The Hibbert Journal* 18/2 (1920) 209–24. Reprinted in *A Revolution of the Spirit: Crisis of Value in Russia, 1890-1924*, edited by Bernice Glatzer Rosenthal and Martha Bohachevsky-Chomiak, 323–37. New York: Fordham University Press, 1990.

———. *Lektsii po entsiklopedii prava*. Moscow: A. I. Mamontov, 1916.

———. *Mirosozertsanie Vl. S. Solovieva*. 2 vols. Moscow: Put', 1913.

———. *Religiozno-obshchestvennyi ideal zapadnogo khristianstva v V veke: Mirosozertsanie bl. Avgustina*. Moscow: Tipografiia E. Lissnera i Iu. Romana, 1892.

———. *Religiozno-obshchestvennyi ideal zapadnogo khristianstva v XI veke: Ideia bozheskogo tsarstva v tvoreniiakh Grigoriia VII-go i ego publitsistov—sovremennikov*. Kiev: Tipografiiia S. V. Kul'zhenko, 1897.

———. *Smysl zhizni*. Berlin: Knigoizdatel'stvo "Slovo," 1922. (First edition Moscow: Sytin, 1918.)

———. "Svoboda i bessmertie." *Voprosy filosofii i psikhologii* 17.4, kn. 84 (1906) 368–77.

———. "Toward Characterization of the Theory of Marx and Engels on the Significance of Ideas in History." In *Problems of Idealism: Essays in Russian Social Philosophy*, translated and edited by Randall A. Poole, 124–42. New Haven, CT: Yale University Press, 2003.

———. *Trudy po filosofii prava*. Edited by Igor I. Evlampiev. St. Petersburg: RKhGI, 2001.

———. "Uchenie B. N. Chicherina o sushchnosti i smysle prava." *Voprosy filosofii i psikhologii* 16.5, kn. 80 (1905) 353–81.

———. *Velikaia revoliutsiia i krizis patriotizma*. Rostov, 1919.

———. "V seobshchee, priamoe, tainoe i ravnoe." In *Smysl zhizni*, by Evgenii Trubetskoi, edited by A. P. Poliakov and P. P. Apryshko, 299–303. Moscow: Respublika, 1994.

Trubetskoi, Sergei N. "O prirode chelovecheskogo soznaniia." In *Sobranie sochinenii Kn. Sergeia Nikolaevicha Trubetskogo*, edited by Lev M. Lopatin, 1–110. Vol. 2. Moscow: Tipografiia G. Lissnera i D. Sobko, 1908.

———. "Psikhologicheskii determinizm i nravstvennaia svoboda." In *Sobranie sochinenii Kn. Sergeia Nikolaevicha Trubetskogo*, edited by Lev M. Lopatin, 111–33. Vol. 2. Moscow: Tipografiia G. Lissnera i D. Sobko, 1908.

———. "Vera v bessmertie." In *Sobranie sochinenii Kn. Sergeia Nikolaevicha Trubetskogo*, edited by Lev M. Lopatin, 348–417. Vol. 2. Moscow: Tipografiia G. Lissnera i D. Sobko, 1908.

Valliere, Paul. "Introduction to the Modern Orthodox Tradition." In *The Teachings of Modern Christianity on Law, Politics, and Human Nature*, edited by John Witte Jr. and Frank S. Alexander, 503–32. Vol. 1. New York: Columbia University Press, 2006.

———. *Modern Russian Theology. Bukharev, Soloviev, Bulgakov. Orthodox Theology in a New Key*. Grand Rapids, MI: Eerdmans, 2000.

———. "Theological Liberalism and Church Reform in Imperial Russia." In *Church, Nation and State in Russia and Ukraine*, edited by Geoffrey A. Hosking, 108–30. London: Macmillan, 1991.

———. "Vladimir Soloviev." In *The Teachings of Modern Christianity on Law, Politics, and Human Nature*, edited by John Witte Jr. and Frank S. Alexander, 533–75. Vol. 1. New York: Columbia University Press, 2006.

2

Evgenii Trubetskoi's Search for Peaceful Political Renewal

Eric Lohr

Evgenii Nikolaevich Trubetskoi is rightly best known for his philosophy. But he was also a respected and important political figure in the era from 1904–1917, when Russia lived through two liberal revolutions and a *coup d'état* by the Bolsheviks. Trubetskoi was in many respects in the middle of it all. He nearly always found himself in the middle of the political spectrum, trying one way or another to create a vibrant and broad moderate political center that could make the new post-1905 constitutional monarchy work. It was in many ways a very pragmatic and flexible role for the idealistic philosopher to take. But it was also a deeply principled position that was grounded in firm beliefs in human rights, the rule of law, and—undergirding it all—a conviction that the fundamental dignity of the individual was the bedrock of the entire moral and legal system. These core principles were for Trubetskoi not subject to compromise. This article gives an overview of his political career, assessing the strengths and weaknesses of his overall political philosophy and activity, and focusing on how he navigated between his political pragmatism on the one hand and his core beliefs on the other.

In many ways, Evgenii Trubetskoi's political career was unlikely. Few aristocrats from exalted ranks like the Trubetskois engaged in working for pay or public service to the degree that he did. But his father Nikolai Petrovich's family had relatively limited means due to family misfortune at the gambling table, his father's lack of profitable pursuits, and his father's generosity in the pursuit of his love of music (most notably as founder and benefactor of the Moscow Conservatory).[1] Evgenii and his brothers lived

---

1. See Trubetskoi, *Vospominaniia*, 44–45. Their older brother Petr Nikolaevich

comfortably, but did not have unlimited means for a social life of leisure. At a young age, Evgenii and his elder brother Sergei (by one year) dropped out of the demanding, expensive, and intellectually deadening social scene to study and work. Their world was philosophy, literature, music, and the arts—without much political engagement. As students, both questioned the religious faith that their devout mother instilled in them and they swung toward radical secular ideas. But both worked their way back to faith through philosophical reasoning already in their late teens.[2] They were optimists who believed in Progress and were seekers of truth and moral answers not only to the eternal philosophical and religious questions, but also to the secular questions of their time. But from a young age, both rejected positivism and sought to bring morality, religion, and idealism into their political philosophies and practices. Along with this, the Trubetskoi brothers were particularly influenced by their reading of Alexei Khomiakov and Yuri Samarin (the latter of whom was close to the family). Altogether, these various influences contributed to the most distinguishing characteristic of Evgenii and his brothers: the search for some broad unifying principle that could unite everything into one greater, all-embracing philosophy that was particularly Russian yet grounded in universal principles.

This brings us to arguably the most important influence in Evgenii's intellectual (and derivatively, also political) life: Vladimir Soloviev. Soloviev spent many weeks and months at the Trubetskoi estate and was a huge influence on all of them. The Trubetskois shared in his search for the principle of "all-unity" (*vseedenstvo*) in their philosophy, religion, and politics. But they viscerally disagreed with Soloviev's argument that all-unity (or at least the principle of unification based on shared values) could only be achieved through reunification of the Christian churches. This is a philosophical and theological topic for experts on those themes. For the purpose of this essay it is enough to say that in politics, no theme was more powerful than Evgenii's search for unity, to transcend, unite, and overcome divisions among political groupings.[3]

Evgenii taught law and philosophy from 1886 to 1905 in Iaroslavl and Kiev. He developed an interesting philosophy of law based on the idea that natural law is tempered by historical circumstance and the notion that positive law can evolve under autocracy, monarchy, dictatorship, or democracy, but that the trend over time is toward global convergence

---

received most of the remaining family inheritance (from Nikolai Petrovich's first wife Liubov Orlov-Denissov). Petr Nikolaevich provided monetary assistance to his brothers during their studies.

2. See Dosekin, *Evgenii Nikolaevich Trubetskoi*, 19–20.
3. See Trubetskoi, *Vospominaniia*, 113.

toward natural law.⁴ This legal philosophy was not uncommon among liberal juridical philosophers at the turn of the twentieth century. He and his brother both deeply believed that the historically evolved authorities and society could understand each other and cooperate. However, by the turn of the century, Evgenii was among a group of juridical thinkers who turned against positivist and evolutionary traditions of legal thought (as for example, those espoused by the influential Nikolai Korkunov) and toward neo-Kantian notions of natural right and even the idea of revolution in order to base Russia's political order on *a priori* natural law.⁵ Their path toward active and open political activity seems to be in some sense an outgrowth of the family's sense of *noblesse oblige* and quiet sense of responsibility to society.⁶ More immediately, it likely grew out of Sergei Nikolaevich's involvement in student affairs. He began to intervene through articles and involvement in student affairs both to try to promote moderation among students, and to protect students from punishment for their political activities.⁷ Sergei, in fact, became the first elected rector in the history of Moscow University in August 1905.⁸

Evgenii also was deeply involved in university affairs and developed a profound respect among students—so much so that he could say unpopular things and exert real influence on their political positions. He used this political capital in several instances to convince students to end political demonstrations and return to the classroom. In the years leading to the 1905 revolution, he and his brother also had some limited success in preventing government punishment of students for participation in demonstrations by conscripting them into the army.

While both loved their philosophy more than anything, both felt they had a moral and civic obligation to use their social position to push the tsar toward reforms and keep society from falling into violent chaos.⁹ The brothers became involved in the zemstvo movement through their membership in the "Beseda" group and as participants in the series of gatherings of the radical-liberal Union of Liberation, the more moderate Zemstvo Constitutionalists, and the independent zemstvo activists.¹⁰ Due to what Miliukov saw as

---

4. See Polovinkin, *Kniaz' E. N. Trubetskoi*, 33–34.

5. For a fine essay by a contemporary, see Gessen, "Vozrozhdenie estestvennogo prava," and for more on Gessen, see Lohr, "Ideal Citizen."

6. See Troubetzkoy, *Bygone Years: Minuvsheye*, 55.

7. See Anisimov, "Kniaz' S. N. Trubetskoi."

8. See Namestnikova, "Sergei Nikolaevich Trubetskoi."

9. See Polovinkin, *Kniaz' E. N. Trubetskoi*, 35–36.

10. See Emmons, "Beseda Circle."

Trubetskoi's universally held "unimpeachable moral authority," the zemstvo congress of May 24–25, 1905 chose Sergei Nikolaevich to bring a petition to the tsar appealing for deep reforms.[11] It was a key moment in the 1905 revolution, but the tsar's half-hearted response offering the so-called Bulygin consultative duma did not go far enough to keep up with the rapidly escalating demands of the opposition in the context of rapidly growing strikes, demonstrations, and agrarian uprisings. In this period, while trying to convince the tsar to grant concessions, the Trubetskois turned quite clearly toward embrace of revolution in order to establish a constitutional monarchy.[12] Evgenii played an active role in the *de facto* creation of the Party of People's Freedom (later renamed the Constitutional Democratic party—the KD, or Kadet Party after the Russian initials) in the summer and in the formal establishment of the party at its convention on October 12–18, 1905.

Sergei decided that one of the best ways for him to pursue his agenda was by founding and editing a new weekly newspaper, *Moskovskaia nedelia*, in May 1905. The opening issue declared: "The press should, above all to the degree it is able, serve the matter of internal and external peace." He thought that "the country [wa]s thirsty for peace."[13] The censors did not agree: the first issues were seized and the issue was not published until after Sergei's sudden and untimely death on September 29, 1905. That first issue included strong, barely veiled calls for constitutional reform, including a letter from Sergei Kotliarevskii from Paris warning that French public opinion would not allow the French government to provide financial support to Russia unless deep reforms were implemented.[14]

From the start, Evgenii was deeply involved in the production of the paper, and he became the founder and editor of its continuation under the title *Moskovskii ezhenedel'nik*, the first issue of which was published on March 7, 1906. The opening issue started with Evgenii's passionate defense of equal individual political and civil rights for all citizens and outlined a clear vision of a form of Russian national identity that was grounded in that liberal principle.[15] Along with that, he argued that democracy had to be deeper than simple mechanical institutions, rules, and majorities.

11. Miliukov, *Vospominaniia*, 289, cited in Dosekin, *Evgenii Nikolaevich Trubetskoi*, 29.
12. See "Pamiati S. N. Trubetskogo," 3–7.
13. "Pamiati S. N. Trubetskogo," 3–7.
14. See "Pamiati S. N. Trubetskogo," 3–7.
15. See [Editorial], "Obnovleniia Rossii." In this case and others to follow, I cite the unsigned editorials in this way. There was an editorial board, but as editor-in-chief, Evgenii wrote nearly all the editorials and was the final authority signing off on them. So one may treat these articles as expressing Evgenii's point of view.

Returning to a touchstone in his writings, he passionately claimed that the principle of universal, direct, secret and equal voting was grounded in the notion that man is the image and expression of God, and as such was absolutely inviolable. This was the core of the reason he could never really cooperate with or accept the position of the Octobrists, who were willing to go along with all the compromises of the initial 1906 electoral system, and then with its sharp restriction in 1907 that swung it even more in the direction of unequal and indirect voting to favor landlords, clergy, and the bourgeoisie over peasants, workers, and others.[16]

Moskovskii ezhenedel'nik quickly became a personal tribune for Evgenii, his brother Grigorii, and a number of other moderate liberals. It was funded by the remarkable Margarita Morozova, a figure at the center of *fin de siècle* philanthropy and philosophical life, and an intellectual in her own right. Her work with Evgenii in the offices of *Moskovskii ezhenedel'nik* was passionate in more ways than one.[17] Evgenii published weekly ruminations on the politics of the week in several pages "from the editor." It is like a weekly political blog. Evgenii largely kept his philosophical and religious views distinct from his politics. The views he expounded in his weekly editorials and articles were quite consonant with the Right KD party group and had some overlap with the more liberal Octobrists.

By late 1906, Evgenii came out in strong support of the Party of Peaceful Renewal (*Partiia mirnogo obnovlenii—PMO*), and *Moskovskii ezhenedel'nik* became known as a kind of unofficial paper of the party.[18] In his November 4, 1906 editorial, Evgenii outlined the reasons for his embrace of the party. He personally expressed "great sympathy towards the wing [of the KD Party], with whom [he was in] complete solidarity," and noted that although he voted for the full KD list in the prior elections, now he found his "core fundamental principled differences" with the left wing to be too great to remain in the party. The single most fundamental and inviolable principle in politics for him was the unconditional acceptance of the absolute value of the human person, a principle that for him required an absolute rejection of violence. More than anything else, his disillusionment with the KD party was grounded in its failure to reject cooperation with groups to the left that endorsed terrorism, assassination, and violence. It was also the main reason he could not work with the Octobrists, whose leader Aleksandr Guchkov openly endorsed field courts martial and violent government methods of repression. He also had problems with the KD endorsement of

---

16. See [Editorial], "Vseobshchee," 40–41.
17. See "'Nasha liubov' nuzhna Rossii.'"
18. See Trubetskoi, "Partiia 'Mirnogo obnovleniia.'"

the nationalization of land, preferring the PMO platform of promoting peasant land ownership and private property. More immediately, he shared the PMO renunciation of the Vyborg manifesto, issued by 200 deputies (including 120 KDs) after the tsar's dissolution of the first duma. It called for civil disobedience, the evasion of taxes and military service, and demanded a full constitutional regime. He wanted the KDs and everyone to accept the rules of the new constitutional order and strive to make it work. Vyborg became a shorthand in his articles for the opposite approach.

On the other hand, he declared the Octobrist party to be too close to the government and too willing to compromise key principles to be considered a constitutional party. Unlike the Octobrists, he declared that the PMO would not compromise and firmly opposed any anti-constitutional steps of the government, such as refusal to legalize constitutional parties, submit the budget for confirmation, etc. The party would not recognize a ministerial government and would only support a constitutional one.[19] In the campaign prior to elections to the second duma, the PMO moved much closer to the KDs than to the Octobrists. *Rech'*, the newspaper of the KD party, welcomed the move, declaring that the PMO had become a true opposition party. By December, the PMO was working with the KDs on local level agreements to avoid candidates from the two parties taking votes from each other. But the PMO held out against a national agreement with the KDs: Evgenii explained that the PMO focused on principles first, agreements second.[20] In a programmatic article in *Moskovskii ezhenedel'nik*, Evgenii's brother Grigorii Nikolaevich stressed that beyond the specific policies of the party, the paper's editors were drawn to its constructive spirit, which was born not in revolutionary opposition to the government but rather in the halls of the duma, where deputies cooperated in a pragmatic search for ways to make the new constitutional monarchy work. Thus, he asserted, the PMO had from its birth a fundamentally different attitude toward politics than the KDs and other parties.[21]

Russian newspapers had a tradition of writing summaries of the previous year and predicting themes for the new year in their first January issue. Evgenii's January 1907 editorial in this genre was stark, stating that "it was a difficult year of blood spilled on the right and left, a year of unprecedented hopes, and destroyed illusions." He warned that the KD insistence of allying with or trying to win votes from the left was foolish in the context of broader polarization. While the noble assemblies, zemstvos, and city dumas were

19. See G. Trubetskoi, "Partiia mirnogo," 1–11.
20. See Trubetskoi, "K voprosu o soglasheniiakh."
21. See Trubetskoi, "Kak slozhilas."

turning right, the pre-election assemblies were turning left. He worried that the center would not hold and feared the government would use the polarization as an excuse for more violent repression.[22]

Evgenii's response to the victory of the KDs in the second duma elections was "neither unhappy nor enthusiastic" and as the KDs moved left and the socialist parties in the duma made it as unworkable as the first, he and *Moskovskii ezhenedel'nik* moved to the right. In May, for the first time, he called on the duma to find a *modus vivendi* with the government to avoid its dissolution. When the government dissolved the parliament and promulgated a new, much more conservative and restrictive electoral law for elections to the next duma, he was angry, but not only with the government. He raised some of the themes that would be at the center of his writings in 1917, drawing on *Revelations* to conclude that government and revolutionaries were both to blame, that "he who lives by the sword, dies by the sword," essentially blaming the revolutionaries' intransigence for the government's violent response.[23]

During the summer of 1907, Trubetskoi warmed considerably to the Octobrists, claiming that they now were more fully a constitutional party than they had been. He also approved of the KD turn toward more realistic centrist policies.[24] In August, he even claimed that the PMO would no longer need to exist if these trends continued.[25] From 1907–1910, *Moskovskii ezhenedel'nik* continued to critique the government for its repressive measures, but it generally toned down its criticism of the Octobrists. In 1906, Evgenii's brother Petr was elected to the State Council as a relatively liberal Octobrist, perhaps helping to temper Evgenii's critiques of the party.[26]

While Evgenii did not contribute to the *Vekhi* compilation in 1909, he was close to all the contributors and hosted articles by many of them in his weekly paper.[27] He had contributed an essay to *Problems of Idealism* in 1902 and shared the attitudes of the group—especially their biting critique of the intelligentsia for its unwillingness to work for gradual change within the existing political system.[28] The paper's critiques of government policy gradually shifted from domestic to foreign policy.

22. See Trubetskoi, "Novogodnie perspektivy."
23. See [Editorial], "Izmor ili revoliutsiia."
24. See Trubetskoi, "Kadety i Oktiabristy"; Trubetskoi, "K voprosu o edinoi khristianskoi partii."
25. See Trubetskoi, "Kadety i Oktiabristy," 11.
26. See Korros, "Activist Politics."
27. See Shatz and Zimmerman, *Vekhi*.
28. See Poole, *Problems of Idealism*.

This brings us to one of the distinguishing characteristics of the Trubetskoi brothers—their patriotism and nationalism. Randall Poole's 2006 article lays out the complexity of Evgenii's search for a liberal Russian nationalism. His vision was of a liberal, popular Russian patriotism that carried no hatred or resentment for others, but rather had a Herderian respect for other national cultures. He often contrasted this vision to official Russian nationalism, especially as it developed during World War I. His polemics with Struve, Ern, Bulgakov, and Berdyaev showed him to have a much more critical view of nationalism than theirs. It always had to be constrained by moral and legal principles. He strongly opposed viewing the state as the highest principle as Struve seemed to sometimes express it.

The Trubetskois' nationalism gave them respect further to the right along the political spectrum than many of their KD colleagues enjoyed. But it also had a dark side. The brothers were influenced by Slavophile ideas from a young age. After the all-consuming 1905 revolution had settled down, Evgenii and his brother Grigorii began to engage with Neoslav ideas, publishing many articles by one of the leaders of the group, Aleksandr Pogodin.[29] Grigorii developed a particular interest in the Balkans, writing extensively about issues there, often criticizing the government for its lack of support for Slavs in the region.[30] Evgenii became the chair of the Society of Slavic Culture, one of the leading groups propounding Neoslav ideas.[31] The Neoslav movement began in Prague with the strong support of the Young Czech movement as a response to the aggressive pan-German movement and as a call for Slavs to unite for their own civilizational alternative. The movement tried to overcome the traditional hostility between Catholic Poles and Orthodox Slavs, but it also carried with it a predilection for a more forward policy in the Balkans, encouraging the Russian tsar to stand firmly against Austria, Germany, and the Ottomans on the side of the Slavs.

There is some dispute among scholars about the Neoslavism of Evgenii and Grigorii. There is no question that they had affinities with the Neoslav position and supported a more aggressive stand in the Balkans and against Austria-Hungary and Germany prior to the war. Dominic Lieven argues that for Grigorii Nikolaevich it was a means to maintaining a balance of power.[32] Although Evgenii left commentary on foreign policy in

29. See Pogodin, "Politika Rossii." For an overview, see Fischel, *Der Panslawismus*.

30. The Neoslavs were closely watched by the police. When Evgenii expressed a particularly harsh criticism at one meeting in 1908, the police intervened and shut it down. He followed this up with a blistering attack on the government in *Moskovskii ezhenedel'nik* for its lack of national sentiment. Trubetskoi, "Revoliutsiia v 1908 godu," 5.

31. See Poole, "Religion."

32. See Lieven, *Russia*, 91–101.

Moskovskii ezhedel'nik almost entirely to his brother, it is apparent that they shared a common set of views; as chair of the Society of Slavic Culture, Evgenii seems to have seen Neoslavism as something more than simply a Realpolitik response to Pan-Germanism.

In the opening issue of *Moskovskii ezhenedel'nik* for 1909, he noted that while the Right, KDs, and Octobrists could not speak with each other on most issues, the Slavic issue was one that could unite them all. He bitterly denounced the government for treating the Slavic movement like "an internal enemy," for censoring articles and closing down gatherings if too much enthusiasm was expressed (referring obliquely here to a Panslav meeting he hosted that the police broke up). The article uses the Slavic issue as an example of how the government was undermining support by refusing to allow civil society and national sentiments to be expressed freely: "Thus the role of the opposition has become more significant. It must fight against the antipatriotic reaction and become a creator of popular Russian self-consciousness. If the government divides the nation, the opposition should unite it."[33]

His plea for the opposition to become more national was in part a plea for a positive form of nationalism that recognized national difference, respected Polish autonomy, and defended the rights of Jews (defined in opposition to narrow chauvinistic forms of nationalism that he abhorred).

Interestingly and importantly, he and his brother explicitly tackled the most important and divisive national question of all: Poland. They sought reconciliation through a project of autonomy within the Russian empire. Evgenii penned a programmatic article arguing that "The Road to Constantinople Runs through Warsaw." That is, if Russia wanted to re-take Constantinople from the Turks, she had to start by winning the loyalty of her own Slavic subjects in Poland.[34] Grigorii was particularly active on this issue, drafting the declaration to the Poles and working with a close friend of the brothers, Foreign Minister Sergei Sazonov. When Sazonov was replaced in 1916, an opportunity was lost.

The brothers' foreign policy ideas could be seen as consonant with Evgenii's broad and generous Herderian approach to nationality. He saw the Neoslav movement as fundamentally emancipatory; once freed from their empires and allowed to form liberal nation-states, the world would be freer and safer. It was a kind of proto-Wilsonian vision at its best.

But if one reads the voluminous correspondence of the brothers with some of the more extreme Neoslavs, and even their occasional arguments

---

33. Trubetskoi, "Revolyutsiya v 1908 godu," 5–7.
34. Mankoff, "Russia," 90; D'iakov, *Slavianskii vopros*.

with Struve and some of the other leading "liberal imperialists," one does not find a whole lot of pushback against less tolerant and more aggressive approaches. Grigorii in particular had very close personal relationships with leaders in Bulgaria and Serbia, and with Aleksandr Pogodin and other more aggressive Neoslav publicists. As Randall Poole concludes:

> As far as the question of Trubetskoi's defense of Russian claims to Constantinople is concerned, clearly his main motivation was to take advantage of the popularity of this particular war aim to enlist the idea of Sophia in promoting a more liberal nationality and foreign policy. But in doing so, he may well have also betrayed his own principles.[35]

This overarching vision really had no place for Muslims and openly called for a policy that could mean war against Turkey and/or Austria-Hungary. For all the liberal framing of their positions, the brothers still supported a risky policy of confrontation with Austria in the Balkans and the ultimate war aim of conquering Constantinople. (Foreign Minister Sazonov even secretly nominated Grigorii Nikolaevich to be the future Russian commander of the planned postwar Russian occupation zone of Constantinople.)[36] Although there were many other factors, the Trubetskois helped to narrow the options of the regime and to some degree made the outbreak of WWI more likely. Once Russia entered the war, Evgenii Nikolaevich promoted Neoslav war aims that made any exit from the war more difficult. In a popular published lecture in December 1914, Evgenii Nikolaevich linked the war aim of conquering Constantinople to the family affinity for the notion of Sophia, Divine Wisdom. His notion develops the idea of a free association of nations united in their Christianity. Restoring the actual church Hagia Sophia in Constantinople was part of a vision he had of restoring the concept of Sophia to the world. He argued that WWI could be an emancipatory war for Slavic nations (perhaps others too, but he focused on Slavs); in the world of new, free Slavic and Orthodox nations, Constantinople could be restored as a spiritual beacon.[37]

The Trubetskois' strong support of the war aim of annexation of Constantinople was a factor in the catastrophic decisions of the Provisional

35. Poole, "Religion," 213. On the other hand, it is worth noting that Evgenii was by no means alone in this: Pavel Miliukov, leader of the KD party, also shared the dream of conquest of Constantinople, a dream which wrecked his brief tenure as Foreign Minister only two months into the first Russian Republic in 1917 and did a great deal to undermine the prospects for its survival. See Nabokov, *Provisional Government*, 62.

36. See Schmitz, "Grigori N. Trubetzkoy," 171–72. In his memoirs, Grigorii described the news of his future appointment to be the fulfillment of a lifelong dream.

37. Trubetskoi, *Natsional'nyi vopros*.

Government to not only stay in the war, but to launch the June Offensive that was the most important cause of the collapse of the new liberal republic, paving the way for the Bolsheviks.

On balance, Evgenii's political impact was mixed. He tried valiantly to support and create a vibrant center and make the new constitutional monarchy work. He eloquently opposed violence, supported liberal values, and brought religion into politics in a liberal way. He was able to transcend the different worlds of nobility, intelligentsia, politics, and regime in a way that almost no one else could. In my view, he was correct in his rejection of KD tolerance of revolutionary violence on the left and Octobrist acceptance of state violence on the right. In a counterfactual world without the 1917 Bolshevik coup, Evgenii Nikolaevich could well be counted today among the great founding fathers of a democratic Russian state, and a modern liberal Orthodox Church.

But there were some serious flaws in his politics: attempts to transcend rather than engage in politics of compromise and coalition building may have done as much to undermine as to build a unified constitutional liberal political force. While his writings and speeches had influence, his practical political work left a mixed legacy. Although his peers elected him to the State Council in February 1907, he did not use the position to further his views, compiling a very poor attendance record and resigning in 1908. After leaving the KD party, his gambit through the Party of Peaceful Renewal to build a vibrant center did not succeed in building a single party committed to nonviolence and to making the new constitutional order work. However, it could be argued that his vision of an Octobrist party less beholden to the government and a KD party less linked to the parties to their left did come to pass, in a sense achieving his primary goal and making it unnecessary to continue the Party of Peaceful Renewal.

The Trubetskoi brothers helped bring the leaders of the Octobrist and KD parties to agree on a forward policy in the Balkans and in favor of the ultimate conquest of Constantinople, policies that ended catastrophically in World War I and the fatal decision to continue with the offensive of June 1917. The verdict on Trubetskoi's political engagement is mixed; his position was interesting, original, grounded in his Christian philosophical ideals, and I would argue, an effective diagnosis of the main threats to the young constitutional monarchy. Whether it was effective is another question. And in the end, it was all undermined by the tragic flaw of his position in foreign affairs.

Bibliography

Anisimov, Aleksandr I. "Kniaz' S. N. Trubetskoi i Moskovskoe studenchestvo." *Voprosy filosofii i psikhologii* 81 (1906) 146–96.

D'iakov, Vladimir A. *Slavianskii vopros v obshchestvennoi zhizni dorevoliutsionnoi Rossii*. Moscow: Nauka, 1993.

Dosekin, Egor S. *Evgenii Nikolaevich Trubetskoi: obshchestvennyi i politicheskii deiatel'*. Samara: Gosudarstvennyy Institut kul'tury, 2014.

[Editorial]. "Izmor ili revoliutsiia." *Moskovskii ezhenedel'nik* 19 (May 19, 1907) 3–9.

———. "Obnovleniia Rossii." *Moskovskii ezhenedel'nik* 1 (March 7, 1906) 1–4.

———. "Vseobshchee, priamoe, tainoe i ravnoe." *Moskovskii ezhenedel'nik* 2 (March 15, 1906) 39–41.

Emmons, Terence. "The Beseda Circle, 1899–1905." *Slavic Review* 32.3 (1973) 461–90.

Fischel, Alfred. *Der Panslawismus bis zum Weltkrieg*. Stuttgart: Cotta, 1919.

Gessen, Vladimir. "Vozrozhdenie estestvennogo prava." *Pravo* 10 (1902) 475–84; 11 (1902) 533–47.

Korros, Alexandra Shecket. "Activist Politics in a Conservative Institution: The Formation of Factions in the Russian Imperial State Council, 1906–1907." *The Russian Review* 52.1 (1993) 1–19.

Lieven, Dominic C. B. *Russia and the Origins of the First World War*. New York: St. Martin's, 1983.

Lohr, Eric. "The Ideal Citizen and Real Subject in Late Imperial Russia." *Kritika: Explorations in Russian and Eurasian History* 7.2 (2006) 173–94.

Mankoff, Jeffrey. "Russia and the Polish Question, 1907–1917: Nationality and Diplomacy." PhD diss., Yale University, 2006.

Nabokov, Vladimir. *The Provisional Government*. New York: Wiley, 1970.

Namestnikova, Irina A. "Sergei Nikolaevich Trubetskoi i Moskovskii universitet." PhD diss., Moscow University, 2000.

"'Nasha liubov' nuzhna Rossii . . .': Perepiska E. N. Trubetskogo i M. K. Morozovoi." *Novyi mir* 9.821 (1993) 172–229; 10.822 (1993) 174–215.

"Pamiati S. N. Trubetskogo." *Moskovskaia nedelia* 1.2 (May 12, 1905) 3–7.

Pogodin, Aleksandr. "Pochemu politika Rossii dolzhna byt' slavianskoi?" *Moskovskii ezhenedel'nik* 3 (January 17, 1909) 9–18.

Polovinkin, Sergei. *Kniaz' E. N. Trubetskoi: Zhiznennyi i tvorcheskii put'*. Moscow: Sintaksis, 2010.

Poole, Randall A. *Problems of Idealism: Essays in Russian Social Philosophy*. Edited and translated by Randall A. Poole. New Haven: Yale University Press, 2003.

———. "Religion, War, and Revolution: E. N. Trubetskoi's Liberal Construction of Russian National Identity, 1912–20." *Kritika: Explorations in Russian and Eurasian History* 7.2 (2006) 195–240.

Schmitz, Sophie. "Grigori N. Trubetzkoy: Politik und Völkerrecht, 1873–1930." PhD diss., University of Vienna, 1971. https://digitalcollections.hoover.org/objects/62203.

Shatz, Marshall S., and Judith E. Zimmerman, eds. *Vekhi: Landmarks: A Collection of Articles about the Russian Intelligentsia*. Armonk, NY: Sharpe, 1994.

Troubetzkoy, Serge E. *Bygone Years: Minuvsheye*. Translated by Vera Bouteneff, edited by Eugene Sokoloff. USA: Self-published, 2004.

Trubetskoi, Evgenii N. "K voprosu o edinoi khristianskoi partii." *Moskovskii ezhenedel'nik* 44 (November 10, 1907) 25-34.

———. "K voprosu o soglasheniiakh." *Moskovskii ezhenedel'nik* 40 (December 23, 1906) 5-8.

———. "Kadety i Oktiabristy." *Moskovskii ezhenedel'nik* 28 (June 21, 1907) 3-12, *Moskovskii ezhenedel'nik* 30 (August 4, 1907) 3-11.

———. *Natsional'nyi vopros: Konstantinopol' i sviataia Sofiia*. London: Faith, 1916.

———. "Novogodnie perspektivy." *Moskovskii ezhenedel'nik* 1 (January 6, 1907) 5-17.

———. "Partiia 'Mirnogo obnovleniia.'" *Moskovskii ezhenedel'nik* 33 (November 4, 1906) 5-14.

———. "Revolyutsiya v 1908 godu." *Moskovskii ezhenedel'nik* 1 (1909) 1-14.

———. *Vospominaniia*. Sofiia: Rossiysko-bolgarskoe izdatel'stvo, 1921.

Trubetskoi, Grigorii N. "Kak slozhilas' partiia mirnogo obnovleniia i kakiia zadachi ona presleduiut." *Moskovskii ezhenedel'nik* 40 (December 23, 1906) 9-25.

3

Evgenii Trubetskoi's Idealist Grounding of the Religious Meaning of Life

Kåre Johan Mjør

This article discusses the idealism of Evgenii Trubeskoi in light of what is considered his magnum opus: *The Meaning of Life* (*Smysl zhizni*), published in 1918 in the context of war and revolution.[1] The reason why this topic is worth exploring further is that this is not merely a philosophical text, deepening the then still young, yet already firm Russian tradition of idealist philosophy. It is also a very religious work, an expression of Christian faith that actively situates itself within an Orthodox tradition. In this respect, it was also a contribution to what we may today recognize as a Russian tradition: Among its main predecessors we can include Vladimir Soloviev's *Lectures on Divine Humanity* (1877), Sergei Bulgakov's *Philosophy of Economy* (1912) and Nikolai Berdyaev's *The Meaning of Creativity* (1916). These were all explicitly religious works that at the same time started not from the moment of personal experience of the divine or from collective participation in the church, but with philosophical, discursive reasoning. As we shall see, Trubetskoi's *Meaning of Life* follows this pattern.

Scholars have previously noted the religious underpinning of the understanding and reception of philosophical idealism in Russia. According to Randall Poole, Russian neo-idealists believed that "Kantian transcendental idealism entailed a transcendent ontological reality."[2] This article examines more closely how, in the case of Evgenii Trubetskoi, an idealist philosophical position led to the confirmation of a religious worldview. How

---

1. The research on which this article is based has been funded by the Swedish Research Council, project number 2014–01254.
2. Poole, "Reception of Kant," 323.

did Trubteskoi combine philosophical discursive reasoning and idealist grounding on the one hand with religious experience and Christian revelation on the other? Why were idealism and religious devotion two sides of the same coin, according to the late work of Trubetskoi?

Russian Idealism

Late imperial Russia saw a new wave of interest in idealism. It coincided more generally with an anti-positivist reorientation in European thought of the late nineteenth century, as described in Stuart Hughes's classic account, *Consciousness and Society*.[3] For Sergei Bulgakov, for instance, idealism offered a means to defend ethics and metaphysics as true philosophical issues, confronting thereby their rejection by materialist and empiricist thinkers.[4] In Russia, however, the idealist revival was more than an antipositivist reaction, as noted. It would gradually involve a deeply philosophical justification of personhood, which idealists saw as rooted in transcendent being.

By implication, the movement in Russia known as "from Marxism to Idealism" meant also—at least for the most famous, or canonized, philosophers in retrospect—a turn to Christianity. This is particularly evident in the case of former Marxists such as Nikolai Berdyaev, Sergei Bulgakov, Semen Frank, and Peter Struve. The idealist movement led to a "religious renaissance," to evoke Nicholas Zernov's term.[5] Thus, late imperial Russia saw several idealist philosophical projects that at the same time were religiously framed—idealism was also understood by many as a Christian philosophy, or at least as resonating with Christianity.

Since the turn from Marxism to idealism meant in many cases also a further turn to Christianity, it is tempting to see, as some have done, idealism first and foremost as a passing stage in a broader story of precisely a "religious renaissance." But this would be misleading for two reasons. First, as noted, several thinkers combined idealism and religiosity, seeing the two as different aspects of the same thing. As the case of Trubetskoi will show, Russian religious philosophy remained idealist. Second, not all Russian idealists of the early twentieth century saw the truth of idealism as a confirmation of transcendent being. Russian idealism of the early twentieth century was a heterogeneous landscape and thus not necessarily a landmark on a teleological road to a philosophical-religious worldview, though this may have been

3. Hughes, *Consciousness*, 33–66.
4. Evtuhov, *Cross*, 58.
5. Zernov, *Religious Renaissance*, 131–64, describes them as "four notable converts." Zernov's classic work paid less attention to idealism as such.

the case for some of the canonized names of the "Russian religious renaissance," who came to develop a religious worldview further on. In any case, "idealism" involved several trajectories.[6]

Modern idealism, as it gained prominence in the early nineteenth century, meant most basically that the world or reality is the creation of the mind, of consciousness. The world is the "concrete actualization of concepts whose proper home is the mind."[7] This is a common idealist assumption that the Russian thinkers took over from Fichte, Hegel, Schelling, and even Kant—in an idealist understanding of him (see below). All their criticism of Hegel and preference for Schelling notwithstanding, the most basic assumptions of the Russian thinkers discussed here were commonly idealist, and this brought them ultimately together with German idealism as a whole, not in opposition to it.

A thinker who explicitly philosophized on the meaning of idealism in late imperial Russia was Sergei Trubetskoi, a close but younger friend of Soloviev and Evgenii's brother. He was one of the key members (the others being Nikolai Grot and Lev Lopatin) of the Moscow Psychological Society, which was established in 1885. In two seminal articles in the society's journal, *Questions of Philosophy and Psychology*, Sergei Trubetskoi outlined an idealist conception of philosophy, according to which nothing can be said to exist outside of consciousness. The first article, "On the Nature of Human Consciousness" (1889–1891), proposed a collectivist understanding of consciousness as the most appropriate. Trubetskoi went far in grounding this idealism in language as the commonly shared medium of our consciousness. In the second article, "The Foundations of Idealism" (1896), Trubetskoi seems to have abandoned explicit collectivism as a foundation for idealism, but still emphasized that consciousness is not to be understood as individual, subjective consciousness ("my brain")—consciousness for Trubetskoi was something common and universal.[8]

Above all, idealism as understood by Trubetskoi implies that the relationship of subject and object is something that exists for consciousness: "The world of phenomena, as it appears to us, is above all a fact of consciousness . . . We do not know any reality outside of consciousness."[9] And all phe-

---

6. Plotnikov, "Filosofiia 'Problem idealizma,'" 6, who refers to Semen Frank's self-criticism of his own early idealism. See also Evtuhov, *Cross*, 58, who describes idealism as a "passing stage" for Bulgakov, and Poole, "Religion," 198. The teleological view of early Russian idealism may be found in Zernov's work, who, as noted, largely ignores idealist philosophy when narrating the "Russian religious renaissance."

7. Sprigge, "Idealism." See also Singer, *Hegel*, 70.

8. Gaidenko, *Vladimir Solov'ev*, 143–44.

9. Trubetskoi, "Osnovaniia idealizma," 598–99. All translations from Russian editions are my own.

nomena, as real objects, are subject to the "law of consciousness." Trubetskoi developed his argument in dialogue with Kant rather than with subsequent German idealists.[10] Trubetskoi argued that Kant's categories of time and space were universal categories. Likewise, we have to "assume" (*dopustit'*) that causality is a "general logical condition of reality." Thus, idealism for Trubetskoi does not entail asserting the ultimate subjectivity of, e.g., the logical nature of reality—it is objective and universal, and yet ideal (i.e., of consciousness). These were the conclusions that Kant did not draw, Trubetskoi adds. In other word, we must have faith in the objective existence of reality as such and its inherent features such as time, space, and causality. In addition to "assumption," Trubetskoi evokes the notion of *faith* as a precondition for this world outlook—"confident faith in the reality of the world."[11] We have to have faith in outer reality. Although this faith cannot be proven fully in empirical terms, the world of external objects or phenomena would be mere personal illusions without such faith.

Idealism and Christianity

The idea of faith as an epistemological foundation had previously been put forward by Vladimir Soloviev. We encounter it towards the end of his doctoral thesis, *Critique of Abstract Principles*. He referred to it as faith in the "narrow sense of the word," i.e., faith in "that which is." "Faith" here means first and foremost trust in the existence of things, and in existence more generally; that what we observe is not merely the product of our mind. Faith is the "affirmation of unconditional existence."[12]

While working on this thesis, he delivered, beginning in 1877, his *Lectures on Divine Humanity*. The first lecture starts off by defining religion—in keeping with the etymology of the term—as "the connection of humanity and the world with the absolute principle and focus of all that exists."[13] The "absolute principle" is in turn equated with the "divine principle." At the same time, this connection is not merely given, it just as much represents a task. Soloviev's lectures tell the story of how humanity in the past has responded to the absolute or divine principle, be it in the discovery of ideas in Ancient Greece or in the world religions of Buddhism, Judaism, and (early) Christianity. This process, however, is not completed. The main remaining task for humanity is the further integration of all of humanity *and* the integration of

---

10. Poole, "Reception of Kant," 325, emphasizes the Kantian origin of this position.
11. Trubetskoi, "Osnovaniia idealizma," 599–604.
12. Solov'ev, "Kritika otvlechennykh nachal," 726.
13. Solovyov, *Lectures*, 1.

humanity with the divine principle. The culmination will be the creation of a new universal Christian culture. It will come to expression in cultural work, and more specifically as an ethical project, but it is also the work of the mind. For central to Soloviev's philosophy at this moment, in works such as *Lectures on Divine Humanity* and *Philosophical Principles of Integral Knowledge* (also 1877), was the human faculty of "intellectual contemplation" (*umstvennoe sozertsanie*), which he took over from Schelling and which refers to philosophical speculation that draws on experience, while not being limited to sense data.[14] The creation of a new Christian culture would be dependent on this kind of thought. For Soloviev idealism became a philosophical framework for understanding cultural creativity and hence reinterpreting the Orthodox anthropological idea of deification, where divine likeness is seen as attained in the domain of culture and ethics.

The idealist grounding of religion—or actually of several religions but ultimately of Christianity—as a worldview prompting humanity to positive work was taken over by Sergei Bulgakov in his *Philosophy of Economy* of 1912. The primordial principle for Bulgakov was *life*: In life there is an identity between human beings and nature, between subject and object, a perspective that makes labor, our everyday strivings, meaningful. Bulgakov, furthermore, likens this philosophy of identity (Schelling) with Christianity, both of which Bulgakov describes as a "philosophy of identity" as well as a philosophy of "incarnated spirit."[15] For Bulgakov and Schelling, Christianity as well as other mythologies of Divine Wisdom offer complementary perspectives on humanity in the world.

We may also add Nikolai Berdyaev to this list. It is true that his *Meaning of Creativity* (1916) opens by describing a much more negative view of the "world" as compared to Soloviev and Bulgakov: Human beings are captured by the necessity of the material world. However, the power of thought enables our liberation. "Philosophy as a creative act," which is the title of the book's opening chapter, makes the human being a creator of the positive antidote to the "world"—a creator of "cosmos."[16] And what ultimately enables this creation is our likeness to the Creator. Since we are created in God's image and likeness, we are able to create.

Evgenii Trubetskoi was a follower but also a critic of Soloviev. Particularly pronounced was his rejection of what he saw as Soloviev's "Russian Messianism," which was adopted by Bulgakov and Berdyaev. He deemed their exaggerated belief in Russia's vocation too nationalist in

---

14. See Mjør, "Metaphysics," 15–21.
15. Bulgakov, *Philosophy of Economy*, 38, 57, 84, 88.
16. Berdyaev, *Meaning*, 21–56.

its juxtaposition of Russia to the West. However, Trubetskoi also recognized that Russia possesses a "mission"—as does every (Christian) nation. Distinguishing *messianizm* from *missionizm*, he preserved national differences instead of calling for their sublation in a universalist project of theocracy and the unification of the Christian churches, as did Soloviev.[17] Trubetskoi was an anti-utopian thinker, but he nevertheless criticized utopianism within a Christian providentialist framework.[18] As we shall see, his anti-utopianism did not mean a rejection of tasks for the future, even those of world historical significance.

"The Meaning of Life" as an Idealist Project

Trubetskoi's *The Meaning of Life* (1918) was a response to the experience of war. It raises the question of whether life has meaning under such circumstances. The term itself was loaded with profundity by Trubetskoi: "Meaning" (*smysl*) for Trubetskoi means the "absolute significance [*bezuslovnoe znachenie*] of something."[19] Hence meaning in this sense is not subjective; it is the same for all, and is described by Trubetskoi in Platonic terms as "unchangeable and immovable."[20] At the same time, Trubetskoi repeatedly describes meaning thus conceived as an "assumption" (*predpolozhenie*). Meaning for Trubetskoi is trans-psychological or even transcendental, but it is also something that we actively request. We search for meaning behind our own personal impressions and ideas. We cannot but assume that there is such a meaning, because without it, it would be impossible for us to orient ourselves in the world.

Trubetskoi defines meaning also as "content," "truth," and even "meaning-truth" (*smysl-istina*). Whatever definition, meaning, truth and content cannot be separated from consciousness. Meaning/truth as content is also *thought*. What exists is thought, or—since thought is always about something—the *content of consciousness*. This is where Trubetskoi's idealist position—closer to modern German idealism than to Plato—becomes particularly evident. By the same token, meaning/truth is not only transcendent but also immanent: It is not a mere copy of some transcendental world or ideas. Rather, to arrive at truth means to actively confirm a correct, truthful thought or idea forged by us. "The search for the truth

---

17. See Trubetskoi, "Staryi."
18. See Poole, "Utopianism," 58; Poole, "Religion," 201.
19. Trubetskoi, *Smysl zhizni*, 5.
20. Trubetskoi, *Smysl zhizni*, 8.

means the attempt to find the absolute consciousness in my consciousness and my consciousness in the absolute."[21]

Since truth is thought on the one hand and truth is not subjective on the other, Trubetskoi postulates also, as we saw in the previous quotation, a level of "absolute" or "all-encompassing consciousness" or "thought." We are confident that our individual thought is part of an absolute consciousness, and the search for truth is a search for a correspondence with the absolute consciousness. Again, Trubetskoi stresses this is a metaphysical "assumption": "Our thought lives by means of this assumption of absolute thought: to forsake it would have meant to forsake any thinking and consciousness."[22] According to Trubetskoi, such a forsaking of absolute thought is logically impossible since it would imply a judgment that presupposes the knowledge of absolute truth. Knowing the absolute along these lines, therefore, is described by Trubetskoi as a "revelation in the broad meaning of the word."[23] It is philosophical revelation.

Our cognition and knowledge are therefore correlated with this—assumed—transcendental, collective consciousness. Trubetskoi demonstrates this graphically in his text by emphasizing the prefix s-/so- in the Russian word for "consciousness," suggesting thereby that it may also mean "co-knowledge" (*so-znanie*), i.e., shared knowledge. "Meaning" is likewise "co-thought" (*s-mysl*). For Trubetskoi these terms underline the connection with something outside ourselves, the indebtedness of our mind to the absolute, or it being grounded there. Igor Evlampiev has pointed out that Trubetskoi insisted that the absolute has to be understood as thought, whereas Soloviev defined it as the "existent" (*sushchee*), without specifying that it is thought. This enabled Trubetskoi to include non-being, i.e., that which is not yet, in the absolute, since it may be an object for thought.[24]

The Option of Christianity

This is the idealist framework that Trubetskoi establishes for his philosophical quest for the meaning of life. And it is the idealist framework, and the intuition of unity that it enables, that warrants in turn that such a meaning exists—that there is something firm outside ourselves and our own misery and suffering. In our minds we become confident that we are part of a larger whole that is at the same time positively given. This also

21. Trubetskoi, *Smysl zhizni*, 11–13, 17.
22. Trubetskoi, *Smysl zhizni*, 20.
23. Trubetskoi, *Smysl zhizni*, 163.
24. Evlampiev, *Russkaia filosofiia*, 200.

underscores that meaning exists both in and as thought. Ultimate reality is the creation of the mind, and it is also the connections produced by the mind that makes reality meaningful.

Trubetskoi does not refer to "God" in the Introduction. And yet *The Meaning of Life* emerges as a deeply Christian work in that it contains far more Biblical quotations than references to philosophers, but above all in that it formulates a Christian worldview—which is nevertheless grounded in a philosophical, and more specifically in an idealist framework. Having established a philosophical foundation on the basis of human intuition, Trubetskoi proceeds to ideas, or to meaningful "content."[25] He considers three different options, three different attempts to make life meaningful: The "Indian," which is ascetic and "negative" in its attitude to the world; the "Greek," which is vitalist and thus "positive"; and finally the Christian approach, defined by Trubetskoi as the conquering of death and transfiguration of mortal life. And in keeping with the idealist worldview Trubetskoi concludes that life becomes truly meaningful through Christianity alone. The meaning of life is found at the intersection between the joyous life of (Ancient) Greece and the ascetic practices of India, and this is precisely what Christianity according to Trubetskoi accomplishes. Thus, it does not reject the other options, but makes a "synthesis" of them that acknowledges their "partial truth."[26] Trubetskoi seems to be following Soloviev here, who in *Lectures on Divine Humanity* also saw Christianity as a dialectically-historically unfolding synthesis of Buddhism, the Greek worldview, and Judaism. Clearly, there is also a Hegelian understanding of history at work here.

Also adopted from Soloviev is the concept, and assumption, of the "unity of all" (*vseedinstvo*). This unity, the "fullness of life" on both an individual and a collective level, is presented as the goal towards which humanity should strive. We understand it as a duty (*dolzhnoe*). The intuition of a meaning of life is, hence, the intuition, the metaphysical assumption, that there exists such as thing as the "unity of all." The absolute is the integral unity of all.[27] And it is the Christian worldview that according to Trubetskoi allows us to discover this unity in full and that therefore prompts us to strive for fullness. The absolute idea is not only about what "exists" (*sushchee*): it is also the divine intention (*Bozhii zamysel*) about what should be, an intention that applies to humanity directly. As noted above, the absolute for Trubetskoi is thought, the implication being that it is both reality and a

---

25. Trubetskoi, *Smysl zhizni*, 37.
26. Trubetskoi, *Smysl zhizni*, 60, 69.
27. See Evlampiev, "Problema," 44.

project. Trubetskoi's providentialist understanding of history corresponds to this belief in the human contribution to all-unity.

Hence, the philosophical quest for the meaning of life is also a religious quest for Trubetskoi. And Christianity is understood by Trubetskoi—again following Soloviev—as the religion of divine humanity, which bestows upon humanity the providentialist task of participating in God's creation (*tvorchestvo*), conceptualized by Trubetskoi as a process of an extended creative act (*tvorcheskii akt*). The human role is formulated by Trubetskoi in a more modest way than by Soloviev, Bulgakov, and Berdyaev: The human being "participates" in this plan as a "mediator" and "channel." According to Trubetskoi, God sees the human being as a "friend," whereby he plays on the similarity in Russian between the words for "other" (*drugoi*) and "friend" (*drug*), so that the task for the human being becomes to develop from "other" to "friend." The relationship between the divine and human is, or should be, a "friendship," and a genuine friendship is possible since humanity is free to reject it. The human being is a free "collaborator" in a divinely conceived project. Another term that is part of the same rhetorical repertoire is "co-participant" (*souchastnik*). The human being is a co-participant in the "creative act" that aims at perfectibility—a creative act that stretches out in and is enabled by time (history).[28]

This idea of divine-human collaboration through creativity, then, is also Trubetskoi's understanding of deification (*obozhenie, theosis*). Like the works of Soloviev, Bulgakov, and Berdyaev referred to above, *The Meaning of Life*, too, is a book that seeks to reinterpret the traditional Christian-Orthodox idea of deification. Deification for Trubetskoi means perfection of creation, involving the realization of "God's image" as the divine intention to be discovered and accepted as a task.[29] For Soloviev and Bulgakov it was *wisdom* that above all connected God and humanity. In order to characterize this purpose of history Trubetskoi, too, evokes the notion of Sophia, but in comparison to Soloviev and Bulgakov, Trubeskoi pays more attention to grace as a precondition for deification. In Trubetskoi's view, Soloviev and Bulgakov went too far in seeing the fulfillment of creation, or the end of the world, as the task of humanity alone. He criticized Soloviev for depicting the utopian ideal of the "Kingdom of God" as an exclusively human project. By the same token, he maintained the traditional Orthodox distinction between God and world, seeing the philosophy of Soloviev as too pantheistic and gnostic. However, there is a flipside to this. As Berdyaev pointed out in his review of Trubetskoi's Soloviev book, Trubetskoi, by distinguishing so

28. Trubetskoi, *Smysl zhizni*, 53, 81, 84.
29. Trubetskoi, *Smysl zhizni*, 84, 104.

firmly between the heavenly and earthly spheres, theologically legitimizes the secularization of culture. The rejection of pantheism leads to deism, Berdyaev claimed. For Trubetskoi, however, this makes humanity free to choose a Christian life.[30] For as Ludwig Wenzler has pointed out, the religious (Christian) interpretation of the meaning of life does not follow in a compulsory way from Trubetskoi's idealist framework, but is an option that, in his view, offers an understanding of the fullness of life and thus represents the better alternative.[31]

Christianity as an Idealist Project

Trubetskoi sees deification as achieved both in the human mind and in human action filled with creative "energy." Towards the end of the work, Trubetskoi mentions culture, science, art, and social activity as examples of how human beings may work towards their own deification, but action, and creative action (*tvorcheskoe delo*), means for Trubetskoi first and foremost "serving" (*sluzhenie*)—of humanity, the homeland or the closest human beings. It is through serving that humanity may reveal God's image on earth.[32] However, all this presupposes the activity of consciousness. And *The Meaning of Life* is a work that emphasizes the work of consciousness in order for life to become meaningful. The human being becomes a carrier of absolute thought by seeking the absolute through its cognitive acts.

> This [human] consciousness represents all-unity in potentiality; and as far as it recognizes and acquires truth it becomes all-unity in reality. Thus is the image and likeness of that all-unified (*vseedinoe*) consciousness accomplished in the human being, which carries within itself everything and is the truth about everything. This is the earthly likeness of the Almighty.[33]

Thus, deification for Trubetskoi is fulfilled in action but begins in our consciousness. "The thought of Christ [*Mysl o Khriste*], who appeared in flesh, expresses for the Christian the *main* task of culture—the ground that it is called to incarnate in life."[34] The divine intention is revealed for consciousness, becoming thereby human knowledge (*so-znanie*). This

---

30. Trubetskoi, *Mirosozertsanie V. S. Solov'eva*; Berdiaev, "O zemnom i nebesnom utopizme," 51–52.
31. Wenzler, "Poniatie," 30, 32.
32. Trubetskoi, *Smysl zhizni*, 212, 219–20.
33. Trubetskoi, *Smysl zhizni*, 135.
34. Trubetskoi, *Smysl zhizni*, 212.

depends on the human recognition of itself as a "friend" and "active participant in the creative act." The awareness and acceptance of this role and position, then, enables the human realization of the "image of the Creator." Religion means to connect, Trubetskoi reminds his readers (even more explicitly than Soloviev did)—to connect, in the mind, with the absolute and with other human beings.[35]

Trubetskoi proclaims that there is a "coincidence" (*sovpadenie*) between philosophical or "natural" revelation and religious revelation of the absolute truth of the Bible. For Trubetskoi logic reflects Logos. The form of thought is the form of Truth. In contrast to Berdyaev, he sees discursive thought in positive terms as an expression of the absolute. "The calling of human thought is to live in the atmosphere of the eternal Word that creates the world and to be the instrument for its revelation." In fact, Christianity is for Trubetskoi a religion that confirms the significance of the logical form of thought. A Christian philosophy, which is what Trubetskoi engages in himself, is justified by "the active participation by the human mind in attaining knowledge of God." And as with Soloviev, Trubetskoi, too, sees the contemplation of ideas as crucial for realizing them and thereby attaining the goal of divinized humanity: "Divine humanity is the discovery of the genuine idea-entity for the entire humanity."[36]

Trubetskoi's focus on consciousness is noteworthy in a work that is otherwise held to be informed by a "Platonic orientation."[37] This was how Vasilii Zenkovsky described Trubetskoi's philosophical project. While Trubetskoi's quest for meaning has indeed a Platonic character, its idealism is first and foremost of a modern kind. We should keep in mind that the topic of the book is the *meaning* of life. Hence it is a question of perception, of how to enable a meaningful perspective on life. This is also what idealism offers: to attain a firm ground by means of our mind, a point from which different options for how life may be perceived as meaningful may be considered.

An Apocalyptic Work?

The context of *The Meaning of Life* was catastrophic, and Trubetskoi, like so many other of his contemporaries, saw the catastrophic events around him as signs of the times, signifying an imminent end. At first glance, the

35. Trubetskoi, *Smysl zhizni*, 135, 192.
36. Trubetskoi, *Smysl zhizni*, 187, 212, 216. Berdyaev expresses his negative view of "discursive thought" several times in his autobiography, see Berdyaev, *Dream*, 211, 219, 289.
37. Zenkovsky, *History*, 806.

conclusion of the work seems to confirm the prevailing apocalyptic mood of Revolutionary Russia and the expectation of a rapidly approaching divine judgment. The kingdom of God is close, Trubetskoi proclaims. However, *The Meaning of Life* also displays an opposite tendency. The experience of crisis should foster, Trubetskoi believes, positive work. And the "Second Coming" will not take place until humanity has sufficiently prepared for it—in a positive sense. It needs to reach the sufficient level of maturity (*sozret'*).[38] And although Trubetskoi criticized Soloviev's understanding of Divine Humanity as a utopian human project, *The Meaning of Life*, too, announces that there will be no "end of world" without human preparation for it. Thus, Trubetskoi's own philosophy was not devoid of utopianism. On this basis, the apocalyptic situation in which this work was written, and which it even reinforces discursively, cannot be said to signify the end of history; rather, humanity was seemingly very far from attaining divine likeness at the time of its writing. This made it all the more important to write *The Meaning of Life*, a work that called for a fundamental spiritual reorientation and a recognition of the crucial importance of logical thinking in order to accomplish ethical tasks.

The leads us to the final point that this article would like to raise: Trubetskoi is often considered "more Orthodox" in comparison with the predecessors mentioned earlier in this article: Vladimir Soloviev, Sergei Bulgakov, Nikolai Berdyaev, and others.[39] He was more faithful to the classic dogmas of Orthodox theology and toned down to some extent the emphasis the others placed on human creativity and culture as an expression of divine likeness. Trubetskoi's understanding of deification was more modest, while at the same time emphasizing the importance of tasks, without which the divine intention will not be accomplished. However, Trubetskoi's idealism was anything but traditionally Orthodox. It was a response to modernity and a response that made active use of the possibilities of modernity. Without making any claims about his personal religious experience, I have in this chapter tried to argue that Trubetskoi's belief in a religious meaning of life, as it appears in his final philosophical work *The Meaning of Life*, was an answer to a quest that was handled by means of logical, discursive and dialectical reasoning, and by the solutions offered by idealist philosophy. It is a work that hereby confirms Charles Taylor's

---

38. Trubetskoi, *Smysl zhizni*, 214, 217. Trubetskoi's formulations towards the end of *The Meaning of Life* leave it open, in my view, whether the "Second Coming" is to be read concretely or symbolically, i.e., as referring to humanity's attaining of an ethical goal of divine origin.

39. See Evlampiev, "Problema," 12, 41, 47.

description of the "secular age" as a situation where religiosity and belief have become one option among many.[40]

Bibliography

Berdiaev, Nikolai A. "O zemnom i nebesnom utopizme (Po povodu knigi kn. Evgeniia Trubetskogo 'Mirosozertsanie Vl. Solov'eva')." *Russkaia mysl'* 9 (1913) 46–54.
Berdyaev, Nicolas. *Dream and Reality: An Essay in Autobiography*. Translated by Katharine Lampert. New York: Macmillan, 1951.
———. *The Meaning of the Creative Act*. Translated by Donald A. Lowrie. New York: Harper, 1955.
Bulgakov, Sergei. *Philosophy of Economy: The World as Household*. Translated by Catherine Evtuhov. New Haven: Yale University Press, 2000.
Evlampiev, Igor I. "Problema soedineniia zemnogo i bozhestvennogo v filosofskom tvorchestve E. N. Trubetskogo." In *Evgenii Nikolaevich Trubetskoi*, edited by Sergei M. Polovinkin and Tat'iana G. Shchedrina, 10–57. Moscow: ROSSPEN, 2014.
———. *Russkaia filosofiia v evropeiskom kontekste*. St. Petersburg: RKhGA, 2017.
Evtuhov, Catherine. *The Cross and the Sickle: Sergei Bulgakov and the Fate of Russian Religious Philosophy*. Ithaca: Cornell University Press, 1997.
Gaidenko, Piama P. *Vladimir Solov'ev i filosofiia Serebrianogo veka*. Moscow: Progress Traditsiia, 2001.
Hughes, H. Stuart. *Consciousness and Society: The Reorientation of European Social Thought, 1890–1930*. New York: Vintage, 1958.
Mjør, Kåre Johan. "Metaphysics, Aesthetics or Epistemology? A Conceptual History of *tvorchestvo* in Nineteenth-Century Russian Thought." *Slavic and East European Journal* 62.1 (2018) 4–25.
Plotnikov, Nikolai S. "Filosofiia 'Problem idealizma'." In *Problemy idealizma*, edited by Modest Kolerov, 5–60. Moscow: Modest Kolerov and "Tri kvadrata," 2002.
Poole, Randall A. "The Neo-Idealist Reception of Kant in the Moscow Psychological Society." *Journal of the History of Ideas* 60.2 (1999) 319–43.
———. "Religion, War, and Revolution: E. N. Trubetskoi's Liberal Construction of Russian National Identity, 1912–1920." *Kritika: Explorations in Russian and Eurasian History* 7.2 (2006) 195–240.
———. "Utopianism, Idealism, Liberalism: Russian Confrontations with Vladimir Solov'ev." *Modern Greek Studies Yearbook* 16.17 (2000–2001) 43–87.
Singer, Peter. *Hegel*. Oxford: Oxford University Press, 1983.
Solov'ev, Vladimir S. "Kritika otvlechennykh nachal." In *Sochineniia*, 581–831. Vol. 2. Moscow: Mysl', 1988.
Solovyov, Vladimir. *Lectures on Divine Humanity*. Hudson, NY: Lindisfarne, 1995.
Sprigge, Timothy L. S. "Idealism: German Absolute Idealism." In *Routledge Encyclopedia of Philosophy*. DOI. 10.4324/9780415249126-N027-1.
Taylor, Charles. *A Secular Age*. Cambridge, MA: Belknap, 2007.
Trubetskoi, Evgenii N. *Mirosozertsanie V. S. Solov'eva*. 2 vols. Moscow: Medium, 1995.
———. *Smysl zhizni*. Moscow: Respublika, 1994.
———. "Staryi i novyi natsional'nyi messianizm." *Russkaia mysl'* 3 (1912) 12–15.

40. Taylor, *A Secular Age*, 1–22.

Trubetskoi, Sergei, N. "Osnovaniia idealizma." In *Sochineniia*, 595–717. Moscow: Mysl', 1994.

Wenzler, Ludwig. "Poniatie 'smysl zhizni' v filosofii Vladimira Solov'eva i Evgeniia Trubetskogo." *Voprosy filosofii* 11 (2007) 21–32.

Zenkovsky, Vasily V. *A History of Russian Philosophy*. Vol. 2. Translated by George L. Kline. London: Routledge & Paul, 1953.

Zernov, Nicolas. *The Russian Religious Renaissance of the Twentieth Century*. London: Darton, Longman & Todd, 1963.

4

Vladimir Soloviev and Evgenii Trubetskoi

A Survey of an Intellectual Relationship about Theocracy, Freedom, and Divine-Humanity

JEREMY PILCH

In a recently published biographical study of Sergei Trubetskoi, there is a photo of him and Vladimir Soloviev. It depicts the two men standing together, Soloviev with an avuncular arm round Trubetskoi's shoulder.[1] This indication of friendship and mentoring on the part of Soloviev is equally valid as an expression of Soloviev's relationship to the slightly younger Prince Evgenii Trubetskoi. The latter first met Soloviev in the winter of 1886–1887 at the Moscow home of the philosopher Lev Lopatin. He recalls the meeting in his posthumously published memoirs, explaining that they were immediately shouting at each other, in a heated argument about Soloviev's theocratic project. United by a common belief in *Bogochelovechestvo*, however, "as the principle of the communal life of the Church, the content and goal of universal history," the heat of the argument subsided and they ended the evening laughing and joking like old friends as they indeed remained, although the arguments about the relationship of Orthodoxy to Catholicism and the papacy always returned, only to be followed by a swift and deep reconciliation.[2]

Trubetskoi explains in the opening of his 1913 work on Soloviev that he was unable to write a reflection for the 1901 collection of reminiscences about the religious philosopher which his brother compiled because of "a

---

1. Ermishin, *Kniaz' S. N. Trubetskoi*, 111.

2. Trubetskoi, *Vospominaniia*, 192–93. This book is reprinted in Trubetskoi, *Iz proshlogo. Vospominaniia*.

kind of powerful obstacle" which did not allow him to separate himself from his mentor.³ He was unable to distinguish his own worldview from that of Soloviev. Up to 1913, he explains, "all my views developed in communion with him, i.e. in part with his influence, in part in a struggle against this influence."⁴ Soloviev's conciliatory attitude to Roman Catholicism, his negative judgment about Eastern Orthodoxy, and his idea of "universal theocracy" always prompted grave doubts in Trubetskoi. These led to

> my studies of the religious-social ideal of western Christianity. . . . The historical task to which I devoted myself in these works (the explanation of the essence of "the theocratic idea" of the western Church), as any attentive reader will notice, led me to a dogmatic result—to a decisive negative judgement about medieval Latin theocracy and to an evaluation of Roman Catholicism in general as a one-sided form of legal Christianity.⁵

This paper will examine these two early works on Western theocracy by Trubetskoi and some connections they suggest with the thought of Soloviev in the last decade of his life. It will conclude by trying to open up the question of theocracy, divine-humanity and liberalism in contemporary terms.

Originating as a master's dissertation, Trubetskoi's work on Augustine is, of course, also an important work in its own right. It is also one example of the still under-appreciated Russian *ressourcement* of the nineteenth century. Beginning in 1841, an ambitious translation programme of patristic writings into Russian was undertaken in the four theological academies in Moscow, St. Petersburg, Kiev, and Kazan. The Latin Fathers were allocated to the academy at Kiev. Fr. Cyprian Kern, in his invaluable reference work on this project, *Les Traductions russes des texts patristiques: Guide bibliographique*, published over half a century ago, reveals that the complete works of Augustine were published in eight volumes under the direction of Afanasii I. Bulgakov between 1879 and 1895.⁶ This is not to say that Trubetskoi was dependent on this translation project, or even necessarily familiar with it, only to situate this work within an increasing body of Russian patristic scholarship. As Myroslaw Tataryn notes, together with this work of translation twelve different studies of Augustine were published between 1870 and 1914.⁷ By no means were these studies all critical of Augustine; indeed, Tataryn concludes that "[t]he nineteenth-century

---

3. Trubetskoi, *Mirosozertsanie Vladimira Solovieva*, vi.
4. Trubetskoi, *Mirosozertsanie Vladimira Solovieva*, iii.
5. Trubetskoi, *Mirosozertsanie Vladimira Solovieva*, iv.
6. Kern, *Traductions*.
7. Tataryn, *Augustine*, 15. Trubetskoi's work is among those mentioned by Tataryn.

Russian presentation of Augustine was not a conscious attempt to establish distance between Russian Orthodox thought and one of the foundation stones of Western theology, but was rather appreciative of his contribution to what was perceived as the common Christian tradition."[8] Like many of these other Russian scholars of Augustine, Trubetskoi read Augustine in the original Latin for his research, and drew primarily upon contemporary German and French scholarship in his evaluation of the great Latin father. In addition, like his brother Sergei Nikolaevich, who had attended Harnack's lectures in Berlin and become friends with the preeminent Protestant historian of dogma, the younger Trubetskoi's theological views were increasingly shaped by liberal Protestant scholarship.

By contrast, Soloviev had been influenced much more by Catholic historical scholarship and exegesis in the 1880s. Nikolai Kotrelev has demonstrated that Soloviev was much impressed by the work of Johannes Janssen (1829–1891), the German Catholic priest and historian, devoting a lengthy article to a review of his work which was published in *Pravoslavnoe obozrenie* in August 1885.[9] In addition, Soloviev's 1886 essay on the *Didache*, the Teaching of the Twelve Apostles, which his brother had translated into Russian, shows him more accurately dating the recently discovered document of the early Church than Harnack. With regard to divine-humanity, or deification, it is worth bearing in mind that Harnack was part of the liberal German school which was sharply critical of this teaching, considering it a Hellenization of Christianity. Therefore, in terms of *Bogochelovechestvo*, Harnack was not a sympathetic influence on the brothers Trubetskoi. Significantly, Soloviev's nephew and biographer calls Trubetskoi "a moderate liberal, a Protestantized Orthodox . . . a typical, solid representative of liberal Orthodoxy."[10] Arguably, Trubetskoi's critique of Soloviev's support of the Papacy can by viewed as informed as much by Protestant criticism as by Orthodox.

In Trubetskoi's assessment Augustine was never able to fully overcome the dualism of his youth. With regard to Augustine's ethical worldview Trubetskoi argues that, "the human element is belittled, doomed to a purely passive role, which is why in his system there is no place for human freedom."[11] Between the two poles of the force of evil in perverted human nature and the invincible force of grace, Trubetskoi claims that for Augustine, "the

8. Tataryn, *Augustine*, 15–24, quotation at 24. Tataryn focuses in particular on the work of Skvortsov, *Blazhennyi Avgustin*, although he also singles out as impressive the work of Guseyev, *Antropologicheskiia*.

9. See Kotrelev, "Eskhatologiia."

10. Solovyov, *Life*, 409.

11. Trubetskoi, *Filosofiia khristianskoi teokratii v V veke*, 17–18.

human being is nothing: his freedom is entirely swallowed up from below or above, everything going into sin or grace."[12] In this analysis Trubetskoi wasn't necessarily drawing on a specifically Slavophile type of Orthodox critique of Augustine. Even those nineteenth-century Russian works about Augustine which were irenic rather than polemical in spirit recognized "very many negative thoughts about our freedom."[13] Interestingly Yves Congar, drawing on the little known and much neglected study of Aurelius Palmieri, suggests that after Soloviev's criticisms of the Slavophiles, which were "to a great extent well founded," the distinctions between the Christian East and West were more accurately defined, with Trubetskoi taking a leading role: "It was towards the end of the Nineteenth Century and following the new ways opened by the Slavophiles, that anthropological differences and religious peculiarities were systematized. Prince Eugene Troubetskoy seems to have been the first to do it with scope and penetration."[14]

At the same time, however, it is hard not to see something of a less irenic approach, characteristic of the Slavophiles, in Trubetskoi's work. In one of very few studies of Trubetskoi which considers closely these two early works by Trubetskoi on Western Christianity, Igor Evlampiev sees Trubetskoi's works as continuing the criticism of Catholic teaching begun by the Slavophiles and argues further that "Trubetskoi's reflections about the shortcomings of Western Christianity had great influence on Russian thinkers at the beginning of the twentieth century, who continued and augmented his criticism."[15] It seems reasonable to think that the origins of the one-sided presentation of "negative" Western anthropology in the work of leading Orthodox scholars from Myrhha Lot-Borodine to Metropolitan Kallistos Ware can be traced in part to Trubetskoi's critique of Augustine and its subsequent influence.[16] Certainly that critique recalls Kireevskii's view in his 1852 essay "On the Nature of European Culture and on Its Relationship to Russian Culture":

> of all the Church Fathers, both early and late, surely no one had so marked a predilection for the logical concatenation of truths

---

12. Trubetskoi, *Filosofiia khristianskoi teokratii v V veke*, 18.

13. Skvortsov, cited in Tataryn, *Augustine*, 20. For a balanced contemporary overview of the theme of freedom in Augustine see the article: Djuth, "Liberty," 495–98.

14. Congar, *After*, 47. Congar draws here upon the chapter on Trubetskoi in Aurelio Palmieri, *Theologia*, 155–59.

15. Evlampiev, "Problema," 37.

16. Typically this is a fruit of conflating a "Western" Catholicism and a Calvinist Augustinianism, or seeing Catholicism as "Western," thus consciously or otherwise adopting Slavophile categories. See Ware, *Orthodox Church*, 212–18; Lot-Borodine, *Déification*, 47–52.

as St. Augustine, most often called the Teacher of the West. Some of his works are like an iron chain of syllogisms, each link fitting seamlessly into the next. Perhaps for this reason he occasionally allowed himself to become too carried away, and for all the outer harmony he failed to notice the inner one-sidedness of his thought, so that in the last years of his life he found himself obliged to write a refutation of his own earlier assertions.[17]

Trubetskoi explains that the attempt to overcome the dualist position of the Manichaean system was the "living nerve of Augustine's philosophy" and in meeting St. Ambrose, he met someone who "personifie[d] in himself the Church not only as an external unity but as an intellectual order, as an organic, interior unity."[18] The Donatist schism prompted Augustine to focus on preserving Church unity above all else; in this way he becomes, according to Trubetskoi, swayed by judicial, Latin sentiments and defends the Church-state alliance against the anti-church and anti-state Donatists. Similarly, the threat of the Pelagian heresy lay

> in the denial of organic social unity and in rebellion against the mystical, organized action of grace. For the sake of the salvation of society this destructive principle must be forcibly curbed and suppressed: for the masses, the collective unity of the Church organism can only be compulsory, forced. This explains the peculiarities of Augustine's teaching about grace.[19]

Thus, in arguing for external Church unity, Augustine "laid the foundations for medieval Catholic theocracy," leaving in his magnum opus the blueprint for this project: "The City of God is that ideal plan, the programme which medieval Catholicism sought to accomplish."[20] In short, Trubetskoi considered Augustine's teaching a false representation of Christianity, a denial of divine-humanity.

In contrast to Trubetskoi, Soloviev did not view Augustine's teaching about grace, or more broadly that of the Western Catholic tradition, an obstacle to divine-humanity. Shortly before returning to Russia in the late 1880s, for example, Soloviev wrote to Eugène Tavernier from Krakow that "he had read Molina's *De Concordia gratiae cum libero arbitrio* and the posthumous work of Cardinal Franzelin *De Ecclesia Christi*."[21] The work of the

17. Kireevsky, "On the Nature," 202.
18. Trubetskoi, *Filosofiia khristianskoi teokratii v V veke*, 40.
19. Trubetskoi, *Filosofiia khristianskoi teokratii v V veke*, 79.
20. Trubetskoi, *Filosofiia khristianskoi teokratii v V veke*, 143–44.
21. Soloviev, "Lettre," 331.

Jesuit Luis de Molina (1535–1600) was a crucial starting point for any post-Reformation Catholic theology of the relationship between grace and free will.[22] Soloviev's sure grasp of the theological themes involved is revealed in Brockhaus-Efron articles about free will that he wrote in the 1890s. Here he praises particularly St. Bernard on the question of free will as well as singling out the position of Francisco Suarez SJ (1548–1617), who developed Molina's ideas further with the idea of congruent grace. *Justification of the Good* reflects the influence of Augustine, as Soloviev himself suggested in response to a review of his work: "[T]he writer points out in a blissful state of ignorance of Saint Augustine, who wrote twenty-two books in justification of Divine Providence, that the justification of the Good is 'against nature.'"[23] Ernst Radlov devoted nearly half his biographical sketch to *Justification*, and addresses a number of significant points including the influence of St. Augustine, especially with regard to free will.[24] For Soloviev's nephew and biographer, Sergei Mikhailovich Soloviev, the final period of Soloviev's life, "beginning with *The Justification of the Good*, recalls the waning years of Augustine, when the bishop of Hippo worked out his doctrine of grace in his struggle with Pelagius." In particular he argues that in the treatise "Soloviev adopts Augustine's position with regard to free will."[25]

An Augustinian treatment of grace and free will is indeed evident in *Justification of the Good*. Towards the end of the work, Soloviev explains the operation of grace in his handling of the conversion of the Roman centurion Cornelius. It is immediately apparent that he accepts the Augustinian notion of prevenient grace: "The specifically-human actions conformable to the grace of God (*and caused by its preliminary influence*) must obviously express man's normal relation to God, to men, and to his own material nature, in accordance with the three general foundations of morality—piety, pity, and shame."[26] A similar acceptance of an Augustinian position is evident in his Brockhaus article on free will with regard to Pelagius:

> In such a way the good is possible for man only by the action of the divine principle, revealing itself in man and though him but not from him. Such action is called *grace*. Already for someone to want the help of grace it is necessary that grace itself has acted

---

22. Trubetskoi does mention the Jesuits in his study of Augustine, seeing "the restoration of the Pelagian principle as the characteristic mark of the theological teaching of the Jesuits." Trubetskoi, *Ideal zapadnogo khristianstva v V veke*, 191.

23. Soloviev, "Sunday Letters," 77.

24. See Radlov, "V. S. Solov'ev," xxxv–xxxvi.

25. Solovyov, *Life*, 491.

26. Soloviev, *Justification*, 378. My italics.

in him; by his personal efforts not only can he not do or fulfil the good, but he cannot even desire or seek it.[27]

It seems reasonable to assume, therefore, that Trubetskoi's work on Augustine did not prevent his mentor from appreciating the work of the great Latin Father and integrating aspects of his thought into his own great work on ethics.

With regard to Trubetskoi's work on Pope St. Gregory VII and eleventh-century Western theocracy, Soloviev wrote a valuable review in which he praises Trubetskoi as a gifted young scholar for this important contribution to recent Russian historical literature. One of the most significant aspects of Trubetskoi's study is that it radically challenged existing notions of Church and state in the Middle Ages. Soloviev explains:

> Usually the struggle of Gregory VII against Henry is presented as a typical example of the antagonism between spiritual power and worldly power. Prince Trubetskoi's extremely convincing images and deductions necessitate a radical change in such a view. Worldly power in our current sense in general did not exist in the Middle Ages, and the German Empire less than any other order could correspond to such an understanding. Ecclesial power and state power equally have a holy character and both also have spiritual sides indistinguishably linked to the material.[28]

The basic thrust of Trubetskoi's work on medieval theocracy is for Soloviev an important corrective to modern accounts of the period, which fundamentally distort it by applying modern categories that make no sense in a historical period when Christianity underpinned everything.

Where Soloviev finds fault with Trubetskoi is largely confined to the specifics of the ecclesial world of medieval Catholicism. For example, he observes that "the medieval understanding about papal power is outlined without sufficient theological accuracy," arguing that Trubetskoi's account of the medieval idea of papal power expressed in the letters of Gregory VII does not sufficiently distinguish between "the interest of personal piety and the interest of the practical tasks of theocracy."[29] "Prince Trubetskoi claims that for medieval believers the Apostle Peter as it were obscures Christ," Soloviev notes, adding that "this may be just with regard to the public side of the Church; here Christ is obscured by Peter, just as Peter in

---

27. Solov'ev, "Retsenziia," 353.
28. Solov'ev, "Retsenziia," 352.
29. Solov'ev, "Retsenziia," 353.

his turn is obscured by the pope."³⁰ But for Soloviev the key thing is what Trubetskoi misses:

> [N]ext to Christ in the middle ages stands not Peter and not the Pope but only the Mother of God. Here is a remarkable and decisive fact: in the "legal" structure of medieval theocracy there is no place for the Madonna and our author does not mention one word about her, it appears, but in the actual medieval religion She is inarguably first.³¹

Soloviev raises a further point regarding Trubetskoi's mischaracterisation of the papal office, which he presents

> as if the rank itself of the pope makes its carrier a holy man. The extent to which this is unfounded is already clear from the fact that the Catholic Church in the middle ages, like now, recognizes some popes as saints, consequently thereby declaring the rest of the popes non-saints.³²

Trubetskoi, of course, expresses similar misgiving about Gregory VII as he does about Augustine. The concluding words of his book are cited by Soloviev in his review and summarize Trubetskoi's overall position:

> So far as Gregory VII and other teachers of the middle ages demand legal order not only inside separate states but also in the international sphere, and so far as they want all peoples to develop into a "peaceful community of truth," they undoubtedly stand on the ground of universal Christian principles. But in so far as the domination of one power, one law over humanity, serves for them as a higher aim, and they equate the "divine kingdom" with the external hierarchical organization and mix the legal order with the order of grace, then their Christianity is a "legalistic" one-sided Christianity.³³

Soloviev sees this overall evaluation as misguided and asks:

> In what way could Gregory VII and other teachers of the middle ages consider papal monarchy as a higher aim? Had they renounced the Christian dogma about the second coming of Christ and about the life of the future ages, where there will no

---

30. Solov'ev, "Retsenziia," 353.
31. Solov'ev, "Retsenziia," 353.
32. Solov'ev, "Retsenziia," 353.
33. Trubetskoi, *Ideal zapadnogo khristianstva v XI veke*, 363.

other power apart from God's and where this divine power coincides with love?[34]

The sort of legalistic prioritizing of papal power over all else that Trubetskoi argues for is nonsensical, according to Soloviev, in view of the eschatological sensitivities of the age. He develops this criticism fully and persuasively:

> These Christians, not excepting Gregory VII, unceasingly awaited the end of the world and the final judgment. It is psychologically impossible in such expectation—the serious character of which our author fully acknowledges—to think and act for the manifestation on earth of any kind of normal order when now or tomorrow "this earth and all its affairs" must burn away. In the view of the people of the middle ages the last times had already arrived, the universal catastrophe had already begun. Who, seeing that a fire had already begun in their house, would begin to think about putting the house in order, about its best furnishing and decoration? But how should one explain the tireless and immense activity of Gregory VII for the sake of the whole Christian world? He himself gives the explanation in the biblical words by which, before his death, he expressed the meaning of his life: "I love truth and hate disorder, for the sake of which I die in exile." He lived not for the accomplishment of any kind of ideal, but because he loved truth and hated lawlessness. *Dilexi justitiam et odi iniquitatem*—here is sufficient motive for the activity of such a man. The truth does not lose its force even on the eve of the final judgment, when there cannot be any talk of an earthly idea. . . . The medieval world felt itself lying deeply in extreme evil and the struggle with this evil was not "an ideal" but simply the moral duty of all Christians. The scope and character of the struggle was defined providentially by the personal situation of each. Called, as he believed, by the personal will of God to be the higher representative of the whole Christian world in these worst of times, Gregory VII had to defend truth in the whole universe, obeying the higher authority given to him—of course not expecting the actual accomplishment of the ideal order on this earth, which for him was a double earthly exile, but which by his conviction he would not have to live through for very long himself.[35]

---

34. Solov'ev, "Retsenziia," 353.
35. Solov'ev, "Retsenziia," 353.

This evaluation of Gregory VII by Soloviev resonates strongly with that much cited apparent contradiction in his own work: between the optimism of *Justification of the Good* and the apocalyptic tenor of his final work which includes the Second Coming of Christ in his superb *Short Story of the Antichrist*.

One should note Soloviev's view of the inappropriateness of the terminology of "religious-social ideal" being applied to the work of the papacy at this time. These expressions, which play a big role in Trubetskoi's work, simply "did not exist in medieval terminology." He adds: "It would still not be a misfortune, if there had existed at that time something which corresponded to their meaning. But there wasn't and couldn't be."[36] The reason is that "in the Christian faith the true order of life or its construction . . . is found precisely only beyond the limits of earthly existence."[37] Soloviev acknowledges that for Christians of modern times, "although also believing in future blessedness but not occupied entirely by the thought of it, there could be a representation about the *relatively* better social order also on this earth." But "for Christians of the eleventh-century there could not be even such a relative and provisional 'ideal' for the reasons our author thoroughly speaks about in his final chapter, namely because these Christians, not excepting Gregory VII, unceasingly awaited the end of the world and the final judgment."[38]

Finally, Soloviev defends the practical activity of Gregory VII as directed "not to a higher aim but to the lower necessities of everyday social life. Among the medieval chaos, in the rule of force and injustice, church power in its worthy representatives needed to have a legal character."[39] It wasn't the legal character of the Church that was the "principal deficiency of the medieval system," Soloviev argues, but "the inescapable collision of two higher powers" and the fact that there was no "third organ of theocracy" to mediate between the king and the pope.

While Soloviev criticizes Trubetskoi for sometimes being anachronistic in projecting modern terminology upon the medieval world system, he commends his analysis of investitures, one of Gregory VII's key areas of reform. Contrary to the mistaken modern interpretation, which presents the struggle of Gregory VII against Henry as a case of antagonism between spiritual power and worldly power, Trubetskoi takes the view that the investiture controversy was "not a struggle between church and

---

36. Solov'ev, "Retsenziia," 352–53.
37. Solov'ev, "Retsenziia," 353.
38. Solov'ev, "Retsenziia," 353. Emphasis in original.
39. Solov'ev, "Retsenziia," 354.

state, but the clash of two forms or two organs of theocracy, a struggle between a royal priesthood and a holy kingdom."[40] The conflict, he says, "was first of all a question about the mutual relationship of the two heads of theocracy—about the rights of holy power over royal, and about the holy authority of royal power."[41]

Given Trubetskoi's trenchant overall opposition to the idea of a unity of Church and state, it is ironic that his recognition of two sacred powers in operation in the Middle Ages resonates powerfully with a groundbreaking 2017 work on medieval history by Andrew Willard Jones, *Before Church and State: A Study of Social Order in the Sacramental Kingdom of St. Louis IX*. This study of medieval society two centuries after St. Gregory VII argues persuasively that "thirteenth-century France was not a world of the secular and the religious vying for position and power, but a world in which the material and the spiritual were totally dependent on each other."[42] Willard Jones attempts to draw out some of the conclusions of his historical research for modern society.

> The story of sovereignty, the story of Church and State, and the story of the religious and the secular are, therefore, totally bound up together as interlacing plotlines in the same meta-narrative. This whole discourse is, I believe, ultimately ideological, an explication of the modern West's legitimacy.[43]

Ultimately a question arises about the very existence of the secular, which is seemingly taken for granted as the status quo in Western liberal democracy.

How are we to regard the thought of Trubetskoi and Soloviev—both aware of the essential falseness of the application of modern terminology to the medieval period—in the light of this tension, namely that *Bogochelovechestvo* cannot fit into the categories of modern political thought and sovereignty? Can divine-humanity be adapted to fit a society where there is a separation of Church and state? Surely, theologically speaking, the idea of the secular is a lie; as Soloviev says in *Justification*, it would be impious to consider anything as existing outside the reach of grace.[44] The whole thrust

---

40. Trubetskoi, *Ideal zapadnogo khristianstva v XI veke*, 1, 94.
41. Trubetskoi, *Ideal zapadnogo khristianstva v XI veke*, 96.
42. Jones, *Before Church*, 2.
43. Jones, *Before Church*, 15.
44. See Soloviev, *Justification*, 4: "[T]hough piety requires us to admit that the power for the realization of the good is given from God, it would be impious to limit the Deity with regard to the means whereby this power can be communicated." For an important rejoinder to Henri de Lubac and John Milbank, and the integralist position more broadly, see Mulcahy, *Pure Nature*.

of the teaching about *Bogochelovechestvo* is that it is—whether one puts the emphasis on it being the Church or universal humanity—the fruit of the Incarnation which has established a new ontological order of being. This is why, after the failure of his 1880s theocratic project, Soloviev still used the term free theocracy, which dates back to *Lectures on Divine-Humanity*, and why he argues in *Justification* that the purpose of the state is to freely serve the Church. Trubetskoi, in his 1913 work on Soloviev, criticizes him for using the term theocracy which typically implies force of some kind. Subsequently, in correspondence with Margarita Morozova, Trubetskoi rejects outright the whole concept of theocracy:

> I believe in the work of God and in the kingdom of God; but "theocracy" is only a human falsification; such an order where God only limits and contains evil, resorting to the worldly sword for this, is still not the kingdom of God; God can rule only *from within* and not from without. I think that external theocracy in the world in the sense of actual Divine-rule cannot and will not be, because it would be a brake on the work of salvation; humanity would rest in it, which would be the end of Christian progress.[45]

Ironically Trubetskoi here offers the perfect prism through which to understand Soloviev's *Justification of the Good*—the establishment of the rule of God from within, a free theocracy embraced through the proper exercise of moral choices. In practical terms this is one way, at least, albeit an extremely optimistic one—and here it resembles the "virtue politics" propounded by John Milbank in Britain—of maintaining the logic of divine-humanity. For Soloviev ultimately everything was directed to building the kingdom of God. The whole sphere of man's social existence can be sanctified, it can become divine-human, it can be deified, but for this to happen it can only be a free act, a free surrender to and cooperation with divine grace and this requires progress in the moral life of humanity on a dramatic scale.

Unlike Soloviev, Trubetskoi appears to push his understanding of *Bogochelovechestvo* into the transcendent sphere, almost to make room for the state. Perhaps here there is a prefiguration of Berdyaev's more eschatological treatment of the theme. Surely though, in this approach there is a danger of denying the very essence of *Bogochelovechestvo*, namely the Incarnation of Jesus Christ, who is "the redeemer of man" and "the centre of the universe and of history" as Pope St. John Paul II describes him, echoing Soloviev, at the beginning of his first encyclical, *Redemptor Hominis*.[46] It is always on the

---

45. Cited in Polovinkin, *Kniaz' E. N. Trubetskoi*, 19.
46. John Paul II, "Redemptor Hominis." Cf. Soloviev: "Christ . . . must subject

basis of the historical reality of the Incarnation that Soloviev builds his theocratic projects, whether ecclesial or ethical. Trubetskoi, on the other hand, seeks to separate church and state and refrains from "incarnational" politics. While the extent to which Trubetskoi's political views could cohere with his philosophical and religious perspective expressed in *The Meaning of Life* is a question beyond the remit of this paper, it goes without saying that his practical action, just like Soloviev's in the 1880s, ended in failure.

Bibliography

Congar, Yves. *After Nine Hundred Years: The Background of the Schism between the Eastern and Western Churches.* Translated at Fordham University's Russian Center with a Preface by Paul Mailleux. New York: Fordham University Press, 1959.

Djuth, Marianne. "Liberty." In *Augustine through the Ages: An Encyclopaedia*, edited by Allan D. Fitzgerald, 495–98. Grand Rapids, MI: Eerdmans, 1999.

Ermishin, Oleg T. *Kniaz' S. N. Trubetskoi: Zhizn' i filosofiia.* Moscow: Sinaksis, 2011.

Evlampiev, Igor I. "Problema soedineniia zemnogo i bozhestvennogo v filosofskom tvorchestvo E. N. Trubetskogo." In *Evgenii Nikolaevich Trubetskoi*, edited by Sergei M. Polovinkin and Tatiana G. Shchedrina, 10–57. Moscow: ROSSPEN, 2014.

Guseyev, Dmitrii. *Antropologicheskiia vozzreniia bl. Avgustina v sviazi s ucheniem Pelagianstva.* Kazan: Kazanskaya Dukhovnaya akademiya, 1876.

John Paul II. "Redemptor Hominis." http://w2.vatican.va/content/john-paul-ii/en/encyclicals/documents/hf_jp-ii_enc_04031979_redemptor-hominis.html.

Jones, Andrew Willard. *Before Church and State: A Study of Social Order in the Sacramental Kingdom of St. Louis IX.* Steubenville, OH: Emmaus Academic, 2017.

Kern, Cyprien. *Les Traductions russes des texts patristiques: Guide bibliographique.* Paris: Éditions de Chevetogne, 1957.

Kireevsky, Ivan. "On the Nature of European Culture and on its Relationship to Russian Culture. Letter to Count E. E. Komarovsky." In *On Spiritual Unity. A Slavophile Reader*, edited and translated by Boris Jakim and Robert Bird, 189–232. Hudson, NY: Lindisfarne, 1998.

Kotrelev, Nikolai. "Eskhatologiii u Vladimira Solovieva. (K istorii 'Trekh razgovorov')." http://www.intelros.ru/index.php?newsid=185.

Lot-Borodine, Myrrha. *La Déification de l'homme selon la doctrine des pères grecs.* Paris: Cerf, 1970.

Mulcahy, Bernard. *Aquinas's Notion of Pure Nature and the Christian Integralism of Henri de Lubac.* New York: Lang, 2011.

Palmieri, Aurelio. *Theologia dogmatica orthodoxa, II, Prolegomena.* Florence: Libreria Editrice Fiorentina, 1913.

Polovinkin, Sergei M. *Kniaz' E. N. Trubetskoi: Zhiznennyi i tvorcheskii put'.* Moscow: Sinaksis, 2010.

Radlov, Ernst. "V. S. Solov'ev. Biograficheskii ocherk." In *Sobranie sochinenii Vladimira Sergeevicha Solov'eva*, vii–li. Vol. 10. Bruxelles: Zhizn' s Bogom, 1966.

Himself to the same law of external being, and, from the centre of eternity, become the centre of history." Soloviev, *Lectures*, 155.

Skvortsov, Konstantin. *Blazhennyi Avgustin kak psikholog.* Kiev: Tip. Gub. Praw., 1870.

Solov'ev, Vladimir. "Retsenziia (*Vestnik Evropy.* Otdel—Literaturnoe Obozrenie, Aprel' 1897), 'Kn. Evgenii Trubetskoi, *Religiozno-obshchestvennyi ideal zapadnogo khristianstva v XI veke: Ideia bozheskogo tsarstva v tvoreniiakh Grigoriia VII-go i ego publitsistov—sovremennikov,* Kiev 1897.'" In *Sobranie sochinenii Vladimira Sergeevicha Solov'eva.* Vol. 12, 351–55. Bruxelles: Zhizn' s Bogom, 1966.

Soloviev, Vladimir. *The Justification of the Good: An Essay on Moral Philosophy.* Translated by Nathalie A. Duddington. New York: Macmillan, 1918.

———. *Lectures on Divine Humanity.* Translated by Peter Zouboff and Boris Jakim. Hudson, NY: Lindisfarne, 1995.

———. "Lettre à Eugène Tavernier de Cracovie (sans date, probablement janvier 1889)." In *La Sophia et les autres écrits français,* edited by François Rouleau, 331–32. Lausanne: L'Age d'Homme, 1978.

———. "Sunday Letters." In *Politics, Law, & Morality,* translated by Vladimir Wozniuk, 65–130. New Haven: Yale University Press, 2000.

Solovyov, Sergei M. *Vladimir Soloviev: His Life and Creative Evolution.* Translated by Aleksey Gibson. Parts 2 and 3. Fairfax, VA: Eastern Christian Publications, 2000.

Tataryn, Myroslaw I. *Augustine and Russian Orthodoxy: Russian Orthodox Theologians and Augustine of Hippo: A Twentieth-Century Dialogue.* Lanham, MD: International Scholars, 2000.

Trubetskoi, Evgenii N. *Filosofiia khristianskoi teokratii v V veke. Uchenie Blazhennogo Avgustina o grade Bozhiem.* Moscow: Librokom, 2012.

———. *Iz proshlogo. Vospominaniia. Iz putevikh zametok bezhentsa. Umozrenie v kraskakh.* Newtonville, MA: Oriental Research Partners, 1976.

———. *Mirosozertsanie Vladimira Solovieva.* Vol. 1. Moscow: Tovarishchestvo tip. A. I. Mamontova, 1913.

———. *Religiozno-Obshchestvennyi ideal zapadnogo khristianstva v V veke. Mirosozertsanie blazhennago Avgustina.* Moscow: Tip. E. Lissnera i Yu. Romana, 1892.

———. *Religiozno-obshchestvennyi ideal zapadnogo khristianstva v XI veke: Ideia bozheskogo tsarstva v tvoreniiakh Grigoriia VII-go i ego publitsistov—sovremennikov.* Kiev: Tip. S. V. Kul'zhenko, 1897.

———. *Vospominaniia.* Sofia: Rossisko-Bolgarskoe Knigoizdatelstvo, 1921.

Ware, Timothy. *The Orthodox Church: An Introduction to Eastern Christianity.* London: Penguin, 2015.

5

"I Am Experiencing a Real Image of All-Unity in You!"

The Reception of Vladimir Soloviev's Philosophy of Love in the "Loving Friendship" of Margarita Morozova and Evgenii Trubetskoi

ANATOLII CHERNYAEV

The "loving friendship" (*liubovnaia druzhba*) of Evgenii Trubetskoi and Margarita Morozova, whose history is known to us due to their preserved correspondence (unfortunately, not yet published in its entirety), is one of the most noteworthy facts—as well as factors—of Russian culture of the Silver Age. From the point of view of the history of philosophy, it is of interest in at least a few respects: first, as an integral moment of the spiritual and cultural movement known as the Russian religious-philosophical renaissance; secondly, as a revealing attempt to realize the ideas of the religious-philosophical renaissance, especially those of its inspirer Vladimir Soloviev, in personal life and love between a man and woman; and finally, as a creative dialogue in the process of which the philosophical works of Trubetskoi were born, written, discussed and, as a result, appeared.

Evgenii Nikolaevich Trubetskoi (1963–1920) came from a famous princely family. In the era of the development of Russian capitalism, the Trubetskois, like so many other aristocratic families, faced impoverishment, so they had to sell the family estate of Akhtyrka, the childhood home of Evgenii and his older brother Sergei. The golden age of the Russian nobility, when life was a continuous holiday with its balls, merry performances in the manor theater and idle literary and philosophical exercises, would forever remain in the past. The princely brothers, like simple commoners, were forced to seriously think about their daily bread and master a profession, which led them to Moscow University. Sergei Trubetskoi, who was more active by nature, became the first freely elected rector of the university in 1905, but died in the same turbulent year from a stroke. Evgenii's academic career was not so rapid: he spent two decades teaching in Yaroslavl and Kiev, and only in 1906 did he receive a professorship at his alma mater, where five years later he was forced to resign in protest against the government's violation of the principles of university autonomy, to which his elder brother had dedicated his last efforts. A bright portrait of Evgenii was left in the memoirs of his younger brother Grigory. According to him, Evgenii

> had some kind of a special simplicity—a gift of the God. He was like a huge uncouth granite boulder. Even in society he always sat as if there were no one around. He was a little like a primeval human. He never concealed any impressions or thoughts. Being alone or in society, he continued to live by the thought absorbing him, and boredom was too clearly written on his face, if the company in which he found himself did not meet his interests. . . . It was hard to imagine a more solid and immediate person, with a happy clear and pure soul.[1]

Evgenii Trubetskoi played a special role in the Russian religious and philosophical renaissance. First of all, he was one of the few closest friends of the harbinger of this intellectual movement, Vladimir Soloviev, who was destined to die not just anywhere but at the Trubetskoi Moscow estate "Uzkoe." In many respects Evgenii was Soloviev's philosophical successor; he was also most actively involved in social and political activities, trying to realize religious and philosophical social ideals. Finally, his relationship with Margarita Kirillovna Morozova (1873–1958) contributed to her sponsorship of major projects, which in effect ensured some institutionalization of the religious and philosophical renaissance. This extraordinary woman had an exceptional role in the history of Russian culture of the Silver Age. The widow of a major Moscow industrialist, Mikhail Morozov, she was one of the richest—not only in material, but perhaps also in spiritual terms—women of Russia. This is how Andrew Belyi captured her image in his memoirs *The Beginning of the Century*:

> She had amazing eyes with a reflection of a sapphire and at the same time of an emerald; she used to wrap herself in her white talma, crouch down on the sofa and listen. . . . We called her "the

---

1. See Polovinkin, *Kniaz' E. N. Trubetskoi*, 14.

lady with the sultan" as a joke; she used to wear a huge hat with a huge sultan and looked like a giant; considering her height and the tone of the "mistress of the salon," she could frighten everyone for want of habit.[2]

Despite the inevitable vicissitudes of their relations, the "loving friendship" between Trubetskoi and Morozova continued intensively from the moment of their acquaintance in 1905 until their forced parting in 1918. At first, they were brought closer by their joint interests and Margarita Kirillovna's range of reading, which, as is clear from their correspondence, included mostly literature on philosophy, theology, the history of the Church, Russian religious thought, and above all the works of Vladimir Soloviev. She wrote to Trubetskoi from a German resort in the summer of 1909, reporting that she had read Soloviev's "The Great Dispute" and found it very good. "All of its basic ideas are so familiar to me from your conversations and articles and are so close to my soul in general that I really treat them like my own thoughts."[3] In his reply Trubetskoi asked: "Why is the train of thought about Soloviev so cast in a letter to you? Because everything that I think is connected with you so much."[4]

It is no exaggeration to say that the whole history of their relationship, as reflected in the correspondence, took shape under the sign of Soloviev: his name is the one most often mentioned by them in various contexts, and the discussion of his ideas often turns into a clarification of their relationship, taking the form of polemics about understanding and evaluating the doctrine of the founder of the metaphysics of all-unity. In turn, this correspondence can be read as a kind of commentary on Soloviev, whose ideas were put to the test of life in the joint experience of the two correspondents. Even their intimate feelings found expression in the language of this philosophy: "I am experiencing a real image of all-unity in you!"[5]—Morozova told Trubetskoi with enthusiasm. While seeing in herself the embodiment of eternal femininity, she strove to share this with her "priceless friend":

> Your work and you yourself need—mine. Really, really need! Not me, I am not talking about myself, but mine, *das Ewig-Weibliche*!

2. Belyi, *Nachalo veka*, 508.

3. "'Nasha lyubov' nuzhna Rossii . . .' Perepiska E. N. Trubetskogo i M. K. Morozovoi," 181.

4. "'Nasha lyubov' nuzhna Rossii . . .' Perepiska E. N. Trubetskogo i M. K. Morozovoi," 183.

5. "'Nasha lyubov' nuzhna Rossii . . .' Perepiska E. N. Trubetskogo i M. K. Morozovoi. Okonchanie," 196.

> But I need yours too! Soloviev was right that only both origins in conjunction represent an integral person![6]

It was this integrity that Morozova and Trubetskoi, inspired by Soloviev's ideas, were trying to achieve. And the misunderstanding between them took the form of a conflict over interpretations of Soloviev's philosophy.

The feeling that broke out between these not very young people turned out to be exceptionally deep and unrelenting (in the year of their acquaintance, Trubetskoi was in his fifties, and Morozova was in her forties). Years passed, but the power of passion and the degree of ecstasy, judging by the letters, remained unchanged. "My whole being is overfilled with you, my precious friend," Morozova wrote to Trubetskoi in 1910, five years after they first met. "How I should be grateful to God that He sends me such magical moments when you do not believe that you live on earth, when you really, really feel that you are flying to heaven?"[7] Two years later:

> This morning I was running around everywhere, I could not stop, I was so happy about the dazzling sun, singing birds, wonderful greenery, and I thought of you with such tender love! . . . So much, infinitely much love in my soul and I feel; I want your soul to feel it too, blossom and smile! . . . Oh, how much beauty, how much music and infinitely wonderful things in the world, and how your sunny, magical image shines in![8]

And here is Trubetskoi's confession ten years after he met with Morozova:

> You cannot imagine how I am drawn to you: it pains me. I remember all of the details of your visit down to the smallest detail and they seem to be teasing me. . . . Finally, Mikhailovsky's pines, an official, feigned and indifferent meeting on the balcony with a handshake, a slow quitting to the coveted room. . . . And only there we are alone suddenly, alone in the whole world, together; and all the dams are broken immediately! . . . Madness; as if I were again twenty or twenty-five years old.[9]

Like all lovers, they had their own cherished places, their special signals, their own secret language and conspiracy, affectionate names they called each other known only by them ("Angel," "Zhenichka," "Margosya,"

---

6. "'Nasha lyubov' nuzhna Rossii . . .' Perepiska E. N. Trubetskogo i M. K. Morozovoi. Okonchanie," 191.

7. "'Nasha lyubov' nuzhna Rossii . . .' Perepiska E. N. Trubetskogo i M. K. Morozovoi," 214.

8. See Keidan, *Vzyskuyushchie grada*, 468–69.

9. Keidan, *Vzyskuyushchie grada*, 644.

"Garmosya"). They committed very extravagant acts for people in their situation. "Did you understand that I met you on the Smolensky market purposely, calculating the time of your departure, and that it had to be, and it had to be my last send-off that only you would understand?!"—asked Trubetskoi.[10] To see her beloved man again, even if only from afar, Morozova, on her part, was ready for real adventures: "I will stop at another hotel, and take someone else's passport."[11]

However, for Trubetskoi, the joy of their relationship was overshadowed by the pangs of conscience he felt as a married man whose Orthodox values neither allowed him to leave his wife nor to cheat on her. Morozova's joy was overshadowed too by the fact that Trubetskoi could not utterly devote himself to her. And, gradually, this plea becomes one of the main leitmotifs in Morozova's letters:

> My precious friend! My magic angel, my welcomed one! How much I love you, how much I adore! All I ask of you is to hear my heart, my soul now! . . . I want one moment, one little moment of joy, of *my* joy in life! . . . I know that only for this moment I will give it all up and take it all out! I will never be afraid of life and of all the hardships! I *know* that I will scoop up such a force, such a joy, such a fire![12]

In response to these cries of her soul, Evgenii Nikolaevich could only offer his beloved a religious moralistic reproach: "Is this conversation about 'one moment' nothing but a self-deception and illusion? . . . However, you already told me somehow that 'one moment' cannot be understood literally!"[13]

> Yes, my dear, *we have to act*; and if it is necessary to act, we have to do *what we must do*, whatever it costs! . . . Who, finally, do I love more—you or God. If I say that I love you most, I declare myself a death sentence: then a cross should be put above me as a human being and as an activist. . . . There is nothing else to say about happiness. . . . After all, happiness is not the goal of life.[14]

---

10. "'Nasha lyubov' nuzhna Rossii . . .' Perepiska E. N. Trubetskogo i M. K. Morozovoi," 179.

11. Keidan, *Vzyskuyushchie grada*, 562.

12. "'Nasha lyubov' nuzhna Rossii . . .' Perepiska E. N. Trubetskogo i M. K. Morozovoi," 205–06.

13. "'Nasha lyubov' nuzhna Rossii . . .' Perepiska E. N. Trubetskogo i M. K. Morozovoi," 207.

14. "'Nasha lyubov' nuzhna Rossii . . .' Perepiska E. N. Trubetskogo i M. K. Morozovoi," 206–07.

Trubetskoi expressed his vision of the admissible form and content of his relations with Morozova in the following words: "I feel the possibility of a bright, good and loving friendship with you in harmony with my conscience and common cause!"[15]

It was not by accident that Trubetskoi expressed his "loving friendship" with Morozova as a fragile hope and assumption. It was impossible to keep their stormy feelings within the bounds of friendship. Periodically it inevitably broke through the moral dams that the prince erected with Sisyphean exertion and constancy. There is indirect but unambiguous evidence about the insanities that occurred in their correspondence: on the one hand, in Morozova's ecstatic memories of "a magical moment . . . when you are flying to Heaven," and on the other—in Trubetskoi's bitter remorse about his wife's worries and his multiple expressions of intent to conquer and atone his sin by prolonged separation from his "beloved Garmosya" or even by ascetic exploits on Mt. Athos.

> *Verochka has recognized everything by herself,* by some kind of clairvoyance, with such accuracy that she even identified the timeframe and directly pointed to last spring, when it happened. . . . I will fast before Easter; and if even then I do not bring to the altar a firm intention to atone my sins, then it will not be my salvation. . . . We have to save both your soul and mine.[16]

> It is impossible to create anything great, or holy, or artistic *with such a huge stone* of conscience. . . . We stumbled together and will rise again together. . . . Only a little bit more religiosity and faith are necessary—*to put a sword between us,* as Siegfried did with Brunhilde. . . . Why do we have to sacrifice this bright and constant joy for a *momentary* joy that leaves a long and unbearably agonizing trace behind.[17]

> *This time* I could not handle a wave of pleasure. I could not handle a wonderful evening with the stupefying smell of hay, with the incredible beauty of nature, and most of all—with your charm! Well, there is nothing to despair of, let us be cheerful and firm, we will not lose courage and indulge "horror."[18]

---

15. "'Nasha lyubov' nuzhna Rossii . . .' Perepiska E. N. Trubetskogo i M. K. Morozovoi," 218.

16. "'Nasha lyubov' nuzhna Rossii . . .' Perepiska E. N. Trubetskogo i M. K. Morozovoi. Okonchanie," 177.

17. "'Nasha lyubov' nuzhna Rossii . . .' Perepiska E. N. Trubetskogo i M. K. Morozovoi. Okonchanie," 207–8.

18. "'Nasha lyubov' nuzhna Rossii . . .' Perepiska E. N. Trubetskogo i M. K. Morozovoi. Okonchanie," 208.

And in 1915—the year which marked a decade of his relationship with Morozova—Trubetskoi states that they both are burdened by the "large and long accumulated weight of sin."[19]

It is obvious that the most important watershed for Trubetskoi and Morozova with respect to life and love, their experience and deep understanding, was exactly at that point. The misunderstanding between them required an articulated reflection and well-founded position. Its expression was not limited to the epistolary genre alone. The reflection of these circumstances took place in the prince's philosophical works, which thus can be regarded as the philosophical emanations of this love. But before we turn to the historical-theoretical level, let us dwell on some psychological aspects of the issue. As is known, after the death of her husband many men courted Morozova. Among them was Pavel Milyukov—a famous historian and politician, who turned out to be the rival of Trubetskoi for a while. Elena Polyanskaya, who was Morozova's closest friend and confidante, compared these two men with the heroes of Ivan Goncharov's famous novel; in response, Morozova wrote: "About Oblomov and Stolz you are right and wrong at the same time. In everyday life it is so, and Stolz could give a lot to me, but he could never give me those special things, that only *he* can give."[20]

The comparison between Trubetskoi and Oblomov might seem unexpected and strange; in fact, the prince, unlike this literary character, was never one to lie on a couch for days on end. Rather he led an effective life, working actively: he taught, wrote books, was engaged in scholarship, politics and journalism, and traveled extensively. It can be assumed that the "Oblomovism" of Trubetskoi, which was observed by Polyanskaya and recognized by Morozova, concerned not his whole nature but rather the behavior peculiar to him in certain situations that required decisiveness, for example, in his relationships with women. In this regard Morozova failed to achieve drastic changes and after another five years she reproached Trubetskoi, by his own admission, for "Hamletism,"[21] i.e., for passive inaction. The same assessment was given of Trubetskoi's potential as a politician. At the end of 1905, after the publication of the imperial manifesto on October 17 and the appointment of Count Sergei Witte as prime minister, Trubetskoi received an invitation to the post of Minister of Education. However, the appointment did not take place because the prince gave the count the impression of being a person who was impractical and indecisive: "The Absolute Hamlet of the Russian Revolution."[22]

19. Keidan, *Vzyskuyushchie grada*, 628.
20. Keidan, *Vzyskuyushchie grada*, 47.
21. "'Nasha lyubov' nuzhna Rossii . . .' Perepiska E. N. Trubetskogo i M. K. Morozovoi," 206.
22. Vitte, *Vospominaniya*, 70.

Unexpected confirmation of the fact that some irrational fear prevented Trubetskoi from acting decisively in the right situation and from even fully expressing his feelings can be found in his letter to Morozova of July 26, 1912, where he retells his dream:

> My darling—come into my soul for a moment and try to understand that all of its feelings which are dearest to you are beaten and squeezed. Only yesterday I had an unusually bright dream depicting it better than any words could. I myself am in Moscow coming to you in the usual way—not walking, *but running*. Here is Povarskaya street already, here is Arbat Square. My heart beats happily because I feel that there you are living on Znamenka and are hiding behind the door, ready to jump at me all of a sudden. And then a delight, a stream of feelings, a stream of words, tears of joy. And my heart starts to ache, I feel a spasm as I run forward uncontrollably. And suddenly, something painfully agonizing burns through me. I hear the coachman's rumble on the pavement behind me and feel with every fiber of my soul that *it is her*. I do not see her, but I *feel* this sick, exhausted, feverish look of her swollen eyes.... I have a moment to dive into the yard near you on Znamenka, I am hiding behind some kind of stone; but I feel that nothing could hide me at all: by some kind of "second vision" she sees me through the stone.... My dear friend, really, this dream—is all of my present inner life. My soul is running, rushing to you, to heartache: but the fact that I am not going to you is the same as hiding behind the stones.[23]

The things perceived by Trubetskoi himself during the night as cowardice, as "hiding behind the stones," in daylight become clear as the impossible task of recognizing and fighting sin:

> The sublime, precious and sinful things are messed up and intertwined so much here that it takes superhuman effort to understand where one begins and another ends! ... It is hard for me because when I see you a terrible force of feeling rises inside of me ... my chest is about to explode from the internal pressure.... Just to wish that there was no sin is not enough to save me and our relationship; I have to take some effective measures to control myself.... I need God's help.... What if I go to Athos and spend part of the summer there in prayer![24]

23. Keidan, *Vzyskuyushchie grada*, 476.

24. "'Nasha lyubov' nuzhna Rossii...' Perepiska E. N. Trubetskogo i M. K. Morozovoi. Okonchanie," 181–82.

Relying only on God's help, Trubetskoi confessed not only his own impotence to change the current situation but sought to subordinate Morozova to the same logic of pious quietism while preaching to her a spiritual love which revealed itself in joint self-denial and cross-bearing: "our whole upcoming task now is to bear the cross. And through this cross you and I won't drift apart from each other but will be even closer."[25]

In fact, a sense of hesitation can be observed in Trubetskoi's suggestions in this regard: at times he believes that between him and Morozova there could be possible some kind of passionate but sinless spiritual love "in harmony with conscience and common cause," that their relationship represents a special "sanctity" which offers spiritual illuminations, inspires creative achievements and accomplishments for the benefit of society. This pattern is reminiscent of Vladimir Soloviev's philosophy of love, which considered the love of a man and a woman as a theurgic activity with a universal meaning and as a way of approaching the absolute. But in this Soloviev insisted on the need for abstinence from sexual intercourse. An example of the consistent application of the principles of Soloviev's philosophy of love was the marriage of Alexander Blok and Liubov Mendeleyeva. However, Trubetskoi and Morozova were not meant to approach the embodiment of this ideal. Gradually, the prince reaches the grim conclusion that their love cannot be sinless: "What should I do and how should I fight this mighty, tender, passionate but still sinful love! . . . And others are going to Calvary."[26]

But Morozova strongly refused to accept Trubetskoi's quietism and his virtuous model of "loving friendship." First, she did not want to acknowledge her feelings and their relationship as sinful:

> You are *depressing me deeply with your wrong assessment of our relationship*. . . . There is no way that it is based *only* on *egoism* and *sin*. Who was your *living and real* helper in all of your endeavors and ideas? Who *sacrificed everything* to provide your business, to surround you and bring your soul together with the others? Who offered and gave to you all of the *width, depth and beauty* of the feeling, *that you never had*, otherwise you would never have left V. A.? Who is the *true spiritual half* of you? . . . *Is there really only a sin? From what we should seek salvation? What do I ruin?* There is no way that all of this could be considered as evil, sinful and falling.[27]

25. "'Nasha lyubov' nuzhna Rossii . . .' Perepiska E. N. Trubetskogo i M. K. Morozovoi. Okonchanie," 189.

26. Keidan, *Vzyskuyushchie grada*, 633.

27. "'Nasha lyubov' nuzhna Rossii . . .' Perepiska E. N. Trubetskogo i M. K. Morozovoi. Okonchanie," 179.

But later Morozova acknowledges explicitly and fearlessly: "Though my love and my wishes are sinful, and I know that it is so, but I also know that living like that I will do much more good things in my life."[28] At the same time, she desperately needs the "magic moments" alone with her beloved one; and in the eyes of Morozova it possesses "sanctity":

> I deeply believe in the sanctity and fruitfulness of these moments for everything in life! But you do not! You are always thinking, always reasoning, you never give yourself selflessly, you are always halfway! ... If we will have some moments of a total oblivion and selflessness, and will live with all of our being, only then will we save our spirits high, and, most of all, will we save the freshness, responsiveness and sensitivity of our souls ... here must be the moments of unity, harmony and merging.[29]

And there is no contradiction: when Morozova confesses that her love is sinful, she draws on her correspondent's value system; and when she speaks about sanctity of "moments of unity and merging," she expresses her own conviction. The prince cannot bear to say that he loves a woman more than God. But for Morozova, a juxtaposition like that is literally impossible because in her opinion God and her beloved could not be separated from each other: God creates through being loved, and love provides knowledge of God: "God always was speaking to me through you!"[30] "Could it be anything else except my love for 'him' to do wonders and open my soul to God."[31] Morozova is ready to sacrifice even the immortality promised by religion for an opportunity to be with her beloved: "I do not need immortality, I need only Zhenichka"—these words were remembered by Trubetskoi subsequently.[32]

In her argument with the prince, Morozova invokes Vladimir Soloviev as an ally in support of the righteousness of her attitude. She uses the concepts of Soloviev's philosophy:

> You are evasive and winding up in "your own," and you are not rushing to the "eternal feminine" origin of love and creativity. If it were not for the most intimate, soulful things in Soloviev's work, those closest to my soul, I would not be afraid that much!

28. "'Nasha lyubov' nuzhna Rossii . . .' Perepiska E. N. Trubetskogo i M. K. Morozovoi. Okonchanie," 196.

29. "'Nasha lyubov' nuzhna Rossii . . .' Perepiska E. N. Trubetskogo i M. K. Morozovoi. Okonchanie," 196.

30. "'Nasha lyubov' nuzhna Rossii . . .' Perepiska E. N. Trubetskogo i M. K. Morozovoi," 210.

31. Keidan, *Vzyskuyushchie grada*, 469.

32. Keidan, *Vzyskuyushchie grada*, 569.

> ... If I did not believe that even Russia needs our love, could I protect it with such force! ... It is not the cross that I deny, I require an attention to life and love.[33]

Morozova's appeal to Soloviev's ideas is not surprising because, as already mentioned, her communication with Trubetskoi was marked by the founder of the metaphysics of all-unity, and the discussion of his works had contributed to their growing closer together during the initial period of their acquaintance and remained an important part of it throughout. This was confirmed in their letters to each other; Morozova frequently used the conceptual framework of Soloviev's philosophy to express her thoughts, worries and most intimate feelings. In turn, in these years Trubetskoi was working on his fundamental study, *Vladimir Soloviev's Worldview*. This work was not the last dedicated to Morozova personally. The author confessed to her that his work "affects the meaning of my relationship with you." Thus, as was rightly noted by Alexander Nosov, "only she could understand the reality that stands behind the philosophy of Eros, promoted by Trubetskoi."[34]

Trubetskoi shared his thoughts about his book with Morozova while writing it. He sent her each finished chapter. However, when it came to chapters fifteen and sixteen, the prince started to feel a special thrill: "Today I have sent to you my chapter fifteen and now I am waiting *with trembling* for you to read, to live and feel it; *as if our entire future depends on it!*"[35] And then: "Yesterday I have finished one of the most significant chapters—'The Meaning of Love.' . . . I am afraid of how you would take mine, right or wrong?"[36]

His worries were justified since in the mentioned chapters Trubetskoi severely criticized the key sections of Soloviev's philosophy: the doctrines of universal theocracy and of the meaning of love. Moreover, the common denominator of this criticism was the conclusion that "the same mistake is repeated in the doctrine of the 'meaning of love' as in the idea of 'universal Theocracy'—the attempt to include in the Kingdom of Heaven the interim and dying form of an earthly life; to put new wine into old bottles."[37] Trubetskoi's criticism of Soloviev's philosophy of love was particularly harsh

33. "'Nasha lyubov' nuzhna Rossii . . .' Perepiska E. N. Trubetskogo i M. K. Morozovoi. Okonchanie," 195.

34. Nosov, "Istoriya," 93.

35. "'Nasha lyubov' nuzhna Rossii . . .' Perepiska E. N. Trubetskogo i M. K. Morozovoi. Okonchanie," 186.

36. "'Nasha lyubov' nuzhna Rossii . . .' Perepiska E. N. Trubetskogo i M. K. Morozovoi. Okonchanie," 205.

37. Trubetskoi, *Mirosozertsanie Vl. S. Solov'eva*, 588.

and even emotionally charged: "He interprets the Kingdom of God itself as some kind of immortalized romance."[38] In conclusion, Trubetskoi branded Soloviev's conceptions of theocracy and philosophy of love as utopian dreams: "Soloviev's doctrine of a sexual love is literally a utopia, unprecedented and impossible."[39]

It is safe to say that the sixteenth chapter of *Soloviev's Worldview* was not just Trubetskoi's attempt to dot all the 'i's in understanding the complicated question of Soloviev's philosophy of Eros, but at the same time it was a peculiar response to Morozova's claims against him. The difficult relations between Morozova and himself had served as a major subject of his research: "How many times have I told you and have I wrote in my 'Soloviev' that love is not only a feeling: it is more than that."[40]

> The full value of love—is in another world! But, Lord, how it is difficult! What a feat love requires; and what a lie—is love without a feat.[41]

Those words from Trubetskoi's letters to Morozova could be considered as the quintessence of Trubetskoi's own doctrine of love, one which emerged in his polemics against Soloviev and his follower Morozova. Of course, she could not fully agree with the parts of Soloviev's doctrine in which he claims the need for sexual chastity, but she shared the main idea of this philosopher—the sacralization of earthly love, its image as a way of achieving perfect being. Trubetskoi, in turn, considered this kind of comprehension of love as utopianism, relying on the development of this concept in Pavel Novgorodtsev's works.

Trubetskoi's fears were confirmed. Morozova reacted indignantly to those texts, moving on from criticism of his constructs to even more intensive attacks on Trubetskoi himself:

> Everything in my soul is protesting against your perception of the world! . . . It is definitely not Novgorodtsev's little brain that could judge the great and immortal souls and minds. All of them were utopians. And Soloviev was great and created his immortal doctrine only when he was a utopian. When a sexual love is great, is it justified? Only when it is utopian (it is your phrase), and, to me, it is "wonderful" and "crazy" from an everyday point of view. . . . I am sure that the world is unhappy not

---

38. Trubetskoi, *Mirosozertsanie Vl. S. Solov'eva*, 583.
39. Trubetskoi, *Mirosozertsanie Vl. S. Solov'eva*, 587.
40. Keidan, *Vzyskuyushchie grada*, 546.
41. "'Nasha lyubov' nuzhna Rossii . . .'. Perepiska E. N. Trubetskogo i M. K. Morozovoi," 220.

> because it is not bearing a cross, because I know that it is, but because there is not enough love in it! And love is the only thing that works miracles and resurrects things here on Earth. . . . You have become very ossified in your just Christianity and virtues over the last 48 years. Perhaps it is irreparable and hopeless! You are telling me "pleasant" things in every letter, "warm words"! I need fire or nothing. . . . You do not deserve love, but I kiss you anyway. Write to me![42]

Despite the fact that Trubetskoi had not fully lived up to the expectations of Morozova, she recognized herself as his indispensable companion; she believed in his special spiritual calling and tried to convince the philosopher of this. According to Morozova, in Russia after Alexander III, a new real life had begun; now it was not enough just to think of life; it had to be actually lived, and created. In this situation "a human who has become a little bit psychic" can do a lot for the spiritual resurrection of Russia: "This is the deed and the truth that I await from you."[43] Trubetskoi should have done the things that the Slavophiles and Soloviev did not do.[44]

> My Angel, I am calling you, I am begging you to hear me and believe me that in the current time you are the one not dead, and not talentless, and not muddled! You are the one who could say the living word, the one that could have relevance and influence and authority! . . . You, you, you are the only one. I am begging you to console me—do not ever stop, do not give up, do not worry about anything! Your life is beautiful and full of meaning.[45]

Regarding her beloved as the most significant Russian philosopher, the successor of Vladimir Soloviev, the continuer of his "universal work," Morozova tried with all her power to provide him with the highest platform, to make him the leader of the Russian "Christian community." That is why Morozova helped to finance the creation of the Constitutional Democratic Party, which Trubetskoi helped to found, and sponsored *Moskovskii ezhenedel'nik* (Moscow Weekly), which Trubetskoi edited. She also financed the Vladimir Soloviev Religious-Philosophical Society, which Trubetskoi helped to direct; the meetings of this society took place in Morozova's mansion in the Prechistenka area. But her biggest project was the religious and

42. Keidan, *Vzyskuyushchie grada*, 467–68.
43. "'Nasha lyubov' nuzhna Rossii . . .' Perepiska E. N. Trubetskogo i M. K. Morozovoi. Okonchanie," 202.
44. Keidan, *Vzyskuyushchie grada*, 432.
45. Keidan, *Vzyskuyushchie grada*, 529.

philosophical publishing house *Put'* (The Way). Formally Trubetskoi had the same rights on the editorial board as the other members and founders (Nikolai Berdyaev, Sergei Bulgakov, Vladimir Ern), but in contested situations his opinion was decisive as it was always favored by Morozova. Such situations were not rare because the prince had his fair share of aristocratic arrogance. Morozova always supported his high self-esteem: "I am so proud of you," she wrote to the prince in a private letter. "I am so glad when I see how you are smarter, nobler, much more talented than everyone at all times and in all places."[46]

Morozova's confidence in Trubetskoi's higher mission was so strong that he himself never questioned it, but at the same time he never thought he was worthy of such a spiritual mission because of his insufficient "purity of heart":

> You demand of me that I rise higher than the people whose light I see and feel! As for me, I see it—and could not do that at the same time. I have a wound of Amphortha—that is my pain and suffering.[47]

Indeed, under the professor's frock-coat Trubetskoi always had the nature of a leader, a public figure, a politician; and not by chance both of his dissertations were devoted to the problem of theocracy, to the analysis of the role of Christianity in politics and its interaction with a secular government.[48] This problem was also the focus of his attention in his two-volume work, *Vladimir Soloviev's Worldview*. The revolution of 1905 reawakened the Russian intellectuals. They started to dream of the realization of the most daring projects of the social reorganization of Russia; it was time to move from abstract reflections about the religious and social ideal to attempts to implement it in modern life. Trubetskoi was in the middle of these events too. He sat in the Duma and on the State Council, established political parties and topical periodicals, and worked as a journalist actively and successfully, tirelessly publishing leading editorial articles in *Moskovskii ezhenedel'nik* for several years.

His years dedicated to the exhausting fight on the socio-political front did not bring the desired results, only fatigue and disappointment. In 1911 Trubetskoi wrote an article with an eloquent title, "Over the Broken Trough," in which he declared "the collapse of the Russian revolution, the collapse of

---

46. "'Nasha lyubov' nuzhna Rossii . . .' Perepiska E. N. Trubetskogo i M. K. Morozovoi. Okonchanie," 198.

47. Keidan, *Vzyskuyushchie grada*, 551.

48. See Trubetskoi, *Ideal zapadnogo khristianstva v V veke*; and Trubetskoi, *Ideal zapadnogo khristianstva v XI veke*.

the Russian Constitution, the collapse of attempts to create a 'strong and efficient center,' the collapse of all attempts to create something remotely decent and plausible in our state and public life." But even a negative experience can be a useful lesson, and "sitting over the broken trough always predisposes one to philosophical reflection."[49] Trubetskoi did not renounce his program of Christian social action, but he suggested that direct social and political work and topical journalism were not enough. As a result, a decision was made to close *Moskovskii ezhenedel'nik* and to continue the activity in a fundamentally different format—the publishing of religious and philosophical literature by *Put'*.

> Thought should be purified and deepened to a profound spiritual influence. New spiritual forces should be born. . . . As I understand it, publicism shall be supplied by philosophy and deep religious understanding! That is, philosophy is the first task, and publicism is the second or even third.[50]

There is no doubt that Trubetskoi expressed his sincere conviction in these words from his letter to Morozova, but it should be noted that this was not the main reason for the closure of *Moskovskii ezhenedel'nik*, nor was it financial difficulties (as claimed by Morozova's public statements). The decision to close *Moskovskii ezhenedel'nik* was actually forced, but due to completely different circumstances: by the middle of 1910 the feelings between Trubetskoi and Morozova began to "flare up in a huge fire" and the prince made a decision to put down this "fire" by going abroad for the whole winter, perceiving this as his personal "Athos," as a cross or a "sacrifice at both sides, quite conscious and voluntary."[51] Morozova was forced to agree with this "sacrifice" and in connection with this pointed out the need to cease publication of *Moskovskii ezhenedel'nik*.[52] Indeed, without Trubetskoi continuing its publication lost meaning, because every week he spent a lot of time in the editorial office, secluding himself there with Morozova, which in turn was a matter of concern for Vera Aleksandrovna, the wife of the prince.

Already in 1913, evaluating the results of the *Put'* publishing house's activity, Trubetskoi expressed satisfaction, recognizing both the accomplishments of its founder and his own contribution:

49. See Gollerbakh, *K nezrimomu gradu*, 63.
50. "'Nasha lyubov' nuzhna Rossii . . .' Perepiska E. N. Trubetskogo i M. K. Morozovoi," 216.
51. "'Nasha lyubov' nuzhna Rossii . . .' Perepiska E. N. Trubetskogo i M. K. Morozovoi," 207.
52. "'Nasha lyubov' nuzhna Rossii . . .' Perepiska E. N. Trubetskogo i M. K. Morozovoi," 210.

> All this time I was busy with nothing else but *Put'*, i.e., you eventually, because it was exactly you who was the real assembler of *Put'*; and you were moved by love—your love for me. . . . You assembled all this and in your dear *Put'* everything that is now most significant in Russian religious thought was gathered.[53]

But Morozova saw a task that was much larger and went far beyond the current activities associated with the publication of books and meetings of the Vladimir Soloviev Religious-Philosophical Society. From her point of view, the continuation of the work of the great philosopher was to serve not only and not so much a theoretical discussion of his heritage but most of all the practical realization of his idea of "Christian politics."

Russia's entry into the First World War at first contributed to the rise of patriotic sentiments in Russian society, and in religious and philosophical circles it was perceived as a long-awaited beginning of the realization of the country's spiritual and historical mission. In August 1914, against the backdrop of these truly apocalyptic experiences, Morozova wrote to Trubetskoi:

> An especially huge moment is coming! I am talking about Christian politics; I do not know how to express it in a better way. Now we need hard work, we need to influence, to guide thought and feeling! Everything is now in such chaos, everything in our minds has turned, huge spiritual work will be needed. You can strike while the iron is hot better than anyone else! . . . Your talent, your soul—it was always very, very necessary, and now is just the moment that corresponds to your temperament and direction! The religious moment, the super-political, supranational, idealistic moment! It has to be hot, searing the hearts of men with righteous words. It is necessary to give satisfaction to the confusion of the soul, to resolve restless thought! To mention the new future, new path![54]

Many Russian philosophers reacted with enthusiasm to the First World War and in the first years of the war they actively spoke in the press and from various platforms, explaining the providential significance of the war and the "world task of Russia."[55] Particular diligence in this regard was shown by philosophers grouped around Morozova's projects. The loudest voice belonged to Vladimir Ern at a meeting of the Vladimir Soloviev Religious-Philosophical Society in Moscow, in which he deduced German militarism from German philosophy and culture: "The German madness

---

53. Keidan, *Vzyskuyushchie grada*, 561.
54. Keidan, *Vzyskuyushchie grada*, 587.
55. See Vanchugov, "Filosofstvovanie," 232–45.

passes through scientific, methodological, philosophical forms, finally flipping out in militaristic rampage."[56]

As if responding to Morozova's call, Trubetskoi did not remain apart from the intellectual movement dedicated to understanding the war. His creative activity acquired a journalistic sharpness again. In November–December 1914, together with his follower the philosopher Ivan Ilyin, the prince made a tour of the cities of Russia giving public lectures: "The War and the World Challenge of Russia"; "The Patriotic War and Its Spiritual Meaning"; "The National Question, Constantinople and St. Sofia," and others. In his collection, *The Meaning of War* (1914), Trubetskoi found positive meaning in the recovery of national identity brought about by the war, in the realization of the value of Russia's nature, history and culture.

This national pride was reflected in the prince's philosophical work. During the war, he wrote *Metaphysical Premises of Knowledge: An Attempt at Transcending Kant and Kantianism*. He expressed the book's task in a letter to Morozova: "Now it is time to expose all this hopeless and fruitless recent German philosophy! . . . This yoke has to be thrown off the Russian youth."[57] But, actually, "transcending Kant" mostly required the same Kantian methods.[58] At the same time, Trubetskoi wrote a book in which he finally expounded his own "positive" philosophy: *The Meaning of Life*. On its pages, he points out that the semblance of patriotic enthusiasm will be deceptive if "there is no main, religious staple, which alone can impart a character of indestructible integrity to the people's life."[59] Thus, it turns out that it is precisely to Trubetskoi that we are indebted to the phrase "spiritual staples" which is so popular nowadays.

Like most of Russian society, Morozova met the February 1917 revolution with enthusiasm, which she hurried to share with Trubetskoi:

> A lot of beautiful things have happened; Russia will not turn back again. But what lies ahead? . . . This Renovated Russia needs you more than ever! You will have to conquer the freedom of spiritual Russia and establish and strengthen its true spiritual path.[60]

---

56. Ern, "Ot Kanta k Kruppu," 317.

57. Keidan, *Vzyskuyushchie grada*, 656.

58. According to Alexey Kruglov, "The weakness of Trubetskoi's research and of his task of overcoming Kant is in his proclamation of the immanent analysis of the 'historical Kant' and the actual fight against the neo-Kantian Kant and the neo-Kantians themselves. . . . As a result, Trubetskoi's struggle, to quote Kant himself, is often with his own shadow." Kruglov, "Filosofiia Kanta," 304.

59. Trubetskoi, *Smysl zhizni*, 210.

60. Keidan, *Vzyskuyushchie grada*, 670–71.

Indeed, Trubetskoi after the revolution was no longer directly involved in politics, but rather in spiritual activity and church work. First, he was elected as a delegate to the All-Russian Congress of the Clergy and Laity, which, at the prince's initiative, accepted an appeal to the army and navy on the need to continue the war. Then Trubetskoi became a member and deputy chairman of the All-Russian Local Church Council of 1917–1918 and took an active part in the preparation of conciliar declarations on the relationship between the Church and the state, the meaning of which amounted to the claim that "in the conditions of everyday Russian life, complete separation of the Church is impossible. The Church must be in alliance with the state, preserving independence and self-determination in its inner life."[61]

The last letter from Trubetskoi to Morozova, dated August 1918, was written on the eve of the prince's departure from Moscow. During the Civil War, he joined the Whites and, together with the remnants of Denikin's army, found himself in Novorossiysk. He died there of typhus in 1920, not having left his native land. The story of his "loving friendship" with Margarita Morozova has endured not only because their correspondence is a masterpiece of the epistolary genre in Russian culture. Their painful, barely satisfied passion did not remain completely sterile: the child of its sublimation was not only the publishing activity of *Put'*, but, to a large extent, the entire religious-philosophical renaissance whose organizational and material support would have been much more modest and possibly marginal without it. According to the historian Vladimir Keidan, this is "a rare example of how the drama of 'illicit love' was turned into a creative source which fed a whole religious-philosophical and social movement with its energy."[62]

Bibliography

Belyi, Andrei. *Nachalo veka*. Moscow: Soyuzteatr, 1990.

Ern, Vladimir. "Ot Kanta k Kruppu." In *Sochineniya*, 308–18. Moscow: Pravda, 1991.

Gollerbakh, Evgenii. *K nezrimomu gradu: Religiozno-filosofskaya gruppa "Put'" (1910–1919) v poiskakh novoi russkoi identichnosti*. Edited by Modest Kolerov. St. Petersburg: Aleteiya, 2000.

Keidan, Vladimir. "Na putyakh k gradu zemnomu." In *Vzyskuyushchie grada. Khronika chastnoi zhizni russkikh religioznykh filosofov v pis'makh i dnevnikakh*, edited by Vladimir Keidan, 5–52. Moscow: Yazyki russkoi kul'tury, 1997.

Keidan, Vladimir, ed. *Vzyskuyushchie grada. Khronika chastnoi zhizni russkikh religioznykh filosofov v pis'makh i dnevnikakh*. Moscow: Yazyki russkoi kul'tury, 1997.

61. See Gollerbakh, *K nezrimomu gradu*, 27.
62. Keidan, "Na putyakh k gradu zemnomu," 36–37.

Kruglov, Alexey. "Filosofiia Kanta v issledovanii kn. E. N. Trubetskogo." In *Evgenii Nikolaevich Trubetskoi*, edited by Sergei Polovinkin and Tatiana Shchedrina, 266–309. Moscow: ROSSPEN, 2014.

"'Nasha lyubov' nuzhna Rossii . . .' Perepiska E. N. Trubetskogo i M. K. Morozovoi." Edited by Alexander Nosov. *Novyi mir* 9 (1993) 172–229.

"'Nasha lyubov' nuzhna Rossii . . .' Perepiska E. N. Trubetskogo i M. K. Morozovoi. Okonchanie." Edited by Alexander Nosov. *Novyi mir* 10 (1993) 174–215.

Nosov, Alexander. "Istoriya i sud'ba 'Mirosozertsaniya Vl. S. Solov'eva.'" In *Evgenii Nikolaevich Trubetskoi*, edited by Sergei Polovinkin and Tatiana Shchedrina, 565–93. Moscow: ROSSPEN, 2014.

Polovinkin, Sergei. *Kn. E. N. Trubetskoi. Zhiznennyi i tvorcheskii put'*. Moscow: Sinaksis, 2010.

Trubetskoi, Evgenii. *Mirosozertsanie Vl. S. Solov'eva*. Vol. 1. Moscow: Medium, 1995.

———. *Religiozno-obshchestvennyi ideal zapadnogo khristianstva v V veke: Mirosozertsanie bl. Avgustina*. Moscow: Tip. E. Lissnera i Yu. Romana, 1892.

———. *Religiozno-obshchestvennyi ideal zapadnogo khristianstva v XI veke: Ideya bozheskogo tsarstva v tvoreniyakh Grigoriya VII-go i ego publitsistov—sovremennikov*. Kiev: Tip. S. V. Kul'zhenko, 1897.

———. *Smysl zhizni*. Moscow: Respublika, 1994.

Vanchugov, Vasilii. "Filosofstvovanie v usloviyakh nemirnogo vremeni: postizhenie smysla 'vtoroi otechestvennoi voiny.'" *Istoriya filosofii* 19 (2014) 232–45.

Vitte, Sergei. *Vospominaniya*. Vol. 3. Moscow: Izdatel'stvo sotsial'no-ekonomicheskoi literatury, 1960.

6

The Role of Antinomies in the Theology of Pavel Florensky and Sergei Bulgakov in Light of Evgenii Trubetskoi's Critique

TIKHON VASILYEV

My research primarily concerns the study of Sergei Bulgakov's theological legacy. Bulgakov systematically applied the method of antinomies to all aspects of his theological system. It is now generally agreed that Bulgakov appropriated antinomism through the mediation of Florensky.[1] In my article I will point out the main features of Pavel Florensky's teaching about antinomies. We will also discuss how his teaching was adopted in the theology of Father Sergii, and which aspects of this teaching were criticized by Evgenii Trubetskoi. I will not analyze Florensky's attempt to substantiate antinomies in terms of formal logic. This task has been already undertaken by a number of scholars, most successfully by Paweł Rojek in particular.[2] I will focus on the theological and philosophical aspects of antinomism in Bulgakov and Florensky.

Florensky: Truth Is an Antinomy

Although the importance of antinomies has been understood since Heraclitus, they were first dealt with in a methodical way by Kant in his *Critique of Pure Reason* (1781). Florensky thoroughly examined Kant's four

1. See Gallaher, *There Is Freedom*, 69–75; Seiling, *From Antinomy*, 19.
2. See Rojek, *Logic*.

cosmological antinomies in his talk given at the General Meeting of the Council of the Moscow Theological Academy in 1908,[3] and lays out his own vision in *The Pillar and Ground of the Truth* published in 1914.[4] He argues that Kant's antinomies are not really "the antinomies of pure reason" but demonstrate only the contradictions between different functions of reason. He concludes that while Kant's idea of the possibility of antinomies is "the deepest and most fruitful,"[5] his arguments appear to be insufficiently substantiated. For Florensky, truth itself is an antinomy.[6] He expounds his own understanding of the antinomic structure of human reason and offers "a formal logical theory of antinomy."[7] The antinomical approach is especially appropriate when it comes to religion. He writes:

> The mysteries of religion are not secrets that one must not reveal. They are not the passwords of conspirators, but inexpressible, unutterable, indescribable experiences, which cannot be put into words except in the form of contradictions, which are "yes" and "no" at the same time. They are mysteries that transcend meaning. That is why, when it is expressed in church hymns, the rapture of the soul is inevitably enveloped in the shell of a distinctive play of concepts. The whole liturgy, especially the canons and stichera, is full of this ceaselessly exuberant wit of antithetic juxtapositions and antinomic affirmations.[8]

Father Pavel links the idea of dogma with antinomy, something which is inconceivable to the rational mind.

The teaching about Sophia plays a very significant role in both Florensky's and Bulgakov's theology. In this respect, they were influenced to a certain degree by Vladimir Soloviev. However, both of them criticized Soloviev for what they thought was excessive rationalism. Therefore, antinomism can be said to be the point of divergence between Bulgakov and Florensky, on the one hand, and their predecessor Vladimir Soloviev, on the other.

The sophiological doctrine of Vladimir Soloviev became the target of Florensky's criticism in his fundamental *The Pillar and Ground of the Truth*.

---

3. See Florensky, "Kosmologicheskie antinomii I. Kanta."

4. See Florensky, *Pillar*, 106–23, 411–14.

5. Cf. Schelling, "Immanuel Kant," 7: "The old cheerful Parmenides, as he was described by Plato, and the dialectician Zeno would have gladly recognised him [Kant] as their friend, had they seen his beautifully elaborated antinomies, these permanent triumphs over dogmatism and the eternal propylaea of true philosophy."

6. Florensky, *Pillar*, 114.

7. Florensky, *Pillar*, 110–14.

8. Florensky, *Pillar*, 114.

He questions Soloviev's understanding of Sophia, which is based on his interpretation of the Trinitarian dogma.[9] Florensky pursued his line of argumentation by postulating an opposition between Soloviev's formulations and St. Athanasius's doctrine, charging Soloviev with impersonalism and excessive rationality. He reacts to "rationalism" as if it were an offensive word. For him, rationality in theology is unacceptable in principle.

Bulgakov: Antinomy as the "Ill Fate of Reason"

Bulgakov picks up Florensky's critique and notes that Soloviev, while engaging in polemics with Hegel and Schelling in attempting to construct his own system, seemingly on the basis of theology and Christianity, "unexpectedly draws near them, and in general sins by the excessive rationalism in his theology."[10] It is a system, and it is "sinful."

Indeed, in *The Philosophical Principles of Integral Knowledge* (1877), Soloviev speaks in a very Hegelian way about "integral knowledge" and its philosophical stages. He refers to it as "free theosophy":

> Obeying the general law of historical development, philosophy passes through three main stages.... *The first stage* is characterized by the exclusive predominance of mysticism, which retains in a latent form or a state of fusion rational and empirical elements (which corresponds with the general predominance of theology). *In the second stage* these elements become isolated, and philosophy disintegrates into three separate currents or types that strive for absolute self-affirmation and consequently mutual negation; here, according to the general disintegration of the theoretical sphere into three branches hostile to each other—theology, abstract philosophy, and positive science—we have one-sided mysticism, one-sided rationalism, and one-sided empiricism. *In the third stage* they arrive at an internal *free synthesis*, which forms the basis of the general synthesis of the three levels of knowledge, and consequently also the universal synthesis of human life.[11]

One can see in this passage the three Hegelian stages: thesis, antithesis and synthesis. By contrast, the idea of antinomy supposes embracing thesis and antithesis without their sublation in synthesis.

---

9. See Soloviev, *Lectures*, Book 3.
10. Bulgakov, *Unfading Light*, 152.
11. Soloviev, *Philosophical Principles*, 72.

Bulgakov echoes Florensky in accentuating the significance of Kant's philosophy in respect to antinomies. He writes:

> Kant's most outstanding service in theoretical philosophy was the ascertainment of the antinomies of the intellect, thanks to which it unavoidably becomes entangled in its own nets. The immanent intellect, which does not know any contiguity with the transcendent world, suddenly becomes transcendent for its own self: it turns out that in its center there is a crack through which its content pours out. True, these antinomies in Kant are felicitously "explained" by reason, but one can consider the competence of the latter in this matter to be doubtful, after the antinomic character of its structure is revealed. What is most important here is that this in no way diminishes the very *fact* of the fatal antinomism in thinking, which plainly shows the inadequacy of thinking to its own proper subject.[12]

Bulgakov explains his own antinomism and gives an antinomic résumé of his system in the second chapter of his *The Icon and Icon-veneration* (1931). He expounds three general antinomies:

I. Theological antinomy (God in himself)

Thesis: God is the Absolute and, consequently the pure NOT, the Divine Nothing. (Apophatic theology)

Antithesis: God is the Absolute-in-Itself in self-relation, the Holy Trinity. (Kataphatic theology)

II. Cosmological antinomy (God in himself and in creation)

Thesis: God in the Holy Trinity has all fullness and all-bliss; he is self-existent, unchanging, eternal, and therefore absolute. (God in himself)

Antithesis: God creates the world out of love for creation, with its temporal, relative, becoming being. The Absolute becomes God for it. He correlates himself with it. (God in creation)

III. Sophiological antinomy (Divine Wisdom in God and in the world)

Thesis: God, unisubstantial in the Holy Trinity, reveals himself in his Wisdom, which is his Divine life and the Divine world in eternity, fullness, and perfection. (Noncreaturely Sophia—Divinity in God)

---

12. Bulgakov, *Unfading Light*, 104. Cf. Seiling, *From Antinomy*, 242.

Antithesis: God creates the world by his Wisdom, and this Wisdom, constituting the Divine foundation of the world, abides in temporal-spatial becoming, submerged in nonbeing. (Creaturely Sophia—Divinity outside of God, in the world).[13]

In short, the first antinomy deals with God in himself as Absolute and Trinity; the second is about the possibility of creation out of nothing and what it might mean for the Absolute God and for his creation; finally, the third antinomy is concerned with the possibility of revelation—how the Absolute God can be known by his creation; are there any grounds for a mutual relationship between God and creation?

Bulgakov also appropriates Florensky's understanding of antinomies and their role in the structure of reason. He writes in the *Tragedy of Philosophy*: "Reason necessarily comes up against antinomies, determining its structure and objectives.... The antinomies which tear apart reason—they themselves build it up and determine it."[14] He argues that antinomies are indispensable to human reason. Their presence points to the damage to all of human nature which comes from the Fall and hereditary sin.[15] And human reason alone, without support from faith, is unable to overcome its existing impairment. Moreover, reason often does not perceive its own limits and does not know where to put a stop to its systematizing activity. Antinomies are therefore, on the one hand, the punishment and ill fate of reason. On the other, they are its remedy and an effective means for it to recognize its own condition and for bringing it back to reality. Although antinomies make it impossible for reason to construct an absolute philosophical system, they not only allow but encourage philosophizing: "Philosophizing is the tragedy of reason which has its catharsis."[16]

One must accept the contradictions of reason, rather than try to annihilate them. Bulgakov states that the resolution of antinomism can be neither in eclecticism, when all contradictions are fused and lose their own identity, nor in dialectics when contradictions are sublated and "explained," but in the philosophical turn to religion and theology.[17]

The history of philosophy is a tragedy. On the one hand, human reason cannot cease its attempts to embrace the world, to explain everything

---

13. Bulgakov, *Icons*, 35–36.
14. Bulgakov, *Tragediia filosofii*, 327–28.
15. See Bulgakov, *Tragediia filosofii*, 316.
16. Bulgakov, *Tragediia filosofii*, 354.
17. See Bulgakov, *Tragediia filosofii*, 387–88. Cf. Bulgakov, *Tragediia filosofii*, 426: "The dogma is the substantial way out for reason, salvation from its antinomies and aporias."

logically, somehow appropriating everything. This activity is natural and wholesome for reason. On the other, the world is not ultimately reasonable, as reason is neither the source of itself nor the only architect of the world. There remains a place for mystery. Bulgakov introduces the notion of wisdom which "demands self-consciousness from reason" to perceive its real boundaries.[18]

Trubetskoi: In Defense of Reason

Having presented the main themes in Florensky's and Bulgakov's teaching about antinomies, we can now turn to Prince Evgenii Trubetskoi's critique of this teaching. This material can be found in Trubetskoi's article, "The Light of Tabor and the Transfiguration of the Mind," which was his response to Florensky's book *The Pillar and the Ground of Truth*.

After indicating the many good points in Florensky's book, Trubetskoi concentrated on the critique of his antinomism. One can say that antinomism is not just one of the ideas in Florensky's book, but one of its central ideas. Trubetskoi notes that for Florensky "the Church is veracity, it is the spiritual law of identity."[19] But what happened to the normal law of identity, which is at the foundation of formal logic and which makes possible coherent thinking? Trubetskoi asks his main question: "Does Florensky believe in the transfiguration of the human mind, or does he simply think that reason must be cut off as a tempting 'right eye'?"[20] He rebukes Florensky for not really "understanding what the transfiguration of the mind is." Trubetskoi maintains that the transfiguration of the mind consists in the healing of the sinful disintegration and in the restoration of integrity.

According to Trubetskoi, Florensky is caught between two opposite understandings of antinomism: 1) Antinomism as a characteristic of the sinful state of fallen reason, or 2) antinomism of the truth itself, which would mean that the true religious dogma is also antinomic.[21] Trubetskoi then points to the overgeneralization of Florensky's statement that mysteries of religion "cannot be put into words except in the form of contradictions, which are 'yes' and 'no' at the same time." Trubetskoi thinks this would make impossible a straightforward answer to the question of whether Christ is risen, and to many other questions which require unequivocal answers. Florensky might perhaps reply that if one is speaking about the Resurrection of Christ in the context of the

---

18. See Bulgakov, *Tragediia filosofii*, 316.
19. Trubetskoi, *Svet Favorskii*, 8.
20. Trubetskoi, *Svet Favorskii*, 10.
21. Trubetskoi, *Svet Favorskii*, 11.

above-mentioned quotation, then it is not about "whether Christ is risen," but about the mystery of Christ's Resurrection. The quotation is, in fact, Father Pavel's commentary on the liturgical text Resurrectional Dismissal Theotokion for the second tone: "All beyond thought, all most-glorious are your mysteries, O Theotokos!" It is clear from this that the idea that *all mysteries* are beyond the mind is found not only in Florensky but in the church hymn, which invalidates Trubetskoi's argument.

Trubetskoi further suggests that Florensky uses the terms "antinomy" and "antinomic" in two different meanings: 1) as a sin of the soul, where the terms mean "contradiction"; 2) in relation to dogma, where it in fact means the union of opposites, but this meaning, according to Trubetskoi, is not properly an antinomy or antinomic.

It is worth noting that later authors generally do not make this distinction, applying the term "antinomy" to dogma without hesitation. In his *Mystical Theology* Lossky makes use of antinomies. For example, he writes that the dogma of the Holy Trinity is "the highest point of revelation" and that it is "an antinomy."[22] Nor can we agree, as some authors argue,[23] that Lossky uses the terms "apophatic" and "antinomic" as synonyms. In fact, there is some inconsistency in Lossky's own works on this point. In his earlier works (e.g., *The Debate on Sophia* and *Mystical Theology*) methodologically the concept of antinomy is subordinate to the concept of apophaticism. However, in his later collection of essays, *In the Image and Likeness of God*, he writes, very much like Bulgakov, about "the antinomy of two theological ways, the positive and the negative, established by Dionysius the Areopagite."[24] The two ways together, not just the way of negation, is what he now calls "an antinomic theology." It is interesting that here the apophatic way becomes subordinate to the concept of antinomy, as in Bulgakov, though Lossky previously criticized him for it.

Nor did a more recent scholar, Piama Gaidenko,[25] who wrote about antinomies in Florensky, make the distinction between antinomy as sin and antinomy as the union of the opposites. According to her, antinomy is, in fact, the union of the opposites.

Father Sophrony Sakharov (1896–1993) was one of the last theologians directly related to the Silver Age. He was named "starets" (elder) and in the near future will be canonized. He wrote the following:

---

22. Lossky, *Mystical Theology*, 46, 65–66.
23. See Gallaher, "'Sophiological' Origins."
24. Lossky, *Image*, 52.
25. See Gaidenko, "Antinomicheskaya dialektika."

The dogmas of the Church represent an utterly concentrated synthesis. They are expressed in short formulations, which are of an absolutely exceptional nature, as they have *antinomy* at their core through the positing of two seemingly contradictory affirmations or denials. For critical reason (or fallen, natural reason) they appear to be an absurdity or logical impossibility.[26]

Father Sophrony takes Personal Being as an example of the antinomies of thought:

> We cannot think of such a Personal Being, Which, being absolutely free in its self-positing . . . does not exclude the absolute objectiveness of its nature, or existence. . . . It is inconceivable for us how it is possible that nature or essence, being an absolutely objective reality, does not pre-exist and predetermine the absolute completeness of the subjective self-positing of the Persons of the Holy Trinity. . . . We cannot imagine such a Being in Which three Persons are different from one Essence or Nature, and Essence from Energy, and Which is at the same time absolutely simple.[27]

Father Sophrony's words suggest that Trubetskoi's approach to the logical content of dogma, as well as his critique of Florensky in this regard, can be seen as somewhat simplistic.

Trubetskoi also points out "the right understanding" of antinomies. First of all, antinomies are said to be rooted in the rational (*rassudochnoe*) understanding of the world. Second, according to him, antinomies constitute a certain hierarchy, which is based on a person's spiritual development. They can be resolved with the power of the human mind. Trubetskoi illustrates how antinomies can be resolved in the second chapter of his book *The Meaning of Life*. The denial of monism in thinking is Florensky's gravest mistake, according to Trubetskoi. To deny monism is not to reject the sin of thought, but to deprive thought of its norm, which is the ideal of all-unity and all-wholeness, constituting the formal state of our reason's likeness to God. Trubetskoi concludes that antinomism understood in this way is not coherent with the religious point of view of Florensky himself. Florensky needs to rid himself of "decadent alogism" to be able to root himself in the the ground of genuine churchliness.[28]

---

26. See Sofrony, *Rozhdenie*, 63–64.

27. Sofrony, *Rozhdenie*, 55.

28. Schneider argues that a careful analysis of how antinomism functions in the thought of Florensky excludes its fideist reading. See Schneider, "Will the Truth," 37–51.

Why did Trubetskoi choose Florensky's antinomism as his major target? Could it be that he wanted to defend his friend and teacher Soloviev from Florensky's attacks? This explanation cannot be altogether dismissed.

Bulgakov: The Philosophy of Language in Defense of Antinomism

Despite Trubetskoi's criticism, Bulgakov continued elaborating on the principle of antinomism in his later works. He opposes the idea of antinomism to the principle of logical monism. Logical monism (such as that of Hegel) posits that human reason has the ability to describe the world fully and sufficiently, giving to any philosophical attempt the spirit and pathos of a system. Bulgakov states that "reason is not the only exhaustive and almighty creator of the world."[29] That is why, according to Bulgakov, any kind of philosophical system is inevitably one-sided and insufficient. He notes that the world unfolds in reason (*razum*), but the source of new knowledge is mysterious. In order to comprehend this mystery, Bulgakov proceeds to analyse the universal form of judgement.[30] He concludes from his analysis that the essence of being is not monadic but triadic, or even triune.

Bulgakov describes the subject as the personal pronoun "I" which is a "verbal mystical gesture" and serves as a foundation for every particular thing. Every judgement necessarily relates subject with object. Hypostasis cannot be grasped by thought and thought is not able to perceive the origin of itself apart from the living witness of life which is expressed in judgement. Any judgement has three aspects to it, which although interconnected are not reducible to each other. These are as follows:

1. pure hypostacity of the I—subject;
2. the nature of the I which reveals itself in the I—predicate;
3. self-awareness or self-relatedness to one's own nature (being or the copula)—self-knowledge and self-affirmation of the I.

The subject and predicate do not indicate logical analysis, deduction or proof but synthesis beyond logic. Bulgakov writes: "Substance is one but at the same time triadic. . . . It exists not only 'in itself' as subject but also 'for itself' as predicate, and at the same time 'in itself and for itself' in

---

29. Bulgakov, *Tragediia filosofii*, 315.

30. "The Thomistic school emphasizes the capital role of judgement in human knowledge. The judgement (affirmation, internal speech, interior word, mental word) appears to be the completion of the cognitive act." Steenberghen, *Epistemology*, 143.

connection as being."³¹ He argues that these are not only the "dialectical moments" which sublate each other, as presented in Hegelian philosophy. The three above-mentioned aspects of judgement exist simultaneously and equally and are as it were the "roots of being," where the law of identity,³² which is the basic law of any reasoning, is not applicable.³³ Here Bulgakov defines the philosophical categories of being (*bytie*) and existence (*suschee*). According to his logic, existence is prior to being as existence is the persistently on-going synthesis between hypostasis and its own nature, its self-disclosure in the act of being.³⁴ One can see that Bulgakov deals with the philosophical problems of the relation between being and existence, transcendent and immanent, and non-conditional beginning and finite existence within the terms of theological discourse.³⁵

He then concentrates on the copula "to be" which, being the main instrument of thought, is completely inconceivable by logic as it links together not equal but different and dissimilar things. Bulgakov writes: "The copula has its origin not in grammar or logic but in ontology; it is the life of existence. . . . It is the bridge which links existence and being, the subject and predicate. Actuality and existence are confirmed by it."³⁶

All of the three moments just discussed are both inseparable and unmingled in their existence. This triunity is, however, inadmissible for a logical approach, which can only accept one source of thought, one starting point for any deliberation. And this is a real antinomy that cannot be overcome. Substance can therefore be defined as the metaphysical triunity expressed in judgement.³⁷ There are many places where Bulgakov expresses his understanding of substance in addition to the above-mentioned passages.

He maintains that "substance is the basis of things in existence" (*osnova suschego*).³⁸ Further, he makes the very important point that substance is spirit: "Substance (i.e. spirit) is an existing tri-unity of subject, object and their being."³⁹ "The copula points symbolically to the nature

---

31. Bulgakov, *Tragediia filosofii*, 319.

32. Some of the earliest uses of the law of identity are found, e.g., in Plato, *Theaet*. 185a, and Aristotle, *Metaph*. IV.4.

33. See Bulgakov, *Tragediia filosofii*, 319.

34. See Bulgakov, *Tragediia filosofii*, 322.

35. See Reznichenko, "K metafizike subiekta," 240.

36. Bulgakov, *Tragediia filosofii*, 325.

37. See Bulgakov, *Tragediia filosofii*, 325. See also 317ff.

38. See Bulgakov, *Tragediia filosofii*, 319.

39. Bulgakov, *Tragediia filosofii*, 325.

of substance . . . it signifies substance as object."[40] "The idea of substance necessarily contains an antinomy: one principle comes true in trinity."[41] *The Tragedy of Philosophy* contains the following description of substance: "Substance is, as it were, an equilateral triangle,"[42] "three inseparable and unmingled moments of substance . . . define substantiality."[43] At the end of his book, Bulgakov concludes: "Substance is a living sentence, which contains a subject and also a predicate and a copula."[44]

The idea of substance as the underlying ground of all phenomena is taken by Bulgakov from modern philosophy. The notion of substance in Descartes is instrumental; it is rather a name than a notion and it does not unite God and his creation.[45] Bulgakov develops Spinoza's classical notion of substance.[46] The difference is that whereas substance for Spinoza is reasonable and comprehensible, for Bulgakov it is inevitably antinomical and is revealed by God as the Christian dogma of triunity. The idea of triunity is precisely that relationship which unites God and creation in a substantial way.

In conclusion, one can say that Trubetskoi's critique influenced later authors who analysed the problem of antinomies in Florensky. In Bulgakov's case, despite the fact that he developed Father Pavel's ideas regarding antinomies, we cannot find in his works formulations like "truth is an antinomy," which is typical of Florensky's *The Pillar and the Ground of Truth*. Nor can we find in him any praise for contradictions or antinomies. Rather, for Bulgakov, antinomy is the tragedy and ill fate of reason. He accepted this as he nonetheless made a serious attempt to oppose the so called "logic of monism" to his own antinomic "logic of Triunity."

Bibliography

Aristotle. *The Metaphysics*. Translated by Hugh Tredennick and G. Cyril Armstrong. Vol. 1. London: Heinemann, 1933–35.

Bulgakov, Sergei N. *Tragediia filosofii*. In *Sochineniia v dvukh tomakh*, 311–445. Vol. 1. Moscow: Nauka, 1993.

Bulgakov, Sergius. *Icons and the Name of God*. Translated by Boris Jakim. Grand Rapids, MI: Eerdmans, 2012.

40. Bulgakov, *Tragediia filosofii*, 368.
41. Bulgakov, *Tragediia filosofii*, 387.
42. Bulgakov, *Tragediia filosofii*, 326.
43. Bulgakov, *Tragediia filosofii*, 329.
44. Bulgakov, *Tragediia filosofii*, 518.
45. See Ivanov, *Metaphizika*, 270.
46. See Spinoza, *Collected Works*, E1D3.

———. *Unfading Light: Contemplations and Speculations.* Translated by Thomas Allan Smith. Grand Rapids, MI: Eerdmans, 2012.

Florensky, Pavel. "Kosmologicheskie antinomii I. Kanta." *Bogoslovskii vestnik* 1.4 (1909) 596–625.

———. *The Pillar and Ground of the Truth.* Translated by Boris Jakim. Princeton, NJ: Princeton University Press, 1997.

Gaidenko, Piama P. "Antinomicheskaya dialektika P. A. Florenskogo protiv zakona tozhdestva." In *Kritika nemarksistskikh kontseptsii dialektiki XX veka: Dialektika i problema irratsionalnogo*, edited by Yurii N. Davydov, 169–80. Moscow: Izdatelstvo MGU, 1988.

Gallaher, Brandon. "The 'Sophiological' Origins of Vladimir Lossky's Apophaticism." *Scottish Journal of Theology* 66.3 (2013) 278–98.

———. *There Is Freedom: The Dialectic of Freedom and Necessity in the Trinitarian Theologies of Sergii Bulgakov, Karl Barth and Hans Urs von Balthasar.* Oxford: University of Oxford, Regent's Park College, 2010.

Ivanov, Oleg. *Metafizika v bogoslovskoi perspektive.* St. Petersburg: Tserkov' i kultura, 1999.

Lossky, Vladimir. *In the Image and Likeness of God.* Crestwood, NY: St. Vladimir's Seminary Press, 1974.

———. *The Mystical Theology of the Eastern Church.* Cambridge: Clarke, 1991.

Plato. *Theaetetus.* In *Theaetetus. Sophist*, translated by Harold North Fowler, 1–258. Cambridge, MA: Harvard University Press, 2014.

Reznichenko, Anna. "'Ya': K metafizike subiekta S. N. Bulgakova v rabotakh 20-kh godov." In *S. N. Bulgakov: Religiozno-filosofskii put': Mezhdunarodnaya nauchnaya konferentsiya, posvyashchennaya 130-letiyu so dnya rozhdeniya*, edited by Alexei Kozyrev and Maria Vasilyev, 218–50. Moscow: Russkii put', 2003.

Rojek, Paweł. *The Logic of Orthodoxy. Pavel Florensky's Theory of Antinomies.* Typescript.

Schelling, Friedrich Wilhelm Joseph. "Immanuel Kant." In *Sämmtliche Werke*, 1–10. Vol. 4. Charlottesville: InteLex, 2013. Electronic ed.

Schneider, Christoph. "Will the Truth not Demand a Sacrifice from Us? Reflections on Pavel A. Florensky's Idea of Truth as Antinomy in the *Pillar and Ground of the Truth* (1914)." *Sobornost* 34.2 (2013) 34–51.

Seiling, Jonathan. *From Antinomy to Sophiology: Modern Russian Religious Consciousness and Sergei Bulgakov's Critical Appropriation of German Idealism.* Toronto: University of Toronto, 2008.

Sofrony, Archim. *Rozhdenie v Tsarstvo Nepokolebimoe.* Moscow: Palomnik, 2000.

Soloviev, Vladimir. *Lectures on Divine Humanity.* Translated by Peter Zouboff and Boris Jakim. Hudson, NY: Lindisfarne, 1995.

———. *The Philosophical Principles of Integral Knowledge.* Translated by Valeria Z. Nollan. Grand Rapids, MI: Eerdmans, 2008.

Spinoza, Baruch. *The Collected Works*, edited and translated Edwin Curley. Princeton: Princeton University Press, 1988.

Steenberghen, Fernand van. *Epistemology.* Louvain: Publications universitaires, 1970.

Trubetskoi, Evgenii N. *Smysl zhizni.* Moscow: AST, Folio, 2000.

———. *Svet Favorskii i preobrazhenie uma. Po povodu knigi sviashchennika P. A. Florenskogo.* Moscow: Put', 1914.

PART II

Philosophy of the Icon

7

The Theology of the Icon

Theological Development in Icon Interpretation in the Twentieth Century

Irina Yazykova

The theology of the icon is a relatively new discipline and its history can be traced back no earlier than a hundred years. This started with the "icon discovery" that took place at the turn of the twentieth century with the restoration of ancient Russian paintings, when old overpainted icons, covered in soot, were unveiled and the world was able to see the beauty of the ancient images. The public response was significant and in great part determined the subsequent direction of the development of Russian icon art in the twentieth century. This was true not only for the church but also secular art, something which is clearly demonstrated by Russian avant-garde painters such as Kazimir Malevich, Kuzma Petrov-Vodkin, Natalia Goncharova, and others. The impact was not limited to Russia and here it is pertinent to name Henry Matisse, who admired Russian icons when he saw them in Ilya Ostroukhov's collection. The church's response to this "icon discovery" was not rapid but gradually it became clear that ancient icons were an inexhaustible source of inspiration. However, it would take time before ancient icon painting could truly reinvigorate church art. It was first necessary to rediscover a vast number of relics and to rethink the meaning of the icon for the Russian Orthodox tradition as well as for Christian culture in general.

Icon painting in Russia had been a traditional art, but with the Petrine reforms it was sidelined. The main vector was now the new European painting.

Reverence for ancient icons remained in the peasant environment as well as amongst traditional believers. For the educated part of Russian society, the icon was of little interest and was considered to be crude and unskillful. However, at the beginning of the nineteenth century, this started to change, first with art collectors and then within academia. Interest continued to grow in the following decades. Many scholars took an interest in the study of ancient icon paintings, including Fedor Buslaev, Dmitry Rovinsky, Georgy Filimonov, Nikolai Likhachev, Nikolai Pokrovsky, Alexander Anisimov, Nikodim Kondakov, and others who appreciated the beauty of ancient icons. In the nineteenth century the historical, archeological, and iconographic approach to icon study prevailed. It is evident why: it was necessary to remove later layers added to the icon in order to perform stylistic analysis. The restoration practice of that time was quite primitive; it included mechanical cleaning and was not immune to added embellishments. However, by the turn of the nineteenth and twentieth centuries, restoration methods had significantly improved. Together with this, important steps had been made in the study of Byzantine and ancient Russian legacies as an artistic phenomenon. These advancements gave remarkable results and went down in history as the "discovery of the icon."

The first scientific approach to cleaning icons was commissioned by Ilya Ostroukhov and financed by the Moscow banker Stepan Ryabushinsky. These two, together with other collectors, decided to arrange an exhibition of Ancient Russian art, timed to coincide with the three hundredth anniversary of the House of the Romanovs that was celebrated in 1913. The exhibition was solemnly opened on February 13, 1913 in the building of the Moscow Business Centre on Varvarka Street.

The exhibition showed that the icon was not merely a striking artistic phenomenon but an entire universe of meanings, ideas, and symbols. And this phenomenon required deeper comprehension. However, by that time, the language of the ancient icon had been lost. Despite the fact that icon painting continued to remain a main form of church art, never leaving temples and houses, much had been forgotten—icons were reproduced formally, often with distortions. The language of the icon was in need of new "reading." It needed to be deciphered.

The first person who noticed this was Evgenii Trubetskoi. Influenced by the exhibition of Ancient Russian art from the collection of Ilya Ostroukhov, he wrote three essays about the icon: "Theology in Colour" (1915), "Two Worlds in Ancient Russian Icon Painting" (1916) and "Russia in Its Icon" (1917). This was the beginning of a new stage in icon rediscovery, and it was connected with philosophical and theological comprehension.

Trubetskoi realized that the discovery of the icon occurred during a critical moment in Russian and world history. It was also not limited to narrow confessional or regional significance but extended to a global one. This was because ancient icon art revealed the eternal meaning of existence to the people of the twentieth century.

In his essay "Theology in Colour," Trubetskoi wrote:

> If indeed the apotheosis of evil is the crown of all human life and all human history, where is the meaning that makes life worth living? I shall not try to answer this question myself. I would rather remind the reader of the answer given by our forebears. They were not philosophers, they were seers, and they put their thoughts into colours, not words. Their painting directly answers our question, for in their lifetime, too, the meaning of life was a burning question. The horror of war that we feel so keenly today was a chronic evil in their times. The countless hordes ravaging Russia were a constant reminder of the "image of the beast." The kingdom of the beast even then tempted people with the same eternal bait: "All these things will I give thee, if thou wilt fall down and worship me" (Matt 4:7). The ancient religious art of Russia grew out of the struggle against this temptation. The old-Russian icon countered it with striking power and clarity by embodying in images and colours the vision that filled their souls—the vision of a different truth of life, a different meaning of the world. I shall try to express in words the gist of their answer, though I know, of course, that no words can convey the beauty and power of their incomparable language of religious symbols.[1]

It is possible to call Evgenii Trubetskoi the pioneer of the icon as a theological phenomenon and the founder of a new learned movement called the "theology of the icon." With this movement a serious study of theological language begins.

The Russian priest and scientist Pavel Florensky also entered the process of the interpretation of icons. In works such as "Reverse Perspective" (1919), "Trinity Lavra of St. Sergius and Russia" (1919), "Church Ritual as a Synthesis of Arts" (*Kramovoe deistvo kak sintez iskusstva*) (1922), "Heavenly Signs: Reflections on Colour Symbolism" (1922), and especially his main work *Iconostasis* (1922), he dramatically widened the range of discourse and thus set it on a new level.

Florensky, with his characteristic research zeal, sought to uncover the metaphysical meaning of the icon. That metaphysical meaning he sees in

---

1. Trubetskoi, *Icons*, 15–16.

everything, including technology. Even substances that are employed in various types of art are symbolic, for they all have their own metaphysical characteristic which relates to different spiritual layer of existence. Proceeding from his theory on the philosophy of the cult, Florensky tried to reconstruct the ancient Russian worldview in which he sees the unity of aesthetics and theology, as well as the synergy of rite and various art forms. Today, Florensky's works often become the subject of criticism for their somewhat gnostic bias, yet it is important to notice his enthusiasm as well as his search after wholeness and beauty.

In 1918, the restorers Grygory Chirikov, Vasily Tulin, Ivan Suslov, and Evgenii Bryagin carried out the restoration of the icon "Trinity." In 1918–1922, Florensky was a member of the restoration committee of the Trinity Lavra of St. Sergius. He was one of the first people who saw the "Trinity" after it had been restored. He was delighted and moved by the icon. He noted, just like Trubetskoi did, that amongst disarray, dissension, internecine feuds, and the overall wildness of Russia and the Tatar raids, the "Trinity" revealed the infinite, calm, indestructible heavenly world. Hostility and hatred are challenged by love and unity. It was celestial harmony that Florensky saw in the eternal silent conversation of the angels—the harmony that is able to cleanse and transform all those living on Earth. Florensky then comes to a striking conclusion: "There exists the icon of the Holy Trinity by St. Andrei Rublev; therefore, God exists."[2]

Analysing the peculiarities of the artistic language of the icon, Florensky coined the term "reverse perspective."[3] With its help, he describes the principles by which icon space is created, principles that are fundamentally different from those used in creating realistic art. Whilst Florensky's description of "reverse perspective" is strictly mathematical, he nevertheless highlights its spiritual meaning, i.e., the creation of sacred space which determines the link between the spectator and the world of symbolic images.

Florensky was followed by the painter and theorist Lev Zhegin, who was also interested in reverse perspective. He was the founder of the group "Makovets."[4] Zhegin was more interested in the artistic and practical meaning and not so much in the sacred and symbolic one. In his work, *The Language of Painting*, he considers the problem of the space-time unity of painting which in an icon is achieved through "reverse perspective," where

---

2. Florensky, *Iconostasis*, 68.

3. Florensky, "Obratnaya perspektiva."

4 "Makovets"—an association of Moscow painters (1921–1927) symbolically named after the hill Makovets, upon which Saint Reverend Sergius of Radonezh founded his monastery.

the vanishing points are the spectators.⁵ Zhegin, analyzing the icon's various types of perspective, discovered an expanding and active space. He does not give any philosophical or theological interpretations to this phenomenon but half a century later it was adopted by Alexei Lidov in order to explain his concept of hierotopy, an issue which will be discussed later on.

In the 1970s, the problem of "reverse perspective" was examined by Boris Raushenbach (1915–2001), one of the founding fathers of the Soviet space programme. He describes "reverse perspective" as a physical phenomenon but one with specific properties. In the direct perspective, there is one point from which the spectator looks at objects. These things become smaller with increasing distance and there is one vanishing point on the horizon. In the "reverse perspective" there could be many observation points with several horizons. The objects seem bigger as they move further away from the spectator and the "vanishing point" is situated within the observer. It appears that the icon is trying to look deep inside the heart of the viewer.⁶ In other words, the physicist portrays the icon as an example of spiritual optics. It is no accident that from studying the perspective Raushenbach moved on to studying theology, without which icon comprehension is not possible. His last works are dedicated to the Holy Trinity.⁷

In the Soviet Union, under the ideological control of the time, conditions were not conducive for developing icon theology and icon painting. Yet, icon research did not stop—there were restoration works, museum engagement, and icon research. This research was done under constant ideological pressure and it was only during the late Soviet period that the constraints weakened.

Icon research developed in emigration circles. A study group of young scientists was formed around one of the most prominent icon specialists—Nikodim Pavlovich Kondakov. After his death in 1925, the group took on the name *Seminarium Kondakovianum* which later, in 1931, was transformed into the Kondakov Archeological Institute. The institute contributed significantly to icon understanding, particularly the theological point of view.⁸

In 1927, the Ancient Rite Christian (Old Believer) Vladimir Ryabushinsky founded the society "Icon," which contributed to icon painting, development, and theoretical research. This society did much to introduce icons to the West.

---

5. See Zhegin, *Yazyk*.
6. Raushenbakh, *Prostranstvennye postroeniya*.
7. Raushenbakh, "O peredache."
8. See *Seminarium Kondakovianum*, 1927–1938.

An important contribution to understanding of icons was made by the prominent Russian emigration theologian Father Sergei Bulgakov, who wrote a small but capacious book called *The Icon and Its Veneration*.[9] The book was written under the influence of conversations with the talented icon painter and thinker Sister Ioanna (Reitlinger), as can be seen from their correspondence.[10] First and foremost, Bulgakov is interested in the dogmatic aspect of the icon. In his book he puts forward questions such as the connection between icon and dogma, canon and work of art, tradition and innovation, and symbolic and artistic language of the icon. His work significantly advanced theological understanding of the icon after the works of Trubetskoi and Florensky.

The emigration experience was also beneficial for icon comprehension. Having found themselves in new conditions Orthodox believers strove to keep their faith as the basis for their identity. They built temples, worshipped in Orthodox liturgy, and tried to rethink anew the heritage of Eastern Christianity, including, of course, the icon. One of the most prominent theologians of the Russian diaspora was Vladimir Lossky, who was among the founders of the neo-patristic movement in Russian theology. Together with his friend Leonid Ouspensky, with whom he taught at the St. Dionysius Theological Institute in Paris, he wrote a work called *The Meaning of Icons*. The book was first published in Switzerland in 1952 in German, before being published in French and English.[11] The Russian edition, however, came out only in 2014. The authors addressed this book primarily to the Western reader, who knew little about icon painting and the history of Orthodoxy, let alone Orthodox theology. Nevertheless, the book is popular amongst Orthodox readers, who in many respects lost understanding of the tradition. When reflecting on the icon as part of the Orthodox Church's legacy, Lossky and Ouspensky show the link between the icon and the liturgy, the annual calendar cycle and understanding of the sacred. For the authors the icon is primarily a manifestation of the Orthodox faith.

After Lossky's death in 1958, Ouspensky continued to develop his theological understanding of the icon. He wrote *Icon Theology of the Orthodox Church*, which was published in French in 1960,[12] with the Russian edition being published after the author's death in 1989. This fundamental work, which remains definitive in this area, analyses the historic path of church art

---

9. Bulgakov, "Icon."

10. See Reytlinger and Bulgakov, *Dialog khudozhnika i bogoslova*.

11. Ouspensky and Lossky, *Der Sinn der Ikonen*; Ouspensky and Lossky, *Meaning of Icons*.

12. Ouspensky, *Théologie de l'icône*.

and the development of icon theology. The book started life as a collection of Ouspensky's lectures that were first printed as articles. Leonid Ouspensky was not only a theoretician, he also painted icons and gave lectures. This practical knowledge is reflected in his book. Ouspensky demonstrated how a true attitude towards the icon was formed, established and sometimes fought for within the church. He shows how icon worship influenced icon painting and how artistic expression reacted to various mystical movements (hesychasm) or theological disputes (on the Trinity). He also shows amongst other things how an icon's style was a reflection of the spiritual state of a historical period. Ouspensky demonstrates in a very vivid way Trubetskoi's thesis on the icon as a speculation in colors.

Alongside Ouspensky worked his talented and like-minded friend and icon painter, the monk Grigory Krug (1906/07–1969). His notes were published after his death in *Thoughts on the Icon*, which expanded theological discourse on the icon.[13] Grigory Krug reflected on how individual iconographies compared with the dogmatic teachings of the Church, hymns, and mystical teaching. He tried to interpret icon images in such a way that every detail expressed the spiritual wisdom of the Church.

Amongst the thinkers of the Russian emigration, it is important to mention the philosopher and professor of the St. Sergius Orthodox Theological Institute in Paris, Pavel Evdokimov (1901–1970). In his book, *The Art of the Icon: A Theology of Beauty*, he juxtaposes the icon as a revelation of another world to secular culture, which is detached from its ontological roots.[14] Evdokimov shows that all the artistic means in the Orthodox icon are directed to revealing a beauty that is not made with human hands and which is imperishable. He also discloses the wealth of the Orthodox icon through the biblical foundations of creativity, using extensive theological and philosophical material, as well as the actions of saints. Following Plato's postulate that "beauty is the radiance of truth," Evdokimov coined the term "the theology of beauty." He tried to discern the place art has in God's plan for the world. It is art, with the icon as its highest manifestation, that is called to remind humans of the finality of things and of their ultimate destiny. Evdokimov writes that the icon

> enlightens the destiny of the world and points to the eschatological union of the earthly and the heavenly. Through both human and material cases, with all their imperfections, the icon suggests perfection in delicate lacy contours. It reminds man

---

13. Krug, *Mysli ob ikone*.
14. Evdokimov, *L'Art de l'icône*. English edition: Evdokimov, *Art of the Icon*.

that his original and permanent vocation is to be the image of God, an earthly angel, a heavenly being.[15]

Evdokimov strove in his works to use evocative language, having the view that one should be a poet in order to do theology.

The Russian diaspora facilitated the introduction of the icon to the West. In the post-war years, interest in icons grew in non-Orthodox circles. It is only natural that icons attracted Catholics in particular and this primarily coincided with the very large interest in patristics—the theological heritage of the Church Fathers. It was Cristoph Schönborn, the Cardinal of Vienna and a brilliant patrologist, who showed the close relationship between the theology of the Church Fathers and the icon. His fundamental work on the topic was published under the title *God's Human Face: The Christ-Icon*.[16] In this book he follows the dynamics of theological disputes during the Ecumenical Councils and shows that the Seventh Ecumenical Council had adopted the dogma of iconodulism (veneration of icons) as a logical conclusion of all previous councils and dogmatic disputes.

> The christological controversies dragged on through centuries. During all this time, the Church never stopped to *profess* the mystery of Christ revealed and yet hidden in the holy face of Jesus. In Nicaea (325 AD), she professed Christ as the consubstantial image of the Father; in Ephesus (431 AD) as the unchanged Word become flesh; in Chalcedon (451 AD) as true God and true man; in Constantinople (553 AD) as "one of the Trinity who suffered for us"; and again in Constantinople (681 AD) as the Word of God, whose human acting and willing was in perfect unison with God's counsel, even unto death. After these long centuries of turbulent, consequential struggles for the profession of the true Christ, our gaze comes to rest to contemplate a quiet image: *the icon of Christ*.[17]

In the twentieth century, interest in the icon moved beyond confessional boundaries. Even Protestants, formerly known for their iconoclastic positions, expressed interest in the icon in a theological and symbolic context. The greatest interest in icons was demonstrated by the Anglicans, something which on the surface can be explained by historic reasons. In 1928, the Anglican-Orthodox fellowship of Saint Alban and Saint Sergius was founded. It actively facilitated the cultural and theological dialogue whose participants were prominent theologians such as Bulgakov,

15. Evdokimov, *Art of the Icon*, 219.
16. Schönborn, *Die Christus-Icone*. English edition: Schönborn, *God's Human Face*.
17. Schönborn, *God's Human Face*, 132.

Florovsky, Zernov and later Metropolitan Anthony of Sourozh. Owing to these joint meetings, the Anglicans discovered the treasures of the Orthodox icon. On the one hand, icons attracted people as works of art and, on the other, the icon enabled non-Orthodox believers to better understand the Orthodox tradition.

It is interesting to note that nowadays the subject of the theology of the icon has been taken up by the prominent Anglican theologian and former Archbishop of Canterbury, Rowan Williams. As a student, he took an interest in Russian culture and Orthodox theology, especially in the mystical theology of Vladimir Lossky (about whom he wrote a dissertation). This enabled Williams to comprehend icons as theology in color. He also took an interest in the subject of praying in front of icons, something which was practically unknown in the Church of England but highly valued by the former archbishop. He even wrote two books on praying with the Christ and Virgin icons.[18]

In post-war Europe, the interest in Orthodox icons is not only theoretical but also practical. Icon workshops have been created, where now it is the Germans, French, Italians—people of various confessions (and not Russian emigrants)—who are learning how to paint icons. Moreover, interest in Russian icons is helping Europeans discover the roots of their own sacred art. It helps them understand the tradition of the first millennium when art was imbued with theology and when, despite the stylistic difference between the East and the West, it could be easily understood anywhere in the Christian world. It only took a few decades after 1945 to create icon painting schools in various countries such as Italy, France, Switzerland and others.

Amongst those who contributed to the Western tradition of icon painting was Igor (Egon) Sendler—the Jesuit, priest-monk of the Byzantine rite, icon painter and theologian. The founder and head of icon painting schools in France, Italy and Switzerland, he painted in temples in *Collegium Russicum* (the Vatican), Meudon and Versailles (France). At the beginning of the 1980s, Sendler wrote a few works where he explained the artistic and theological peculiarities of icon painting. In them he also researched iconography and gave practical advice on the technique of icon painting.[19] He saw the key to icon comprehension in theology and liturgy. Whilst it might appear that his works do not contribute anything new to the understanding of icon theology, as a Catholic who follows the Byzantine style of worship and thus embodies Eastern and Western practice, he believes that the icon

---

18. Williams, *Dwelling*; Williams, *Ponder These Things*.

19. Sendler, *L'icône*; Sendler, *Trasfigurazione*; Sendler, *Icônes byzantines*; Sendler, *L'icona immagine dell'invisibile*; Sendler, *Mystères du Christ*.

is capable of unifying both traditions. It is the icon, he argues, that brings us back to our common source of faith.

There are cases where icon study was the reason for some to convert to Orthodoxy. This was the case with the former Catholic priest Michel Quenot. In the temple where he worshipped in the early 1990s, the icons were painted by the Russian icon painter, Pavel Busalaev. Having started with icon aesthetics, he later moved on to study icon theology and subsequently wrote the book *Window onto the Absolute* (*Fenêtre à Absolut*).[20] In this work the author shows both the artistic and theological aspects of the icon phenomenon to the Western reader. In the 2000s, Michel Quenot converted to Orthodoxy and now worships as an Orthodox priest.

It would be pertinent to mention here Gabriel Bunge, the famous patrologist and former Benedictine monk who converted to Orthodoxy and became head of the Holy Cross monastery in Lugano (Switzerland). His contribution to icon theology was his small but informative book where he analyses Rublev's Trinity.[21] In it the author reveals the icon as a theological and liturgical text which can be understood through meditation and contemplation.

It is clear that not everyone who studies icons becomes an Orthodox believer. The "birthplace" of the icon, despite its Orthodox theology, is the Church of the first millennium. Icons, therefore, transcend confessional boundaries and carry the wholeness of the Christian worldview.

The universality of icon heritage is demonstrated by the icon painting school in the central *Russia Christiana* in Seriate, Italy. One of the pioneers of the school was Egon Sendler. Russian icon painters such as Adolf Ovchinnikov, Archimandrite Zinon (Theodor), Brother Pavel (Beschastni), and others taught at the school. The founder of *Russia Christiana*, Romano Scalfi, used to say that it was Russian Orthodox believers who helped the Italians rediscover their own treasure—the ancient icons of the first millennium before the schism. There are many icons and mosaics in Italy that indicate the deep roots of Western icon art. This, of course, is true of medieval art of other European regions, which provides amazing examples of sacred icon art that convey a holistic perception of the world.

Contemporary icon painting goes beyond the boundaries of the European continent—there are now icon painting schools in America, Australia, New Zealand, and other countries. This begs a question which is intrinsically theological—do icons belong solely to the Orthodox world or are they part of universal heritage of the Church?

20. Quenot, *Fenêtre à Absolut*. English edition: Quenot, *Window on the Kingdom*.
21. Bunge, *Rublev Trinity*.

Let us, however, return to Russia or, more precisely, the Soviet Union. What happened here after 1917? Despite the strict indoctrination there of the communist and atheist ideology, icon research continued. It is true to say that it was a secular science with no place for theology. The Soviet School of Art Studies was based (or so it was believed) on Marxism. There were many iconography scholars such as Mikhail Alpatov, Vladimir Lazarev, Natalia Demina, Engelina Smirnova, and others who wrote a great number of articles and monographs on icons but who had to keep to the Marxist approach. This created a situation where icons were taken out of their liturgical, ascetic, and theological context. It became clear that this approach could not understand the full depth of the icon. Censorship, however, left very little room for maneuver. One of the first researchers who broke the taboo was an outstanding scholar of Byzantium, Moscow State University Professor Olga Popova. She openly started to make connections between icons and their spiritual-historical context as well as their connection with contemporary ideological movements, theological disputes, and spiritual literature (especially of the Church Fathers). Her icon research went beyond the formal analysis permitted by the Soviets. Her works always included a search for theological meaning. For obvious reasons, she was only able to publish her main works in the post-Soviet period.[22]

It is now difficult to imagine how stringent the Soviet ideological censorship was—there could not be even a hint of theology in academic articles and books. Nevertheless, scholars knew that to examine icons thoroughly, mere artistic and aesthetic analysis was not enough—there was too much symbolism in them. The semiotic school was also interested in icons and this can be seen in the works of Boris Uspensky, who analysed the icon's sign structure through the prism of theological and dogmatic texts.[23] Uspensky's contribution to icon research is significant but the semiotic approach is in great part opposed to the theological because the former employs signs and the latter symbols.

In the post-Soviet period, interest in icons grew rapidly, with the disappearance of official ideology and revival of church culture. In the 1990s, many articles and books on icons were published but most of these works were educational and had little to do with research and theology. It became evident that icon theological discourse was far from complete and needed further development.

---

22. Popova, *Les miniatures russes*; Popova, *Russian Illuminated Manuscripts*; Popova, "Le illustrazioni."

23. Uspensky, *Semiotics*.

It is also important to mention the works of Maria Nikolayevna Sokolova (later known as Sister Juliania after she became a nun) (1899–1981). She was an icon painter and one of the pioneers of the revival. With her efforts, the icon painting club at Trinity Lavra of St. Sergius, which she ran between the 1950s and 1970s, helped establish the icon painting school at the Moscow Theological Academy, which has now become a leading center for training in icon painting. Maria Sokolova developed study materials for her students in which she expressed her views and theological vision. There is definitely a difference between her works (which are not systematic) and Uspensky's book. However, she gave her students not only practical advice but also some theological foundations. She followed tradition which helped her go through the difficult years of the Church's persecution. Amongst her teachers were the priests Alexii and Sergii Mechev, Vasily Kirikov (a restorer who took part in the icon rediscovery at the beginning of the twentieth century), and Bishop Afanasi Sakharov (confessor and liturgist). It was with their help that Maria Sokolova developed the solid theological vision of icons which she conveyed to her students. Her works were published in the 1990s and 2000s. They played an important role in helping people to understand the meaning of icons.[24]

At the turn of the millennia, with the appearance of new ideas and concepts, the spectrum of theological understanding of icons has become wider. To name a few of these trends, there is Valery Lepakhin's "iconicity" (*ikonichnost'*), which tries to comprehend the entire Orthodox heritage through the prism of the icon, and Alexei Lidov's hierotopy theory (the science of making sacred spaces), which looks at the icon as a means by which sacred space is created.[25] Both theories have their advocates and opponents.

Lepakhin coined the term "iconicity" (*ikonichnost'*) to designate specific qualities such as: indissolubility into two parts, paradoxicality, applicability to liturgy, *sobornost* (spiritual community), applicability to synergy, symbolism, and canonicity.[26] He also coined the term *ikonotopos*—a space sacralized by man and perceived as an icon.[27]

The concept of *ikonotopos* is close to Lidov's concept of the spatial icon or hierotopy. A spatial icon is an image which the viewer perceives in some specific sacred space. That image is born by means of various symbolic and metaphorical parts being put together. A spatial icon, in

---

24. Iuliania (Sokolova), *Trud ikonopistsa*; Aldoshina, *Blagoslovennyi trud*; Juliania, *Russian Saints*.

25. Lepakhin, *Ikona i ikonichnost'*; Lidov, *Ierotopiya*.

26. Lepakhin, "Ikonichnost' istinnaya i mnimaya," 23–26.

27. See Lepakhin, "Ikonichnost' istinnaya i mnimaya," 28.

the same way as any other icon, acts as a link between earthly reality and heaven. Its image fills the space and manifests itself through various plastic forms (shapes). Various elements can be employed to create that space. Some of them can be stationary, such as architecture, murals, icons, and liturgical objects. Others can be dynamic, such as the liturgy itself, music, light, and even smell. For Lidov, the Christian temple is precisely such a spatial icon.[28] There is a clear link with Father Florensky's cult philosophy and Zhegin's theory of icon space expansion. But here they are perceived through the prism of new contemporary research techniques which include semiotics and structuralism. All this significantly expands the boundaries of theological discourse on icons.

The icon theology which started at the beginning of the twentieth century lost none of its importance at its end. This is demonstrated by the works of such prominent contemporary theologians as Olivier Clement,[29] Metropolitan Kallistos Ware,[30] and Hans Urs von Balthasar.[31] It would be interesting to outline Balthasar's concept here, though space does not permit. His theology of beauty and theo-aesthetics has considerable relevance for icon theology and the subject in general, though he was a Catholic thinker and did not directly touch on the subject of icons.

In the context of this discourse it is also important to note the fundamental work by an Orthodox American theologian, David Bentley Hart. In his book *The Beauty of the Infinite*, he puts forward his concept of holistic beauty which opposes world disintegration, market diktats and cultural degradation.[32] In a certain way, this runs parallel with Balthasar's theory but with a stronger emphasis on the image (*eicon*) as a cornerstone of existence.

Some Western philosophers have turned to icons as a tool which reveals images that are invisible and concealed. One of the most prominent ones is Jean-Luc Marion. In his book, *Idol and Distance*, he opposes the dead god or idol to the living God and Christ as the Father's icon. What Marion sees in icons is our interaction with God, where the image brings us closer to God.[33]

Trubetskoi's works set a new direction for the understanding of icons. It is possible to say today that icon theology is a serious discipline, with its own glossary, methodology, vast bibliography, various schools and theories.

---

28. See Lidov, *Hierotopia*; Lidov, *Ierotopiya*.
29. Clement, *Sillons de Lumière*; Clement, *L'autre soleil*.
30. Ware, *Orthodox Church*.
31. Balthasar, *Glory of God*.
32. Hart, *Beauty*.
33. Marion, *Idol and Distance*.

Moreover, the icon has entered philosophical discourse and is even used as a postmodern concept. This overview is far from being extensive; it only scratches the surface. But even this shows that icon understanding, including its theological comprehension, is as relevant today as it was in the first millennium. There are more discoveries and revelations to come.

Bibliography

Aldoshina, Natalia E. *Blagoslovennyi trud*. Moscow: Moskovskaya Dukhovnaya Akademiya, Isographica, 2001.

Balthasar, Hans Urs von. *The Glory of God. A Theological Aesthetics*. Translated by Andrew Louth et al. 7 vols. Edinburgh: Ignatius, 1982–1989.

Bulgakov, Sergius. "The Icon and Its Veneration." In *Icons and the Name of God*, translated by Boris Jakim, 1–114. Grand Rapids, MI: Eerdmans, 2012.

Bunge, Gabriel. *The Rublev Trinity: The Icon of the Trinity by the Monk-painter Andrei Rublev*. Crestwood, NY: St. Vladimir's Seminary Press, 2007.

Clement, Olivier. *L'autre soleil: Quelques notes d'autobiographie spirituelle*. Paris: Desclée de Brouwer, 2010.

———. *Sillons de Lumière*. Paris: Fates Cerf, 1990.

Evdokimov, Paul. *The Art of the Icon: A Theology of Beauty*. Translated by Fr. Steven Bigham. Knob Hill, CA: Oakwood, 1996.

———. *L'Art de l'icône. Théologie de la Beauté*. Paris: Desclée De Brouwer, 1970.

Florensky, Pavel A. *Iconostasis*. Translated by Donald Sheehan and Olga Andrejev. Crestwood, NY: St. Vladimir's Seminary Press, 1996.

———. "Obratnaya perspektiva." In *U vodorazdelov Mysli*, 43–106. Vol. 2. Moscow: Pravda, 1990.

Hart, David Bentley. *The Beauty of the Infinite: The Aesthetics of Christian Truth*. Grand Rapids, MI: Eerdmans: 2003.

Iuliania (M. N. Sokolova). *Trud ikonopistsa*. Moscow: Sviato-Troitskaya Sergieva Lavra, 1995.

Juliania. *Russian Saints. Russische Heilige. Venäläisiä Pyhiä. Svyatye Rusi*. Translated by Henry Fullenwider. Helsinki: Rista, 2000.

Krug, Grigori. *Mysli ob ikone*. Paris: YMCA, 1978.

Lepakhin, Valerii V. *Ikona i ikonichnost'*. St. Petersburg: Uspenskoye Podvorye Optinoi Pustyni, 2002

———. "Ikonichnost' istinnaya i mnimaya." *Dary* 2 (2016) 21–37.

Lidov, Alexei M. *Hierotopia. Sravnitelniye issledovaniya sokralnikh prostranstv*. Moscow: Indrik, 2009.

———. *Ierotopiya. Prostranstvennye ikony i obrazy-paradigmy v vizantiyskoi kul'ture*. Moscow: Teoria, 2009.

Marion, Jean-Luc. *Idol and Distance*. Translated by Thomas A. Carlson. New York: Fordham University Press, 2001.

Ouspensky, Léonide. *Essai sur la Théologie de l'icône dans l'Église orthodoxe*. Paris, 1960.

Ouspensky, Léonide, and Vladimir Lossky. *Der Sinn der Ikonen*. Bern and Olten: Urs Graf-Verlag, 1952.

———. *The Meaning of Icons.* Translated by Gerald Eustace Howell Palmer and Eugenic Kadloubovsky. Crestwood, NY: St. Vladimir's Seminary Press, 1982.

Popova, Olga. "Le illustrazioni dei manoscritti antico-russi." In *Lo spazio letterario del medioevo. Le culture circostanti*, edited by M. Capaldo, 753–95. Vol. 3. Roma: Salerno Editrice, 2006.

———. *Les miniatures russes du XIe au XVe siècle.* Leningrad: Éditions d'art Aurore, 1975.

———. *Russian Illuminated Manuscripts.* London: Thames and Hudson, 1984.

Quenot, Michel. *The Icon: Window on the Kingdom.* Translated by a Carthusian monk. Crestwood, NY: St. Vladimir's Seminary Press, 1991.

———. *L'icône. Fenêtre à Absolut.* Paris: Editions du Cerf, 1991.

Raushenbakh, Boris V. "O peredache troichnogo dogmata v ikonakh." *Voprosy iskusstvoznaniya* 4 (1993) 232–42.

———. *Prostranstvennye postroeniya v drevnerusskoi zhivopisi.* Moscow: Nauka, 1980.

Reytlinger, Yuliya N., and Sergii Bulgakov. *Dialog khudozhnika i bogoslova.* Moscow: Nikeya, 2011.

Rowan, Williams. *The Dwelling of the Light: Praying With Icons of Christ.* Mulgrave, Victoria: Garratt, 2003.

———. *Ponder These Things: Praying with Icons of the Virgin.* Canterbury: Canterbury, 2002.

Schönborn, Christoph. *Die Christus-Icone. Eine theologische Hinführung.* Wien: Wiener Dom Verlag, 1998.

———. *God's Human Face: The Christ-Icon.* Translated by Lothar Krauth. San Francisco: Ignatius, 1994.

Sendler, Egon. *Les icônes byzantines de la Mère de Dieu.* Paris: Desclée de Brouwer, 1992.

———. *Les Mystères du Christ: Les Icônes de la liturgie.* Paris: Desclée de Brouwer, 2002.

———. *L'icona immagine dell'invisibile. Elementi di teologia, estetica e tecnica.* Cinisello Balsamo, Milan: Edizioni Paoline, 1992.

———. *L'icône, image de l'invisible.* Paris: Desclée de Brouwer, 1981.

———. *Trasfigurazione. Introduzione alla contemplazione delle icone.* Cinisello Balsamo, Milan: Edizioni Paoline, 1987.

Trubetskoi, Eugene N. *Icons: Theology in Color.* Translated by Gertrude Vakar. Crestwood, NY: St. Vladimir's Seminary Press, 1973.

Uspensky, Boris. *The Semiotics of the Russian Icon.* Edited by Stephen Rudy. Lisse: de Ridder, 1976.

Ware, Timothy. *The Orthodox Church.* Baltimore: Penguin, 1963.

Williams, Rowan. *The Dwelling of the Light: Praying with Icons of Christ.* Grand Rapids, MI: Eerdmans, 2004.

———. *Ponder These Things: Praying with Icons of the Virgin.* Brewster, MA: Paraclete, 2006.

Zhegin, Lev F. *Yazyk zhivopisnogo proizvedeniya. (Uslovnost' drevnego iskusstva).* Moscow: Iskusstvo, 1970.

8

The Theandric Dimension of Art in the Eastern Christian Tradition

Teresa Obolevitch

Introduction

When we speak about Eastern Christian art, we first and foremost mean the icon, not only as the best known example of this kind of art, but—in the Eastern Orthodox consciousness—as art *par excellence.* This is because there is more to the icon than just human art; it has a transcendent dimension that reveals not only and not so much the created, earthly beauty, but the uncreated, divine one. It was the debate about icon veneration that took place in the eighth and ninth centuries in the Byzantine Empire that consolidated the Eastern Christian understanding and justification of art as such.[1] Weighty volumes have already been written on the subject of the icon. This paper neither pretends to treat the subject exhaustively, nor to interpret it innovatively. The aim is much more modest: to highlight several aspects of the icon as a work of art of a theandric—i.e., divine-human—nature. Such a context calls for three perspectives: (1) an ontologico-theological one that renders the icon's internal structure, (2) one that reveals the process of painting, or writing, the icon,[2] and (3) the perspective of the reception of the work of art, its interpretation, but above all—the veneration paid to the icon. On none of the enumerated planes

---

1. See Louth, "Orthodoxy and Art," 163–68.

2. Sometimes it is said that an icon is "circumscribed," and not "painted," while some researches claim that these expressions can be used interchangeably. In Greek both senses are captured by the verb *gráphō*; for its semantics, see, Schönborn, *God's Human Face*, 207–10.

does the icon appear as an autonomous work by the artist, but as a product of collaboration or synergy between God and man.

The Ontological and Theological Dimension of the Iconic Art

What is an icon? Etymologically, it is simply an "image" (*eikōn*). However, it is not an ordinary illustration or a photograph of depicted reality, as in the case of a portrait. Icons are not allegories:

> Indeed, it may be that to speak of an icon as "representing" anything is misleading. To be sure, icons are pictures of saints, of events like the Transfiguration, etc. To be sure again, there are conventional signs and techniques which make of icons a language about the objects (events, persons, etc.) shown in them. But the moment we assimilate icons to ordinary sorts of representation, we deny them: we say that they are not what they purport to be.[3]

This special quality of icons makes them perhaps the highest or purest exemplar of a more general ontological feature of reality, which Vasilii Zenkovsky formulates as follows:

> All material things serve as means for expressing a higher truth, a higher beauty. In philosophic terms, this is a *mystical realism*, which recognizes empirical reality, but sees *behind* it another reality; both spheres of being are real, but they are of hierarchically different value; empirical being is sustained only through "participation" in a mystical reality.[4]

The icon is a visible image of the invisible and transcendent reality. This applies to icons of Christ—the incarnate Person of the Holy Trinity—as well as to icons of saints, human beings who lived at a specified time and were endowed with particular physical traits. The icon does not reflect outer features or empirical qualities, but is an illustration and expression of an invisible idea embedded in the divine realm. To cite the words of Fr. Pavel Florensky (1882–1937), an outstanding Russian thinker and one of the first theoreticians of the icon, it must be said that the icon does not reflect the "face" (*litso*), but the countenance (*lik*),[5] that is, the *logos* or the *eidos* of an individual—the

---

3. Frary, "Logic of Icons," 398.
4. Zenkovsky, *History*, 27.
5. See Florensky, *Iconostasis*, 50.

spirit expressed in the body. Immaterial content comes to be expressed by means of material aids (a panel, metal or fabric, paint, wax, etc.). Therefore, it goes beyond the limits of time and space. Ultimately, the icon finds its justification in the Biblical conception of faith: "now faith is confidence in what we hope for and assurance about what we do not see" (Heb 11:1). As Vladimir Weidlé (1895–1979) explained, in the icon it is "not the earthly, but the heavenly, not that which was, but that which is everlasting" that becomes visible.[6] Therefore, the icon has ontologico-theological and eschatological significance: it is "a visible testimony to the invisible"; it is a cataphatic (or positive theological image) of the apophatic Proto-Image—God.[7] "Icons impinge on our consciousness by means of the outer senses, presenting to us the same suprasensible reality in 'esthetic' expressions."[8]

Saint John of Damascus (675–749), a defender of the cult of icons, pondered the following: "How to depict the invisible? How to picture the inconceivable? How to give expression to the limitless, the immeasurable, the invisible? How to give form to immensity? How to paint immortality? How to localise mystery?"[9] In answering these questions, one should stress the fact that the icon is antinomic, which is characteristic of the entirety of the Orthodox tradition.[10] The antinomic Christian truths (e.g., the dogma of the Triune God, or of Christ, one Person having two natures "unconfused, immutable, indivisible and inseparable") are inexpressible in words and came to be expressed in the art of the icon. As Léonid Ouspensky (1902–1987) aptly observed, "The icon participates, so to speak, in the holiness of the prototype, and through the icon we in turn participate in this holiness in our prayers . . . *The icon does not represent the Divine; it points to participation of man in the divine life.*"[11]

The icon describes reality *sub specie aeternitatis*. It is an emanation of God, and so does not stop at itself. This is discerned, inter alia, by Jean-Luc Marion, a contemporary French philosopher who writes the following: "The

6. Veydle, "Pis'ma ob ikone," 15.

7. Lepakhin, *Ikona i ikonichnost'*, 59, cf. 78.

8. Lossky, "Tradition and Traditions," 167; Ouspensky and Lossky, *Meaning of Icons*, 22.

9. John of Damascus, "Apologia," 4 (translation modified).

10. Cf. a statement by Fr. Pavel Florensky: "Truth is truth precisely because it is not afraid of any objections. And it is not afraid of them because it itself says more against itself than any negation can say, but truth combines this its self-negation with affirmation. For rationality, *truth is contradiction*, and this contradiction becomes explicit as soon as truth acquires a verbal formulation. . . . The thesis and the antithesis together form the expression of truth. In other words, truth is an antinomy, and it cannot fail to be such." Florensky, *Pillar*, 109.

11. Ouspensky, "Theology," 37, 39.

icon summons the gaze to surpass itself by never freezing on the visible, since the visible only presents itself here in view of the invisible."[12] According to the teachings of the Church Fathers, the icon always refers to the Proto-Image, the Archetype, which is expressed by the Aristotelian category of relation—*prós tí*. Already Patriarch Nicephorus I (750–829) explained it as follows:

> Similarity is a certain relation placed at the center between two ends or poles: between the likeness and the one to whom it is like. Both are united and connected by the [same] appearance, while both are different as to their nature. And even though both, image and model, are each *different* in nature, they nevertheless do not represent something altogether different, but both represent *one and the same* reality. For through the image, we gain the knowledge of what the model originally looked like, and in this depiction we can behold the *person* of the one so depicted.[13]

On the one hand, the icon has its own nature, but on the other hand one cannot speak about its absolute ontological independence. It is a relative, or correlative being; it exists inasmuch as it belongs to its Prototype and points to it. An icon is never an invention, an act of creation out of nothing. On the contrary, in the spirit of Christian Platonism, it is an artistic testimony to that which already exists.[14] Hence, the source of the icon is not some creative work of a master who is trying to paint/write a religious-themed picture, but God himself who contains perfect models of all creatures, and who, more importantly, manifests himself as the Second Person of the Holy Trinity, who shares his essence/nature (*ousía/phúsis*) and actions (in Greek, *energies* or *enérgeiai*) with the other Persons.

Early Christian writers emphasised that the essence/nature of God is incomprehensible. It cannot be expressed with words, terms, definitions, or any artistic devices. The essence of God (and the Persons of the Holy Trinity) cannot be verbalised or depicted. That which we come to know about God always concerns his actions/energies, that is manifestations, or expressions of the essence.[15] This fact is of fundamental relevance for a proper understanding of the icon. It does not illustrate the essence of God, but it refers to divine energies identified in the patristic tradition with divine names. The same can be said of the icons of saints called "God's friends," which are sanctified thanks to the divine name which features on them (rendered in a

---

12. Marion, *God without Being*, 18.
13. Cit. from: Schönborn, *God's Human Face*, 212.
14. Cf. Papajohn, "Icon Veneration," 83.
15. See, e.g., the classic book by Russian emigrant thinker Vladimir Lossky (1901–1958): Lossky, *Mystical Theology*, 67–90.

graphic form and thus representing the divine energy/action). Saint John of Damascus taught us to "submit to the tradition of the Church in the worship of images, honoring God and His friends, and following in this the grace of the Holy Spirit." Further, he said that anyone refusing to honour and worship such an image as sacred (but not worshipping it as God, of course)

> is an enemy of Christ, of His blessed Mother, and of the saints, and is an advocate of the devil and his crew, showing grief by his conduct that the saints are honoured and glorified, and the devil put to shame. The image is a hymn of praise, a manifestation, a lasting token of those who have fought and conquered, and of demons humbled and put to flight.[16]

Just as the name ("an oral icon") expresses the divine energy, so the written icon (a graphic representation of God's name) symbolises the Prototype, the Proto-Icon that is the Person of Christ and the other divine Persons as well as saints. On the basis of this understanding, Pavel Evdokimov (1901–1970) wrote that "in the pronounced name, through and with the icon, which 'pronounces' in it a silent and visible way, our love carries us to venerate and embrace the grace of the real presence in the very likeness of the icon."[17] Another twentieth-century thinker, Boris Uspensky (1902–1987), expressed a similar view: "An icon without an inscription is invalid, for the inscription tells us what the icon signifies. As a visible sign, an icon must be confirmed with an inscription of a verbal sign.... The verbal sign itself also contains some energy of the proto-image."[18] Such twentieth-century developments in the theology of the icon can trace their roots to the Seventh and Eighth Ecemunical Councils. According to Canon 3 of the Fourth Council of Constantinople (the Eighth Ecumenical Council, 869–870):

> as the words of the Gospel lead us to salvation, so also do the images through their colors produce the same effect, and all, learned and unlearned, can derive benefit there from. The message that comes to us through the written word is also brought home to us through the color of the pictures.[19]

Experts on the icon would refer to it as "contemplation in color" or "theology in color" (Evgenii Trubetskoi, Léonid Ouspensky), as well as "philosophy in color" (Fr. Pavel Florensky, Viktor Bychkov).[20] An icon is a sym-

16. John of Damascus, "Apologia," 6, 22–23.
17. Evdokimov, *Art of the Icon*, 200. See Antonova, "Neo-Palamism," 23–32.
18. "Prolegomena do tematu 'Semiotyka Ikony,'" 1609.
19. "Concilium Constantinopolitanum IV."
20. See Trubetskoi, *Icons*; Florensky, *Iconostasis*, 152–53; Bychkov, *Fenomen ikony*, 258.

bol, but here the "symbol" is not something conventional arising from some agreement, or a creator's invention. In this case a "symbol" is as much as an expression, a manifestation of inner and hidden content with the aid of outer means of expression. In other words, an icon is a special place where divine energy-names are present, God's uncreated grace, a place where divine actions meet human effort. Because of this, the symbolism of the icon is utterly real, enabling participation in divine energies.

> The conception of art which icon painting presupposes, of course, is symbolic. According to this conception, the purpose of art is not to create something out of nothing, but to give artistic witness to what already exists—it is not meant to create realities but the images of realities. A material basis, however, is required for the embodiment of these images which are distinguished from the actual objects themselves.[21]

Alexei Losev (1893–1988), the "last Russian philosopher of the Silver Age," explicated the realistic symbolism of the icon as follows: "Either God somehow *reveals* and manifests Himself—and then both icons and worship are possible . . . or icons are mere idols and do not express God or the saints—then nothing can be said about any God, and complete and absolute positivism and atheism prevail."[22]

The ontologico-theological basis of the icon thus consists in the manifestation of the invisible and unknowable essence of God in divine actions/energies common to all the Persons of the Holy Trinity. Christ, true God and true man, has two natures and, respectively, two actions/energies, the divine and the human.[23] As a perfect image of the Person of the Father (*imago Dei*), Christ is the Icon *sensu stricto*, that is the Proto-Icon—a prototype for all possible icons.[24] Saint Maximus the Confessor (580–662) would cry:

> O mystery, more mysterious than all the rest: God himself, out of love, became man. . . . Without any change in him, he took on the weakness of our human nature, in order to bring salvation to man, and to give himself to us men as the ideal image [hypotyposis] of virtue and as a *living icon of love* and good will toward God and neighbor, an icon that has the power to elicit in us the dutiful response.[25]

21. Papajohn, "Icon Veneration," 83.
22. Losev, *Ocherki*, 899.
23. See Schönborn, *God's Human Face*, 117–22.
24. See Lepakhin, "Ikona i obraz," 32–33; Ozolin, "Theology."
25. Cit. from: Schönborn, *God's Human Face*, 129.

The theandric, divine-human character of the Second Person of the Holy Trinity constitutes yet another, Christological foundation of the iconic image, revealing the divine realm in the worldly sphere, and hence in Church reality. The prototype, Christ, is present in the icon not by way of essence, but by the likeness of the Person-Hypostasis. In other words, the Prototype is not fully present in the icon (which would be the case if we perceived this material object in a magical and idolatrous manner),[26] but only partially. The icon is not a sacrament enabling substantial (as with the Eucharist) but only intentional participation in Christ. This is because it is an image, not a Proto-Image.[27]

The Divine-human Aspect of Icon Creation

The very process of icon creation is also characterised by a theandric dimension; for it is nothing else than prayer, a meeting between God and man. The work of the iconographer (also called isographer) is radically different from the work done by a painter, even one who draws his inspiration from religious themes. Above all, an iconographer must be a believer and accept the Christian Revelation not so much in theory, but primarily in practice, and so he must experience God and be in unmediated contact with him. Because of this, not every work of art painted in accordance with the established iconographic style has been recognised as an icon and accepted for liturgical use or in worship. This can be exemplified with the output of such pre-eminent Russian painters as Mikhail Vrubel (1856–1910) and Nicholas Roerich (1874–1947).[28] Though impeccable in the stylistic and artistic respect, their works raised doubts of a spiritual nature, and some technical devices and intentions, especially the ones employed by Roerich, who was under the influence of Eastern religions, were even regarded as sacrilegious or occult. That is the reason why some of their paintings can be found in museums, and not in Orthodox churches. An iconographer must remain in dogmatic and liturgical unity with the Church, otherwise he does not deserve the title. It is sometimes very difficult to distinguish experimentation and innovation in the creative process from stylisation, vulgarisation, or simplification. Not all specialists view the works of the famous Krakow-based artist Jerzy Nowosielski (1923–2011) as icons *sensu stricto*, even though Church consciousness has included them in the sacral sphere.

26. See Antonova, *Space*, 82–83.
27. See Sendler, *Icon*, 46–47.
28. See Gorbunova-Lomaks, *Ikona. Pravda i vymysly*, 152–64.

The art of the icon is not founded on the artist's individuality, but in Christ, who appears to every iconographer in a unique and inimitable manner. Unlike the secular painter, the iconographer does not adopt an outside stance on his work, but in a way finds himself inside the image he is creating, "presenting the world *around* himself."[29] He displays an attitude of involvement, and not of detachment or alienation. In the process of icon creation, everything has its specific significance, ranging from the material used (a wooden panel, natural dyes) to the painting technique and individual artistic details (i.e., reverse perspective, use of colours, a specific workflow, arrangement of the figures, etc.). It is noteworthy that the iconographer's spiritual experience becomes recorded once and for all. All the copies that will be subsequently made of the original (*podlinnik*), that is the *canon*, will have the same spiritual value as the original icon, even though they may be radically different from it in respect to their artistic or historical value.

As mentioned earlier, an important element in the creative process is inscribing God's name on the icon, whereby it becomes sanctified,[30] that is, removed from secular use. However, the icon does not always bear the artist's initials or signature, because the true Artist and Author is not a human being, but God,[31] who is present and acting in his Church, in the conciliar (*sobornyi*) consciousness. Because of this, many famous iconic masterpieces remain anonymous. While in Western religious painting both the model and the artist are recognisable (e.g., *Sistine Madonna* by Raphael Sanzio),[32] in the icon the whole attention is focused on the Proto-Image.

The Church Fathers used to stress that one cannot get to know God without the Holy Spirit's assistance, which, therefore, is necessary in presenting (and, by extension, in recognising) his image in the icon. Hence, writing an icon is possible thanks to God's inspiration which effects an inextricable connection between the Proto-Image and the image, as a result of which veneration is due to the icon (see further below on this issue).[33] Such outstanding icon painters as Theophanes the Greek and Andrei Rublev perceived

---

29. Uspenskii, "O semiotike ikony," 160.

30. The practice of the sanctification of the icon by a priest was popularised in Russia only in the eighteenth century by Metropolitan Petro Mohyla under the influence of the Western tradition. However, nowadays this is considered to be an integral element in the emergence of the icon and one of the criteria of its authenticity. See Bulgakov, "Icon," 77–80.

31. The custom of signing the icon with the creator's name was originated in Ruthenia only in the seventeenth century. See Kutkovoi, *Kraski mudrosti*, 554.

32. See Dagron, "Holy Images and Likeness," 23.

33. See Lepakhin, "Ikona i obraz," 58.

themselves as mere helpers of the Holy Spirit—the Great Master, or as translators of "supernatural significance into the language of art."[34]

> What appears abstract from a naturalistic standpoint is realistic by the standards of an iconography that seeks a particular kind of transcendent simplicity in form and composition. Icons were meant to recreate a spiritual realm, to paint a world in which temporal beings live eschatological lives.[35]

It is the Holy Spirit who "helps the iconographer to express with the aid of lines and colours that which is inexpressible, to describe that which is indescribable, that is, to present the icon to believing, spiritual eyes, to present a church painting as a divine-human *mysterium*, an antinomic unity of the image and the Proto-Image, a visible image and the invisible original."[36] Understandably enough, the iconographer in the Eastern Christian tradition is considered to be a servant of the Church, and not a craftsman/artist who in his creative process uses his own discretion; this was officially announced during the Seventh Ecumenical Council.[37] Many icon painters—e.g., Alimpy (eleventh-twelfth centuries), Theophanes the Greek (fourteenth-fifteenth centuries), Andrei Rublev (fourteenth-fifteenth centuries)—were declared saints precisely because of their efforts to connect people and God. On the one hand, man "is a being who sees images, *zōon eikonikon*," but on the other hand, a being who creates those images, *zōon poiētikon*.[38]

> Therefore, man's mirroring of images should not be understood in the sense of passive, indifferent reflection. Man actively participates in this iconization of being (just as he actively and creatively realizes the knowledge of being, or logicization). *In and through himself* he finds the icons of things, for he himself is in this sense the *pan-icon* of the world.[39]

It is no wonder then that every stage of icon creation is accompanied by a special prayer, fasting and other ascetic practices. This does not merely serve to express the icon writer's ordinary piety, but it is an integral element of the creative process as synergy between God and man, and by extension a collaboration between divine energies (*enérgeiai*) and human actions/

---

34. Cf. Bychkov, *Fenomen ikony*, 304.
35. Tsakiridou, *Icons in Time*, 207.
36. Cf. Lepakhin, "Ikona i obraz," 63.
37. See Kutkovoi, *Kraski mudrosti*, 558–60, 572.
38. See Bulgakov, "Icon," 43.
39. Bulgakov, "Icon," 43.

efforts (érgon). In the Eastern Christian tradition, it is believed that all icon-writing canons (concerned with the composition, colours, light, symbolism, etc.) are not conventional products of human imagination, but a result of the activity of the Holy Spirit. It is worth restating that an icon painter is merely (or as much as) a co-creator alongside God.

The Theandric Character of the Cult of Icons

An icon is more than just a work of art intended to be admired. Its basic function does not consist in fulfilling even the most noble and sublime aesthetic needs, but in presenting the invisible Image in empirical reality, in connecting heaven and earth, God and man. "There is no doubt that if iconography had created forms of worldly beauty it would certainly not have assisted in the perception and understanding of the mystery of worship."[40] Hence, "the purpose and the ideal of Byzantine iconography is the expression of the category of holiness, which, of course, is not made sensate by the physically beautiful, that is, is not by necessity united to this."[41]

In other words, the icon reflects spiritual, and not sensual beauty, and hence beauty that is integrated with good, according to the ancient ideal of *kalokagathia*. In the Eastern Christian tradition, love of beauty (*philokalía*) was regarded as a synonym for love of wisdom (*philosophía*) and—by extension—holiness. Epiphanius the Wise (fourteenth-fifteenth centuries) called the famous icon painter Theophanes the Greek a "celebrated sage" and a "highly proficient philosopher."[42] An icon is an essence of divine wisdom and a result of a creative unification of human wisdom and divine conception.[43] As Sergei Bulgakov put it, art (viewed as art in the service of God) shares in wisdom to a greater degree than science, which is limited to earthly and logical reasoning.[44]

One should view the icon with the heart's eyes. According to Patriarch Nicephorus's concept, the dynamics of cognition is directed at the outer image (*túpos*) through contemplation of the intelligible image (*eîdos*), and reaches up to the hypostasis of the figure featuring in the icon.[45] The icon

---

40. Kalokyris, "Orthodox Iconography," 43.

41. Kalokyris, "Orthodox Iconography. Prolegomena," 176.

42. See Bychkov, *Fenomen ikony*, 261; Obolevitch, *La philosophie religieuse russe*, 36.

43. See Bychkov, *Fenomen ikony*, 8.

44. See Bulgakov, "Religion and Art," 177.

45. See Pilipenko, "Bogoslovie," 180.

is capable of disclosing the revealed truth and sharing in it;⁴⁶ it is timeless. Thus, the icon serves an important religious function (the one of unifying God and man) also at the final stage of its reception and perception. That is another theandric aspect of the icon. As a unity of the visible and the invisible, it makes for prayer and contemplation of the transcendent sphere. Moreover, the icon is "both a way to follow, and a means; it is itself prayer,"⁴⁷ and hence dialogue between God and man. Orthodox art is a language and a means of Orthodox Church service.⁴⁸ Iconic painting as such and other genres of Christian art emerged as a result of cultural needs.

In the dispute between iconoclasts and icon defenders, which took place in the eighth century, an orthodox concept of the cult of sacred images was devised. In antiquity, a painting or a sculpture embodied a represented individual, and so works of art depicting gods or emperors were held in absolute reverence. By contrast, veneration paid to the icon is described with the aid of the notion of worship or "proskynesis" (*timētikḗ proskúnēsis*). It is a bow different than the cult of "latreia" (*lātréia*)—adoration due to God only.⁴⁹ The cult form of "proskynesis" safeguards against magical or superstitious treatment of the icon. According to Saint Basil the Great (329–379), "honour paid to the image passes on to the prototype,"⁵⁰ which happens only in the order of energy and grace, not substance. Therefore, according to a resolution passed by the Seventh Ecumenical Council of 787, "he who reveres the image reveres in it the subject represented."⁵¹

The cult of icons is also possible thanks to the Holy Spirit, who makes it possible for the Proto-Icon, that is God, to be discerned in the visible image. An icon is not only intended as an instrument for manifesting personal piety. It also has liturgical, and by extension communal significance (*leitourgía*—"a deed of the people").⁵² As it is a conciliar work (which is another argument why in the past the icon was not signed with the author's name), it belongs to the whole organism of the Church. Every liturgical act is of a theandric character. Veneration paid to the icon is not a subjective, psychological or merely human activity, but participation in an objective act of salvation through the agency of the Holy Spirit. The

---

46. Cf. Evdokimov, *Orthodoxy*, 222.
47. Ouspensky, "Theology," 90.
48. See Kalokyris, "Orthodox Iconography," 45–46.
49. See Kitzinger, "Cult of Images."
50. Basil the Great, "On the Holy Spirit."
51. "Concilium Nicaenum II," 784.
52. See Patterson Ševčenko, "Icons in the Liturgy."

icon is not for sensual contemplation, but for encouragement to living communion with the represented reality.

The icon as a theandric work is a guide to the divine realm, a "window on eternity,"[53] a microcosm unifying the divine and the created worlds.[54] While a painting showing religious themes (e.g., one by Leonardo da Vinci or any other Western painter) merely depicts, instructs, reminds, decorates, etc., an icon calls for active participation, passing into a super-empirical sphere.[55] Obviously, this does not happen mechanically, without a committed attitude on the part of the recipient of the work of art. Furthermore, there have been many cases of non-iconic paintings inspiring recipients, or even causing a mystical ecstasy and a radical conversion. By way of illustration, the famous Russian thinker and icon theoretician Sergei Bulgakov went through a profound religious experience (which was instrumental in his abandonment of Marxism) when contemplating the *Sistine Madonna* by Raphael Sanzio at the Dresden Gallery.[56] The painting by the Italian artist was also held in high regard by Fyodor Dostoevsky (1821–1881) and other Russian writers and thinkers.[57] The correspondent for the Polish-language "Kronika" wrote that the divine nature of the *Sistine Madonna* would captivate even an atheist.[58] Still, it is actually the icon that is a privileged place in which to meet God. Unlike the psychologico-pedagogical significance of Western art, it is characterised by an ontological as well as anagogical and mystical dimension.[59] In other words, the icon *always* has *religious* significance and by definition *cannot be secular*. Developed in the Renaissance and later periods, Western art is ontologically *neutral*, and depending on particular factors (a theme, the artist's or the recipient's intention, etc.) it can take on either a secular or religious character. The function of the icon is to *reflect*, with the aid of artistic devices, *God's image in man*,[60] whereas the aim of Western art (post-iconic—so to speak—as Old Christian and medieval art referred to the iconic paradigm) was to *create man's image*, not necessarily with regard to God, and not infrequently

---

53. See Limouris, *Icons*; Quenot, *Window on the Kingdom*.
54. See Fortounatto and Cunningham, "Theology of the Icon," 136.
55. Cf. Lidov, "Ikonichnost' i ikonicheskoe," 25.
56. See Bulgakov, *Unfading Light*, 3.
57. See Pearson, "Raphael"; Jackson, *Quest for Form*, 214–215; Bori, "La Madonna Sistina."
58. See Łysiak, *Malarstwo białego człowieka*, 312.
59. See Kutkovoi, *Kraski mudrosti*, 589.
60. Kutkovoi, *Kraski mudrosti*, 593.

in opposition to him. Every icon is miraculous, at least *in potentio*, as it is capable of transforming and sanctifying man.[61]

Conclusion

Tomáš Špidlík (1919–2010) noted that it is not only the icon, but every form of true art that is in essence religious and theurgic; it is "in a way God's word," constituting—as Mikołaj Stankiewicz (1813–1840) put it—"the first step towards cognition of God,"[62] though the cognition is non-discursive. Still, the theurgic and theandric divine-human character comes to show most profoundly in the case of the icon. As Sergei Bulgakov observed:

> The icon is a work of art that knows and loves its own forms and colors, understands their revelation, governs them, and is obedient to them. But the icon is also a theurgic act in which the revelation of the supramundane is attested in images of the world and the revelation of spiritual life is attested in images of the flesh. In the icon God reveals Himself in man's creative act; in the icon the theurgic act of the union of the earthly and the heavenly is accomplished. Thus, iconography is both a feat of art and a religious feat, full of prayerful and ascetic intensity.[63]

It is noteworthy that the arrangements made during the Seventh Ecumenical Council regarding the icon were concerned with all kinds of plastic arts such as fresco, bas-relief, embroidery and sewing, and the like. Hence, the theurgic and theandric character peculiar to the icon determines the specificity of all Eastern Christian arts. "A temple erected by human hands is a reflection of the temple not erected by hand, that is, the cosmos or creation." It is not examined as a separate work of architecture, but as a whole creation encapsulating the work of the builders, icon painters, masters writing and decorating the liturgical books, craftsmen making liturgical vestments, choristers and such like, and last but not least the ministry of priests. Therefore, a temple is—to cite Fr. Pavel Florensky's words—a "synthesis of arts."[64] Vladimir Lossky explains the point further:

> The different arts entering the composition of a church should form, together with the Liturgy, one whole. There must be perfect conformity between the divine service and the church in

---

61. See Tarabukin, "Filosofiya ikony," 82.
62. See Špidlík, *L'idée russe*, 96.
63. Bulgakov, "Icon," 72.
64. See Florensky, "Church Ritual."

which it is celebrated. Art in the church is liturgical, not merely a frame for the Liturgy, but similar to it both in its content, and in its ways of expression.[65]

Sacral architecture, with its characteristic domes and mosaics, is supposed to lead to the entrance of the heavenly temple, where Christ reigns. Earthly participation in the Eucharist in a sense is mirrored in the chalice-like shape of the dome. The mosaics do not only serve a decorative purpose in the Orthodox Church, but thanks to the play of reflected light they create a spatial image that the believer takes part in. In consequence, the opposition of "image—viewer" dissipates to make room for integration between the true Creator (and the Image), creation, God and man.

Presenting the general characteristics of the icon from an artistic perspective is a far from easy task. There are so many iconic styles (e.g., Byzantine icons are quite different from Coptic icons, which in turn are different from Serbian ones). In Ruthenia and Russia, the icon underwent some evolutionary transformations—from the Old Russian icon, characterised by extraordinary brightness and abundance of light, through early modern Russian icons influenced by Western, and especially Italian, painting (they gravitated towards the realism of the depicted figures), to contemporary, avant-garde icons. Over the centuries, the semiotics of the icon (and by extension the canons concerned with symbolism, composition, use of colour, proportions, depicted scenes, etc.) and the icon-writing technique changed. Still, what has remained unchanged is the belief that the icon is a divine-human inspired work that reflects heavenly beauty and is intended for prayer. Therefore, theandricity is an integral element in iconic painting and Eastern Christian art as such. In it, the ontological and theological dimensions precede the aesthetic aspect; more precisely, the latter aspect, as connected with the category of beauty, relies on the foundation of Divine truth and goodness. In this way, beauty is not treated as a subjective experience conditioned by psychological, historical, cultural and other circumstances, nor is it about "being appealing." It is an objective expression of Beauty in itself. It was for good reason that Fr. Pavel Florensky declared: "There exists the icon of the Holy Trinity by St. Andrei Rublev; therefore, God exists."[66] The aesthetic category of sublimity is also endowed with an objective and nearly literal meaning in Eastern Christian art—the elevation of the human spirit to God, uniting it with him.

---

65. Lossky, "Place of Icons," 239.
66. Florensky, *Iconostasis*, 68.

Bibliography

Antonova, Clemena. "Neo-Palamism in the Russian Philosophy of Full Unity: The Icon as Energetic Symbol." *Sobornost* 34.1 (2012) 16–32.

———. *Space, Time, and Presence in the Icon. Seeing the World with the Eyes of God.* Burlington: Ashgate, 2010.

Basil the Great, Saint. "On the Holy Spirit." Translated by Bl. Jackson. https://www.elpenor.org/basil/holy-spirit.asp.

Bori, Pier Cesare. "La Madonna Sistina di Raffaello nella cultura russa." In *La Madonna di San Sisto di Raffaello. Studi sulla cultura russa*, 11–52. Bologna: Il Mulino, 1990.

Bulgakov, Sergius. "The Icon and Its Veneration (A Dogmatic Essay)." In *Icons and the Name of God*, translated by Boris Jakim, 1–114. Grand Rapids, MI: Eerdmans, 2012.

———. "Religion and Art." In *The Church of God. An Anglo-Russian Symposium by Members of the Fellowship of St. Alban and St. Sergius*, edited by Eric L. Mascall, 174–91. London: Society for Promoting Christian Knowledge, 1934.

———. *Unfading Light: Contemplations and Speculations.* Translated by Thomas Allan Smith. Grand Rapids, MI: Eerdmans, 2012.

Bychkov, Viktor V. *Fenomen ikony. Istoriya, bogoslovie, estetika, iskusstvo.* Moscow: Ladomir, 2009.

"Concilium Constantinopolitanum IV—Documenta Omnia." http://www.documentacatholicaomnia.eu.

"Concilium Nicaenum II—Documenta." http://www.ccel.org/ccel/schaff/npnf214.html.

Dagron, Gilbert. "Holy Images and Likeness." *Dumbarton Oaks Papers* 45 (1991) 23–33.

Evdokimov, Paul. *The Art of the Icon: A Theology of Beauty.* Translated by Fr. Steven Bigham. Redondo Beach, CA: Oakwood, 1990.

———. *Orthodoxy.* Translated by Jeremy Hummerstone. London: New City, 2011.

Florensky, Paul. "The Church Ritual as a Synthesis of the Arts." In *Beyond Vision: Essays on the Perception of Art*, translated by Wendy Salmond, 95–111. London: Reaktion, 2002.

———. *Iconostasis.* Translated by Donald Sheehan and Olga Andrejev. Crestwood, NY: St. Vladimir's Seminary Press, 1996.

———. *The Pillar and Ground of the Truth.* Translated by Boris Jakim. Princeton: Princeton University Press, 2004.

Fortounatto, Marianna, and Mary B. Cunningham, "Theology of the Icon." In *The Cambridge Companion to Orthodox Christian Theology*, edited by Mary B. Cunningham and Elizabeth Theokritoff, 136–49. Cambridge: Cambridge University Press, 2009.

Frary, Joseph P. "The Logic of Icons." *Sobornost* 6 (1972) 394–403.

Gorbunova-Lomaks, Irina. *Ikona. Pravda i vymysly.* St. Petersburg: Satis, 2009.

Jackson, Robert Louis. *Dostoevsky's Quest for Form. A Study of His Philosophy of Art.* Bloomington: Physsardt, 1978.

John of Damascus, Saint. "Apologia of St. John Damascene Against Those who Decry Holy Images." In *St. John of Damascene on Holy Images: Followed by Three Sermons on the Assumption*, 1–54. Grand Rapids, MI: Christian Classics Ethereal Library, n.d. http://www.ccel.org/ccel/damascus/icons.html.

Kalokyris, Constantine D. "The Essence of Orthodox Iconography." *The Greek Orthodox Theological Review* 14.1 (1969) 42–64.

———. "The Essence of Orthodox Iconography. Prolegomena." Translated by Peter Chamberas. *The Greek Orthodox Theological Review* 13.1 (1968) 168–204.

Kitzinger, Ernst. "The Cult of Images in the Age before Iconoclasm." *Dumbarton Oaks Papers* 8 (1954) 83–150.

Kutkovoi, Viktor S. *Kraski mudrosti*. Moscow: Palomnik, 2008.

Lepakhin, Valerii. *Ikona i ikonichnost'*. St. Petersburg: Uspenskoe podvor'e Optinoi Pustyni, 2002.

———. "Ikona i obraz." In *Ikona v russkoi slovesnosti i kul'ture*, edited by Valerii V. Lepakhin, 11–71. Moscow: Palomnik, 2012.

Lidov, Aleksei. "Ikonichnost' i ikonicheskoe." *Dary* 1 (2015) 25–45.

Limouris, Gennadios. *Icons. Windows on Eternity. Theology and Spirituality in Colour*. Geneva: WCC, 1990.

Losev, Aleksei F. *Ocherki antichnogo platonizma i mifologii*. Moscow: Mysl', 1993.

Lossky, Nicholas. "The Place of Icons in the Church." *Sobornost* 6 (1949) 238–41.

Lossky, Vladimir. *The Mystical Theology of the Eastern Church*. Cambridge: Clarke, 2007.

———. "Tradition and Traditions." In *In the Image and Likeness of God*, 141–68. Crestwood, NY: St. Vladimir's Seminary Press, 1974.

Louth, Andrew. "Orthodoxy and Art." In *Living Orthodoxy in the Modern World: Orthodoxy, Christianity and Society*, edited by Andrew Walker and Costa Carras, 159–77. Crestwood, NY: St. Vladimir's Seminary Press, 2000.

Łysiak, Waldemar. *Malarstwo białego człowieka*. Vol. 2. Warsaw: Wydawnictwo Andrzej Frukacz Ex Libris – Galeria Polskiej Książki, 1997.

Marion, Jean-Louis. *God without Being*. Translated by Thomas A. Carlson. Chicago: The University of Chicago Press, 2012.

Obolevitch, Teresa. *La philosophie religieuse russe*. Translated by Maria Gawron-Zaborska. Paris: Les éditions du Cerf, 2014.

Ouspensky, Léonid. "The Theology of the Icon in the Orthodox Church." Translated by Jane M. de Yver Horka. *One Church* 1.28 (1974) 29–44.

———. "The Theology of the Icon in the Orthodox Church." Translated by Jane M. de Yver Horka. *One Church* 2.28 (1974) 83–144.

Ouspensky, Léonid, and Vladimir Lossky. *The Meaning of Icons*. Translated by Gerald Eustace Howell Palmer and Evgeniia Kadloubovsky. Crestwood, NY: St. Vladimir's Seminary Press, 1999.

Ozolin, Nicholas. "The Theology of the Icon." *St Vladimir's Theological Quarterly* 31 (1987) 297–308.

Papajohn, John. "Philosophical and Metaphysical Basis of Icon Veneration in the Eastern Orthodox Church." *Greek Orthodox Theological Review* 2.1 (1956) 83–89.

Patterson Ševčenko, Nanci. "Icons in the Liturgy." *Dumbarton Oaks Papers* 45 (1991) 45–57.

Pearson, Irene. "Raphael as Seen by Russian Writers from Zhukovsky to Turgenev." *The Slavonic and East European Review* 59.3 (1981) 346–69.

Pilipenko, Evgenii. "Bogoslovie vospriyatiya ikony v kontekste pravoslavnoi epistemologii." In *Uchenie Tserkvi o cheloveke: Bogoslovskaya konferentsiya RPTs*, 174–81. Moscow: Sinodal'naya Bogoslovskaya Komissiya, 2002.

"Prolegomena do tematu 'Semiotyka Ikony'. Rozmowa z Borysem Uspienskim. Interviewer Zbigniew Podgórzec. Translated by Julia Ponomariowa. *Znak* 12 (1976) 1600–1616.

Quenot, Michel. *The Icon: Window on the Kingdom*. Translated by a Carthusian monk. Crestwood, NY: St. Vladimir's Seminary Press, 1991.

Schönborn, Christoph. *God's Human Face: The Christ-Icon*. Translated by Lothar Krauth. San Francisco: Ignatius, 1994.

Sendler, Egon. *The Icon. Image of the Invisible. Elements of the Theology, Aesthetics and Technique*. Translated by Fr. Steven Bigham. Torrance: Oakwood, 1999.

Špidlík, Tomás. *L'idée russe: une autre vision de l'homme*. Troyes: Éd. Fates, 1994.

Tarabukin, Nikolai M. "Filosofiya ikony." In *Smysl ikony*, 29–159. Moscow: Izdatel'stvo Pravoslavnogo Bratstva Svyatitelya Filareta Moskovskogo, 2001.

Trubetskoi, Eugene N. *Icons: Theology in Color*. Translated by Gertrude Vakar. Crestwood, NY: St. Vladimir's Seminary Press, 1973.

Tsakiridou, Cornelia A. *Icons in Time, Persons in Eternity: Orthodox Theology and the Aesthetics of the Christian Image*. Farnham: Ashgate, 2013.

Uspenskii, Boris. "O semiotike ikony." *Simvol* 18 (1987) 143–216.

Veydle, Vladimir. "Pis'ma ob ikone. Pis'mo pervoe. Obraz i simvol." *Vestnik Russkogo khristianskogo dvizheniya* 55 (1959) 10–19.

Zenkovsky, Vasilii V. *A History of Russian Philosophy*. Vol. 1. Translated by George L. Kline. London: Routledge, 2006.

9

Between Two Worlds

Philosophy of the Icon in Evgenii Trubetskoi and Pavel Florensky

Ruri Hosokawa

Introduction

In the long history and tradition of icon arts, and especially of their interpretation, Russian religious philosophy in the early twentieth century made its presence felt. This tendency toward the reinterpretation of the icon in philosophy was associated with widespread social interest in icons as artworks in that period in Russia, which can be seen in the appearance of collectors of icon painting, such as Nikolai Likhachev, Il'ya Ostroukhov, and Stepan Ryabushinsky; in the first exhibition featuring Russian icon painting; in the establishment of an association for the study of ancient Russian icon painting in 1913; and in the publication of the collection *The Russian Icon* in three volumes in 1914.[1] The attitude toward the icon, to which Russian religious philosophers at the beginning of the twentieth century had tried to give ontological significance, is distinctive and worth discussing. In this paper, the views of two Russian religious philosophers, Evgenii Nikolaevich Trubetskoi and Pavel Alexandrovich Florensky, will be contrasted to make the ontological views of icons in the early twentieth century clearer.

It may seem strange to attempt to address both Evgenii Trubetskoi and Pavel Florensky in one paper. Although the pair can be considered representatives of Russian religious philosophy in the early twentieth century and both belonged to the Vladimir Soloviev Religious and Philosophical Society,

---

1. Dmitriev, *Ocherki*, 227; Kaizawa, "Pavel Florenskii," 48.

which Trubetskoi co-organized with Margarita Kirillovna Morozova and others in 1905, evidence of positive interaction between Trubetskoi and Florensky is not so clear. In a broad sense, it can be said that both of their philosophies have roots in the same ground, which had been cultivated by Vladimir Sergeevich Soloviev, but their forms of flowering were quite different. Rather, it is better to say that their philosophical views were inconsistent with each other. As is well known, Evgenii Trubetskoi was a close friend of Soloviev, and has often been regarded as the most devoted follower of Soloviev's philosophy.[2] His largest work, *V. S. Soloviev's Worldview* (1913), was devoted to an analysis of Soloviev's philosophy; and Trubetskoi's fundamental interests, such as Christian metaphysics and the development of Christian social philosophy (especially church-state relations) in European history, were borrowed from Soloviev's philosophy.[3] However, the understanding of Soloviev's philosophy among his contemporaries was controversial. Sugiura (2013) pointed out that Trubetskoi, who was a proponent of rationality in thought, opposed Florensky and Sergei Nikolaevich Bulgakov, who advocated antinomy.[4] In fact, there was a series of arguments between Trubetskoi and Florensky occasioned by Florensky's book, *The Pillar and Ground of the Truth* (1914), published by *Put'*, which Morozova established with Trubetskoi. Reading the draft of the book, Trubetskoi soon sent a letter to Morozova in which he aggressively criticized the treatment of antinomies in Florensky's book as "ridiculous—dilettantish."[5] For Florensky, on the other hand, antinomy was "not only a logical contradiction, but also a sign of motion, outside of which any living thing, any living being, and any 'living thought,' that is, intellect [*razum*], cannot exist."[6]

Despite this controversy and conflict of philosophical views, there was a commonality between Trubetskoi and Florensky: both paid great attention to icon painting, contributed to liberating icons from the prevalent view that they were merely relics of history, and valued icons as worthy objects of philosophical contemplation.

2. Nosov, "Istoriya," 75.
3. Evlampiev, "Problema," 10.
4. Sugiura, "E. Trubetskoi," 5.
5. Keidan, *Vzyskuyushchie Grada*, 559; Andronik and Polovinkin, "Logizm," 318. All translation from Russian by Ruri Hosokawa.
6. Andronik and Polovinkin, "Logizm," 317.

The Two Worlds

Before beginning a detailed analysis of the views of Trubetskoi and Florensky, it is necessary to point out a fundamental commonality between their interpretation of icons. Their interpretation is based on the same concept, according to which the icon is considered an embodiment of contiguity between the two worlds, earth and heaven, the terrestrial sphere and the celestial sphere.

Trubetskoi devoted three papers to icons: "A World View in Painting" (1915), "Two Worlds in Old-Russian Icon Painting" (1916), and "Russia and Her Icons" (1918). As the title of "Two Worlds in Old-Russian Icon Painting" shows, Trubetskoi focused on the ontological role of icons as a sign of contiguity of heaven and earth. In this paper he wrote: "They [old-Russian icons] also show us the contiguity and interaction of two worlds, two planes of being: on one hand, the eternal peace of the higher regions; on the other, a world of sorrow, sin, chaos, but thirsting for God's peace—a world that seeks but has not yet found God."[7]

The idea of separation and connection between the two spheres was fundamental for Trubetskoi, and not only for his arguments on icons. Rather, it is related to his philosophy as a whole. According to Evlampiev (2014):

> In his all works, Trubetskoi was drawn to the problem of the correlation between the material values of ordinary human life and the spiritual values to which Christianity beckons, that is, to the problem of the correlation between the earthly and the divine. This is indeed the key to understanding his philosophical works.[8]

It can be said that the study of icons had an importance for Trubestkoi and for his philosophy as a whole, because the icon functions as a visualized contiguity of the earth and the divine.

For the philosophy and life of Florensky, who was an Orthodox priest, icons also played a great role. Florensky served on the Commission for the Preservation of Monuments and Antiquities of the Trinity Lavra of St. Sergius from 1918 to 1920, trying to preserve the monastery's precious materials, which had both historical and spiritual value to the Orthodox faith. In relation to his involvement with the Commission, Florensky was invited to teach Byzantine art at the Moscow Institute of Historical and Artistic Research and Museology. One of his major works on icons, *Iconostasis* (1922), was written in preparation for his Byzantine art course.[9] Focusing

---

7. Trubetskoi, "Two Worlds," 43.
8. Evlampiev, "Problema," 39.
9. Misler, "Biographical Sketch," 23.

on Florensky as art historian, Misler (2002) argued for the importance of icons in his works: "Florensky considered the ideal model or synthesis of the visual arts to be the Russian and Byzantine icon, an identification that is crucial to any understanding of Florensky the art historian and one that cannot be emphasized enough."[10]

Like Trubetskoi, Florensky thought about icons in relation to the idea of the two worlds. Florensky's analysis of icons in *Iconostasis* begins with these sentences:

> In the beginning of Genesis—"God created the heavens and the earth"—we have always recognized as basic this division of all creation into two. Just so, when we pray the Apostles' Creed, we name God as "Maker of all things visible and invisible." These two worlds—the visible and the invisible—are intimately connected, but their reciprocal differences are so immense that the inescapable question arises: what is their boundary? Their boundary separates them; yet, simultaneously, it joins them. How do we understand this boundary?[11]

Considering this question to be the key to any understanding of icons, Florensky developed his view on icons, or iconostasis, from the ontological aspect.

Florensky's analyses of icons are not limited to the fields of art and art history. In "Reverse Perspective" (1920), Florensky's major work on icons alongside *Iconostasis*, he analyzed reverse perspective, which is the major principle of icon painting, sharply criticizing not only linear perspective as a technique of painting, but also the whole European modern worldview, which he thought had its roots in the Renaissance and is based on linear perspective and Euclidean geometry. Although Trubetskoi did not refer to mathematics, the way in which he reflected the ontological analyses of icons and the idea of the two worlds reveal his whole philosophy to be similar to Trubetskoi's.

Coloring of Icons

Trubetskoi paid great attention to colors and the coloring of icons, and this shaped the character of his philosophy of icons. Many pages of his "Two Worlds in Old-Russian Icon Painting" are devoted to analysis of colors and

---

10. Misler, "Art Historian," 31.
11. Florensky, *Iconostasis*, 33.

coloring in icon painting, especially colors of the sky. Trubetskoi confirmed that the colors of the sky in icons show the existence of the other world:

> The artists used color to separate the two planes of being, the heavenly and the earthly.[12] We have seen that these colors come in a great variety, from the red of storm to dazzling sunlight to the brilliance of a luminous apparition. But no matter how variegated the colors that separate the two worlds, they are always celestial colors, in both the direct and the symbolic sense. They are the colors of the real, visible sky, but they have acquired conventional symbolic meanings of signs from the otherworldly sky, that is, heaven.[13]

Trubetskoi explained these colors, which express the sky of the other world, by giving examples: "the glitter of stars, the red of dawn, the reds of nocturnal storms or distant fires; and also the rainbow's many hues; and, finally, the gold of the midday sun."[14]

For Trubetskoi, an especially important color was red, on the background of which the figure of Sophia is depicted. Sophia is associated with red in Trubetskoi's idea, because it is the color which appears when the sky turns from midnight to morning, from dark to light; and by this color, better than any other, the contiguity between the two worlds and the transition from one to the other can be expressed. He wrote:

> The Wisdom [*Premudrost'*][15] embodied in Sophia is the design of God that preceded creation and called all celestial and earthly creatures forth from non-being into being, out of the darkness of night. That is why Sophia appears against a background of night. And this dark background makes her brilliant celestial red absolutely necessary. It is the red of God's dawn emerging from the night of non-being; it is the eternal sun rising over all living things. Sophia is what precedes the days of creation ... red marks the contact of sunlight with darkness.[16]

---

12. The "two planes" [*dva plana*] in this text has a twofold meaning: on one hand, it means the foreground and the background of the icon, and on the other hand, it metaphorically means this world and the next. Trubetskoi intended to say that icon painters divide this world and the other world in a similar way as they divide the background and the foreground by coloring.

13. Trubetskoi, "Two Worlds," 47.

14. Trubetskoi, "Two Worlds," 48.

15. Sophia is the personification of wisdom and is often identified with wisdom in Christianity.

16. Trubetskoi, "Two Worlds," 52–53.

PART II—PHILOSOPHY OF THE ICON

It is remarkable that Trubetskoi focused on the expression of the separation of the two worlds and especially on the transition between them in relation to the colors of the icon of Sophia.[17]

Interest in the colors of icon painting is also to be found in the ideas of Florensky, and there is something here in common with Trubetskoi. For example, the interpretations of gold by Trubetskoi and Florensky almost coincide with one another. Both considered gold to be the color of the sun or the light of the sun itself, and as the origin of all the colors. Trubetskoi argued:

> the mysticism of icon painting is primarily solar, in that word's highest spiritual sense. However beautiful the sky's other colors may be, the gold of the midday sun remains the color of colors and the miracle of miracles. All the others are, so to speak, of subordinate rank, from a hierarchy around it. In its presence, the nocturnal blue disappears; the stars pale, and so does the glow from a fire at night. Even the red of dawn is merely a harbinger of sunrise. Finally, the play of sunrays produces every color of the rainbow, for the sun is the source of all color and all light in the sky and below it. . . . Not one color of the rainbow is denied a place in these images of divine glory, but only the solar gold symbolizes the center of divine life. All the rest are its environment.[18]

Similarly, Florensky wrote of gold:

> The gold is pure, "admixtureless" light, a light impossible to put on the same plane with paint—for paint, as we plainly see, reflects the light: thus, the paint and the gold, visually apprehended, belong to wholly different spheres of existence. . . . Gold, the

---

17. Florensky also analyzed colors that indicate the presence of Sophia in "Celestial Signs," but his analysis of the colors of Sophia goes beyond the discussion of icons: "Contemplated as a work of divine creation, as the first clot of being, relatively independent of God as the darkness of nothingness moving forward to meet the light, i.e., contemplated as moving from God towards nothing, Sophia appears as blue or violet. Conversely, when contemplated as the result of divine creation, as inseparable from the divine light, as the foremost wave of divine energy, as the power of God moving to overcome darkness, i.e., when seen [moving] from the world towards God, Sophia appears pink or red . . . Finally, there is also a third metaphysical direction, neither towards nor away from the light, Sophia outside of her definition or self-definition towards God . . . this aspect of Sophia appears golden-green and translucent emerald" (Florensky, "Celestial Signs," 122).

18. Trubetskoi, "Two Worlds," 48.

metal of the sun, is colorless because it is almost equivalent to the sun's light.[19]

In relation to the expression of gold as divine light, both Trubetskoi and Florensky pointed out the importance of a method called *assist*. According to Trubetskoi:

> In our icon painting this divine gold has a special name, *assist*, and is used in a special way. It never looks like solid gold; it resembles, rather, an ethereal, airy cobweb of fine rays emitted by God and lighting everything around. When it appears in an icon, God is always suggested as its source.[20]

Florensky understood *assist* very similarly to Trubetskoi. He wrote:

> The *assyst* [*assist*] . . . is one of the most conclusive proofs that iconpainting possesses a concretely metaphysical meaning. It is, I suppose, understandable that the historical character of gold-*assyst* seems at a superficial glance to be unvaryingly monotonous; but in its essence, in its intricately refined patterns, the technique changes almost at the historical level from one style of iconpainting to another; thus, this extremely delicate golden network most expressively and conclusively manifests the icon's ontological constitution.[21]

In the same way that Trubetskoi stressed the relation between *assist* and the presence of the Divine, Florensky argues:

> The gold-*assyst* in icons does not articulate the metaphysics of the natural order (though this order is divinely created), but that it instead corresponds directly to the manifest energy of God. Look very closely: in the icon, *assyst* is placed not just anywhere but only upon that which has a direct relationship with the power of God, i.e., upon that reality which is itself not metaphysical even in any special sense but which nevertheless has entered into a direct relationship with God's manifest grace.[22]

It should be emphasized that, for Trubetskoi, the importance of *assist* in an icon is that it serves as a method by which the opposition of the two

---

19. Florensky, *Iconostasis*, 123, 125. Translation of this sentence was corrected by Ruri Hosokawa, according to Florensky, "Ikonostas," 69: "Zoloto, metall solntsa, potomu-to i ne imeet tsveta, shto pochti tozhdestvenno s solnechnym svetom."
20. Trubetskoi, "Two Worlds," 48–49.
21. Florensky, *Iconostasis*, 120–21.
22. Florensky, *Iconostasis*, 128–29.

worlds is expressed. According to Trubetskoi, "The strongest impact is achieved by the use of *assist* where the artists needs to contrast the two worlds, put a distance between the divine and the earthly."[23] It can be said that, for Trubetskoi, the coloring of an icon is the key to separating the two worlds and expressing their opposition, contiguity, and sometimes the transition between them.

The Transition to the Other World

In the color expression of the sky in an icon, especially the expression of transition from dark midnight to dawn, Trubetskoi found the transition from this world to the other. Furthermore, he focused on the expression of spatial motion from the earth to sky. He mentioned the icon on which the prophet Elijah is "ascending in a fiery chariot against a bright red, stormy sky" as a good example of the depiction of spatial motion.[24] According to Trubetskoi:

> His contact with the terrestrial plane of being is indicated by the Russian shaft bow of his horses headed straight for heaven and by the natural, casual way he hands down his cloak from that stormy sky to his disciple Elisha, who remains on earth.[25]

In this analysis of Elijah, Trubetskoi focused on the separation of the icon into the upper side and lower side, which correspond to the other world and this world. Elijah is passing across the boundary between them, from earth to heaven, and his cloak is falling from the sky to the ground. This vertical motion between the ground and sky expresses the contiguity and possibility of transition between them.

There is another example which Trubetskoi gave to explain the relationship between heaven and earth in icon painting: the icon of Florus and Laurus, which Trubetskoi saw as an intermediate style of expression between icon painting and Russian folk art. Of the figures of Florus and Laurus, which are depicted with the characteristics of Russian peasants, Trubetskoi wrote: "While ruling over the horses, they [Florus and Laurus] themselves are guided by an angel, who also appears in the icons... their clear Russian eyes shine with a prayerful fervor that lifts them to infinite heights above this world."[26] In this example, Trubetskoi also paid great attention to the expression of

---

23. Trubetskoi, "Two Worlds," 49–50.
24. Trubetskoi, "Two Worlds," 44.
25. Trubetskoi, "Two Worlds," 44.
26. Trubetskoi, "Two Worlds," 45.

interaction between the two worlds. In addition to the eyes of Florus and Laurus, there are reins held by the angel: They are depicted as vertical lines from the sky to the ground and can be considered an obvious expression of the connection between heaven and earth.

In Trubetskoi's philosophy of icon painting, this vertical motion and structure in icons is quite important, because icons are not independent, but serve as part of a temple and depend on its structure, in which everything aspires to its peak, which symbolizes the Eternal. According to Trubetskoi:

> In intent, a church and its icons form an indivisible whole. Hence the icon is subordinated to the architectural design of the church. This explains the remarkable architectural quality of our religious painting. Subordination to architectural form is felt not only in the church as a whole but in every single painted image. Every icon has its special internal architecture.[27]

Icons, in Trubetskoi's interpretation, are located on the way to Christ in both their visual and symbolic meanings. It can be said that icons embody the process of ascent toward Christ in two ways: on the one hand, icons themselves are embedded in the structure of a church, which directs from the bottom to the top; and on the other hand, as we have already seen in the examples of Sophia, Elijah, and Florus and Laurus, contiguity and transition to the divine world are expressed in each icon visually with the help of coloring and depiction of vertical motion.

Like Trubetskoi, Florensky thought "the Orthodox temple is the way of ascent."[28] However, Florensky thought of icons as iconostasis, and for him iconostasis is not a process of ascent, but a boundary or a wall with windows between the two worlds:

> The wall that separates two worlds is an iconostasis. . . . In actuality, the iconostasis is a boundary between the visible and invisible worlds, and it functions as a boundary by being an obstacle to our seeing the altar, thereby making it accessible to our consciousness by means of its unified row of saints (i.e., by its cloud of witnesses) that surround the altar where God is, the sphere where heavenly glory dwells, thus proclaiming the Mystery. Iconostasis is vision . . . To speak figuratively, then, a temple without a material iconostasis crests a solid wall between altar and temple; the iconostasis opens windows in this wall,

---

27. Trubetskoi, "World View," 25.

28. Florensky, *Iconostasis*, 59. Translation of this sentence was changed by Ruri Hosokawa, according to Florensky, "Ikonostas," 26: "Khram est' put' gornego voskhozdeniya."

through whose glass we see (those of us who can see) what is permanently occurring beyond: the living witnesses to God.[29]

If icons in the idea of Trubetskoi have vertical characteristics, it can be said that for Florensky they have horizontal characteristics as well.

This view of Florensky corresponds to his peculiar outlook on the world. In his book *Imaginaries in Geometry* (1922), which was written in the almost same period as *Iconostasis*, Florensky defined the terrestrial sphere and the celestial sphere, and contrasted them to each other in a mathematical-symbolic way. This book firstly attempted to extend the field of the two-dimensional images of geometry with the latest discoveries in physics and mathematics,[30] but its last chapter is dedicated to Florensky's peculiar view of the universe, in which the Ptolemaic system and Dante's *Divine Comedy* play great roles. The key to separating the two spheres is light. Florensky regarded the velocity of light as a standard, and defined the terrestrial sphere as a world in which every velocity is lower than the velocity of light, and the celestial sphere as a world in which everything moves faster than light. Light itself corresponds to the boundary between the two spheres. In his idea, in the terrestrial sphere everything has the length and mass of real numbers, as we know, but in the celestial sphere everything has the length and mass of imaginary numbers and time flows in reverse: "beyond the boundary, that is, where everything is faster than light, time flows in a reverse sense, so results precede causes."[31] On the boundary between them, or to be more precise, in the limitlessly thin sphere of light, the length of things is equal to zero, the mass of things is infinite, and time there is seen from our sphere to be infinite. The idea of reverse time is also mentioned in Florensky's *Iconostasis*:

> For, indeed, very long sequences of visible time can, in the dream, be wholly instantaneous—and can flow from future to past, from effects to causes. This happens in our dreams precisely when we are moving from the visible world to the invisible, between the actual and the imaginary.[32]

29. Florensky, *Iconostasis*, 62–63.

30. *Imaginaries in Geometry* has the subtitle "An Extension of the Field of the Two-Dimensional Images of Geometry: An Attempt at a New Interpretation of the Imaginaries."

31. Florensky, *Mnimosti v geometrii*, 50.

32. Florensky, *Iconostasis*, 35.

In *Imaginaries in Geometry*, Florensky considered light as the boundary between the two spheres, and in *Iconostasis*, he thought of iconostasis as the boundary between them.

Vladimir Andreevich Favorsky, an engraver and close friend of Florensky, successfully depicted this unique view of Florensky's. At the request of Florensky, Favorsky designed the cover of *Imaginaries in Geometry*. According to Florensky, it "does not simply decorate the book, but is an integral part of its spiritual makeup,"[33] since it helps to make Florensky's view visually clear. The plane of the cover is separated into two sides, right and left. On the left side of the plane, each image is depicted clearly and solidly, representing the sphere of real numbers, the visible world, and the terrestrial world. On the right side, however, everything is depicted vaguely, representing the sphere of imaginary numbers, the invisible world, and the celestial world. A line divides the two sides as a boundary. According to Florensky,

> both sides of the drawing, right and left, are not simply abutted to each other, even if they are qualitatively different, one purely visual, the other visually tactile, but they actually constitute the two sides of a single plane. . . . Both sides of the plane are linked together.[34]

In Florensky's vision, as expressed on the cover of the book, the two worlds, or the two sides of the one world, correlate symmetrically and horizontally, and between them lies the boundary line, which consists of light—or to be more precise, is light itself. This boundary of light, as Florensky explained in *Imaginaries in Geometry*, corresponds ontologically to iconostasis in the book *Iconostasis*, in which iconostasis is regarded not only as the art of light, but also as the metaphysics of light.[35]

Conclusion

In this paper, we have focused on the interpretations of icon painting in the philosophies of Evgenii Trubetskoi and Pavel Florensky. The connection between them is usually mentioned in relation to their philosophical controversy over antinomy. Both share a common concept of the division of the two worlds, which is reflected in their analyses of icon painting: For both Trubetskoi and Florensky, icons show the contiguity between the

---

33. Florensky, "Explanation," 189.
34. Florensky, "Explanation," 194.
35. Florensky, *Iconostasis*, 153.

terrestrial sphere and the celestial sphere. However, their ways of showing the contiguity differ.

Trubetskoi observed the signs of transition from one world to the other in the depictions and expressions of icons: the coloring of the sky, which separates the plane of the icon into two spheres; the vertical separation into the upper side and the lower side; the expression of time transitions in the sky from midnight to dawn, related to the presence of Sophia; and expression of vertical spatial motion between the ground and sky. This division of two spheres and aspiration to ascend correspond with the structure of a temple, in which every being aspires to the peak. In the philosophy of Trubetskoi, icons show processes toward the celestial world in their planes, and at the same time, they are embedded in the whole upward movement of a temple.

In contrast with Trubetskoi, who captured the vertical characteristics of icon painting, Florensky conceived the icon or iconostasis as a boundary consisting of light. In the philosophy of Florensky, the terrestrial world and the celestial world are contemplated horizontally—symmetrically to each other, putting the iconostasis/light between them as a boundary. Seen from the terrestrial sphere, the icon functions as a window opening toward the infinite celestial world, while seen from the celestial sphere, the icon is a reflection of infinity in finite, concrete form.

Bibliography

Andronik (Trubachev), and Sergei M. Polovinkin. "Logizm kn. Evgeniya Trubetskogo i antinomizm Pavla Florenskogo." In *Evgenii Nikolaevich Trubetskoi*, edited by Sergei M. Polovinkin and Tatyana G. Shchedrina, 309–28. Moscow: ROSSPEN, 2014.
Dmitriev, Sergei S. *Ocherki istorii russkoi kul'tury nachala dvadtsatogo veka*. Moscow: Prosveshchenie, 1985.
Evlampiev, Igor I. "Problema soedineniia zemnogo i bozhestvennogo v filosofskom tvorchestve." In *Evgenii Nikolaevich Trubetskoi*, edited by Sergei M. Polovinkin and Tatyana G. Shchedrina, 10–57. Moscow: ROSSPEN, 2014.
Florensky, Pavel A. "Celestial Signs." In *Pavel Florensky: Beyond Vision*, edited by Nicoletta Misler, translated by Wendy Salmond, 113–22. London: Reaktion, 2002.
———. "Explanation of the Cover." In *Pavel Florensky: Beyond Vision*, edited by Nicoletta Misler, translated by Wendy Salmond, 183–96. London: Reaktion, 2002.
———. *Iconostasis*. Translated by Donald Sheehan and Olga Andrejev. New York: St. Vladimir's Seminary Press, 1996.
———. "Ikonostas." In *Pavel Florenskii: Istoriya i filosofiya iskusstva*, edited by Aleksandr A. Guseinov, et al., 9–118. Moscow: Akademicheskii proekt, 2017.
———. *Mnimosti v geometrii*. Moscow: Lazur', 1991.

———. "Obratnaya perspektiva." In *Pavel Florenskii: Istoriya i filosofiya iskusstva*, edited by Aleksandr A. Guseinov, et al., 181–236. Moscow: Akademicheskii proekt, 2017.

Kaizawa, Hajime. "Pavel Florenskii no zoukeigeijutsuron ni okeru higashi to nishi: hyoushou, shintai, jinkaku no shiten kara." *21 seiki COE Program "Slav-Eurasia gaku no kouchiku" kenkyu houkoku shu 21 Slav-Eurasia ni okeru touzaibunka no taiwa to taikou* 1 (2007) 44–71.

Keidan, Vladimir I., ed. *Vzyskuyushchie grada. Khronika chastnoi zhizni russkikh religioznykh filosofov v pis'makh i dnevnikakh*. Moscow: Yazyki Russkoi Kul'tury, 1997.

Misler, Nicoletta. "Pavel Florensky: A Biographical Sketch." In *Pavel Florensky: Beyond Vision*, edited by Nicoletta Misler, translated by Wendy Salmond, 13–28. London: Reaktion, 2002.

———. "Pavel Florensky as Art Historian." In *Pavel Florensky: Beyond Vision*, edited by Nicoletta Misler, translated by Wendy Salmond, 29–93. London: Reaktion, 2002.

Nosov, Aleksandr A. "Istoriya i sud'ba 'Mirosozertsaniya Vl. S. Solov'eva.'" In *Evgenii Nikolaevich Trubetskoi*, edited by Sergei M. Polovinkin and Tatyana G. Shchedrina, 75–113. Moscow: ROSSPEN, 2014.

Sugiura, Shuichi. "E. Trubetskoi 'Vladimir Solov'ev no sekaikan' no kousatsu." *Media and Communication Studies* 64 (2013) 1–20.

Trubetskoi, Evgenii N. "Two Worlds in Old-Russian Icon Painting." In *Icons: Theology in Color*, translated by Gertrude Vakar, 41–70. New York: St. Vladimir's Seminary Press, 1973.

———. "Russia and Her Icons." In *Icons: Theology in Color*, translated by Gertrude Vakar, 71–98. New York: St. Vladimir's Seminary Press, 1973.

———. "A World View in Painting." In *Icons: Theology in Color*, translated by Gertrude Vakar, 13–39. New York: St. Vladimir's Seminary Press, 1973.

10

Between Image and Enigma

On the Philosophical Meanings of "Art History"
(Evgenii Trubetskoi and Others)[1]

Natalia Vaganova

Appealing to ancient iconography was natural among Russian philosophers, but its very first interpretation in philosophical work was, as Alexei Losev ironically observed, "unprecedentedly innovative."[2] In his work *The Idea of Humanity in Auguste Comte*, published in 1898, Vladimir Soloviev pointed out that the icon of Holy Sophia the Wisdom of God was Auguste Comte's *Grand Être*, the "unknown god" of philosophers, found in the faces of the Eternal Feminine for two and a half thousand years.[3]

It should be noted that attempts to explain the idea of the Holy Sophia icon enjoyed a long history in archaeography, dating from the first approach to the subject taken by Evgenii Bolkhovitinov in 1825.[4] Although consensus in these explanations was never achieved, Soloviev's interpretation turned out to be prominent. It did not appeal to the Russian tradition, Byzantine iconography, or biblical exegesis, thus inspiring a totally new direction in subsequent interpretations of this image. Besides his paradoxical desire to connect Old Russian icon painting and Comte's doctrine, his interpretation

---

1. This article was written in 2018 within the framework of the project "Russian religious thought from the second half of the nineteenth century to the beginning of the twentieth century: The problem of German influence in the context of the crisis of spiritual culture," supported by PSTGU Development Foundation.

2. Losev, *Vladimir Soloviev*, 254.

3. See Soloviev, "Idea," 222.

4. See Bolkhovitinov, *Opisanie*.

generated some specific comments. One such comment was made by Trubetskoi: "I remember how the late Soloviev in private conversations liked to point to the striking backwardness of Orthodox theology and iconography, especially with regard to the veneration of Mary, Mother of Jesus, and 'Sophia.'"[5] He also pointed out: "It is well known how much the image of Holy Sophia in Novgorod gave to this teaching."[6]

This is the only reference to Russian iconography in Vladimir Soloviev's works, but later a number of his followers took a keen interest in icons. Trubetskoi was the first to write essays on Russian iconography with the antinomic headlines: "Two Worlds in Old-Russian Icon Painting" and "A World View in Painting." These works, along with Florensky's *Iconostasis*, are considered groundbreaking in the field of the so-called "theology of the icon," but their value can now be considered a historical misconception in terms of art history, as they are full of arbitrary statements and conclusions.

"A World View in Painting" starts with Trubetskoi's impression of a panoramic view of Novgorod in winter, with golden heads of white-stone domes.[7] The Old Russian church dome is onion-shaped, which Trubetskoi considered to be a symbol of a candle flame and an appeal to Heaven in prayer.[8]

One does not have to be a specialist in the history of architecture to see how this and subsequent reflections were far removed from any understanding of the physical nature of dome construction, as well as its historical evolution. If Trubetskoi were in the vicinity of Novgorod today, he would be bitterly disappointed. In recent decades, the domes have acquired their original, historically accurate form after restoration. They no longer resemble onions or candle flames and therefore their appearance does not represent such a pure Russian religious expression, as Trubetskoi saw it.

Many of the thoughts of Russian philosophers on old Russian icon paintings are of a similarly dubious nature. It can be stated that in terms of art they reveal a flagrant dilettantism. They have been much criticized but this has been determined by apologetic positions rather than by aesthetic principles. A summary can be found in John Meyendorff's work, which called Soloviev's and his followers' intuition the most "significant attempt to achieve a synthesis between philosophical idealism and Christian revelation," though

---

5. Trubetskoi, "Svet Favorskii," 293.
6. Trubetskoi, "Svet Favorskii," 293.
7. In fact in Novgorod there are no temples built of white stone. White-stone architecture was found in the Vladimir-Suzdal principality.
8. See Trubetskoi, "World View," 16–17.

they misused iconography and liturgy, artificially equating images and ideas from Christian tradition with those coming from other sources.[9]

However, the philosophical component in appealing to the old Russian icon was neither pointless nor irrelevant. In order to see and assert its significance, we need to abandon ideas like Florensky's "reverse perspective" and similar phantoms as if they really referred to the Russian icon itself, and address the question of the role of such concepts within the philosophies of Soloviev, Trubetskoi, Florensky, and Bulgakov.

First of all, we should take into account that Meyendorff and others who are critical of non-historical appeals to "iconography data" have themselves not escaped the same mistake. Puzzled by the combination of such disparate elements as Byzantine iconography and modern religious doctrines, they completely ignore the nature and direction of the audience's spiritual needs as perceived by Soloviev and his followers. Perhaps only Trubetskoi, writing about Florensky's appeal to the Sophia icon and its connection with Soloviev, touches on the point of these modernizations and their role in creating synthesis:

> All these positions should be regarded not as a new teaching by Father Florensky, but as a genuine attempt to bring people's consciousness closer to the fathers' faith—the old Christian tradition which fortunately managed to become the tradition of Russian religious philosophy. Father Florensky in this respect takes a new and a very important step, which no one could take before him, except for V. Soloviev. He makes an effort to use for religious teaching the centuries-long religious experience expressed in Orthodox Church service and Orthodox iconography.[10]

In this article we will continue Trubetskoi's attempt to reveal the meaning of philosophical art history by concentrating on Florensky's interpretation of the iconography of Sophia, the Wisdom of God, in his book, *The Pillar and Ground of the Truth*.

First of all, we will designate a range of sources that could have been used by Florensky. References to these sources in the footnotes of the book show that he had three types of sources at his disposal. First are verbal descriptions of sophian icons (or the mere mention of their presence in temples) borrowed from different authors. Second are certain images which Florensky saw himself and mentioned in his notes. The final sources are drawings and photos

---

9. Meyendorf, "Tema 'Premudrosti,'" 251.
10. Trubetskoi, "Svet Favorskii," 293.

from different publications. All these materials primarily relate to samples from the seventeenth and eighteenth centuries.

The book also includes illustrations (three outline drawings and one photo) of icons of Sophia the Wisdom of God. At the moment of the book's creation, their dating was limited to the sixteenth and seventeenth centuries, but currently the oldest is dated to the first or middle part of the fifteenth century. And the newest one could not be earlier than the eighteenth century.

An important theoretical source for Florensky was Nikolai Pokrovsky's study, *The Gospel in the Monuments of Iconography* (1892). Here Florensky accepts first a typology of the images of "Sophia" and, second, some principles for analyzing icon composition. Following Pokrovsky, Florensky highlights three major types of sophian iconography, which he defines as the Angel type, the Church type (or Sophia of the Cross), and Virgin Mary type. They are categorized as the Novgorod Sophia, Yaroslavl Sophia and Kiev Sophia, according to locations of the best examples.

Furthermore, Florensky indicates that the three types of sophian iconography have a common spiritual principle: they all had one name and were worshipped as an expression of one idea. While not expressed by means of rational formulations by our ancestors, they were presented according to an iconographic plotline which articulated clear dogmatic ideas. The plot itself, in turn, was a vast religious phenomenon, beloved and national, that had apparent grounds in the historic depths of tradition, according to Florensky.

Florensky partly borrowed Pokrovsky's iconographic method. In particular he drew attention to the formal elements in icon composition that were connected with numeric and color symbolism. In Florensky's interpretation, these elements lend themselves to a kind of a consistent scientific approach applicable to the description of the artistic image.

Equally important in theoretical terms was Georgii Filimonov's "Essays on Russian Christian iconography: Sophia the Wisdom of God."[11] Filimonov supposed that the icon of Sophia the Wisdom of God was a creation of purely symbolic character, free of historical background. That is why its characterization could be modified depending on the context.

We now turn to the analysis suggested by Florensky and to the Novgorod icon of Sophia the Wisdom of God. Following Filimonov, Florensky thinks that connecting the icon of Sophia with the second hypostasisis is an artificial adoption of alter-ideological content, since there is an apparent discrepancy between the content of the image and the way the Fathers of the Church represented the idea of Sophia. Therefore, he excluded

11. Filimonov, "Ocherki," 1–20.

Christological interpretations of the central image in the Novgorod icon from consideration, focusing on different interpretations.

The characteristics of Novgorod-type iconography can be seen as partly correct and partly arbitrary (for example, reference to the correlation between the number of angels and the presence of the figure of God the Father). Sometimes they fail to correspond to reality (a golden eight-pointed star, fire columns under the throne of Wisdom). The same conclusion is true of the symbolic interpretation of the specific image elements that Florensky describes further. His explanation of symbols and signs in the images often seems artificial, trivial and colored by a shade of dilettantism. In general, most of Florensky's findings have a non-historical, modernizing character, yet blaming him for this would be useless. Florensky is not trying to reveal his own logic of iconographic image; rather he is overcoming challenges of a quite different nature and his logic was set on another objective.

As mentioned above, a special role in Florensky's analysis belongs to formal elements that became the dominant and even exclusive method: numbers (three, seven, twelve), geometrical figures, and especially color combinations (red, green, blue):

> Sophia's wings clearly indicate that she has some special closeness to the world on high.... The caduceus... in the right hand is an indication of theurgic power, of *psychopompia*, of mysterious power over souls. The rolled-up scroll in the left hand, pressed to the organ of higher knowledge, the heart, indicates knowledge of shrouded mysteries.[12]

By these formal elements Florensky tries to confirm the ambivalence in the image of Sophia and its identification with the Savior or with the Mother of God, simultaneously distinguishing it from them (mentioned by art historians, e.g., Pokrovsky). In order to do so he uses a sort of symbolic didactics in which every sign in the icon necessarily has to point to something. For example, if one and the same attribute is shared by various figures, this, according to Florensky, marks their internal sophian connection:

> Moreover, the Savior, Sophia, and the Mother of God are clearly distinguished in this composition. Sophia is placed below the Savior, i.e., in a subordinate position, and the Mother of God is placed before Sophia, once again in a subordinate position. The Savior, Sophia, and the Mother of God are therefore in sequential hierarchical subordination. The distinction between nimbuses is also an indication of their inequality. Sometimes, moreover, Sophia, in later icons, also has a cruciform nimbus.... [T]his

12. Florensky, *Pillar*, 270–71.

mixing is highly typical: even though Sophia is an independent figure in iconography, she is clearly so closely connected with Christ and (as we see later) with the Mother of God that she can, through attraction, adopt their attributes and thereby almost merge with the One or the Other, so to speak. A certain kinship between the three Persons is also sometimes revealed in the fact that they are all portrayed with wings.[13]

Such an approach to the artistic image is inclined to excessive rationalization and importunate sketchiness: the icon turns into a kind of mathematical computation, every element of which has its unambiguous sense and strictly defined conceptual framework, and hermeneutics comes down to calculation. As a result, Florensky ignores other substantive and artistic aspects of imagery, transforming them into a kind of enigma that could be solved. For this, one only needs to find out the meaning of each element and the principle connecting them.

Of course, Florensky is justified, first of all, by his reliance solely on the iconographic approach to ancient painting, the only existing one at that time. Second, it should be taken into account that the late icon painting that Florensky generally dealt with is characterized by excessive allegorism, transfer of formal rhetorical acts into image, emphasis on numerical repetitions (seven steps, seven virtues, seven cathedrals), geometrical construction and a common tendency to edification, therefore providing many reasons for rationalist interpretations. The author refers to the images of the seventeenth and eighteenth centuries in his analysis, since his method with its defiantly scientific basis had more to say about them than about the icons painted in earlier periods which lacked these elements. Nevertheless Florensky, basing himself on rather unreliable and completely insufficient grounds, claims that the icon of Sophia is one of the most ancient icons in Russian icon painting and dates it to the eleventh century at the latest, as part of the iconography of the Novgorod type.

Florensky needed to present the icon of Sophia as older than it really was in order to defend the image, which was suspicious from Orthodox point of view. This gave some grounds to consider the sophiological theory as a part of Orthodox tradition. However, antiquity and tradition were unlikely to have absolute value for Florensky. His attitude to the antithesis *antiqui—moderni* is clearly identified in Letter Ten, dedicated to Sophia. The ancient as something valuable is characteristic of Gnosticism. Orthodoxy agrees with it only to some respect. Since Church and personality are *res realiores* and eternal as they are, they pre-exist as well as "after-exist."

---

13. Florensky, *Pillar*, 272.

In this context Florensky, locating the origin of Sophia in the first period of Russian Christianity and rejecting the origin of the idea *ex nihilo* (as coming from a religious void), nonetheless is inclined to simulate the situation where its reception and development in Russian Orthodoxy are connected with a historical void, the absence of any ground or of any religious, cultural, political or other presuppositions:

> It was the rare fortune of the Russian people to receive Christianity before its national self-definition had been fully achieved. Christianity collides in the Russian people neither with a formulated doctrine nor with the rich cult of some other religion; nor does it find deeply rooted moral habits or state aspirations.[14]

However, this very groundlessness and lack of presuppositions guarantee the dogmatic purity and authenticity of the sophian tradition in the Russian Slavonic reality.

> Christianity was received by the souls of children, and the entire further growth of these souls, and their entire inner organization, were accomplished under the direct guidance of the Church. It is quite understandable that the national spirit, formed in this way, cold not fail to be essentially Orthodox.[15]

Thus, the source of the tradition is Revelation itself, while the archetypical specifics of its reception are related to the spiritual constitution of St. Constantine-Cyril, the true "spiritual parent of the Russian people."[16] From the Virgin, chosen by Sophia, or more precisely from Sophia-Virgin herself, Russian Orthodoxy starts with the religious idea in creating Sophia icons and temples. The sophian tree grew in a clean field, free of cultural stratification and of the pagan sources of Greek Byzantine culture.

Undoubtedly, Florensky's appeal to the Russian past in fact implied appealing to the present, and his iconographical interpretations aimed not to account for the existing religion and tradition but for the need to design a new style. The project makes the anachronistic dissonances arising from visual perception quite natural, where icons of the seventeenth and eighteenth centuries seem an intrinsic part of the baroque engravings arranged along the frame of the book and of the author's appeal to Kiev/Novgorod antiquity. The common stylistic context is eventually recognized as an *Art Nouveau* phenomenon. Sophia's icon in such a context is a symbolic concept which is similar functionally and methodologically to many of Florensky's

---

14. Florensky, *Pillar*, 557n695.
15. Florensky, *Pillar*, 557n695.
16. Florensky, *Pillar*, 557n695.

other liturgical-symbolic elements, representing only *naming*, pointers to the idea, and not substances with their own value.

Among the other elements of this project, the icon, as a physical object of worship, stands out as the most recognizable and "energetically" saturated, the most ontologically solid, effectively centering the aggregate will of those who venerate it. As the icon is both a thing of worship and a brilliant work of art, the icon's effect on us grows, and in this regard the icon is incomparable among aesthetic or religious objects.

In sum, we can state that the appeal of the Russian icon to religious thinkers at the turn of the nineteenth and twentieth centuries, and their attempts at philosophical-theological analysis and interpretation, were absolutely justified and very promising. Let us not forget that around this time there was a "discovery of the Russian icon" for a new audience which was previously unfamiliar with it: educated Russian society.[17] Soloviev, Trubetskoi, Florensky, and Bulgakov perceived the icon as a unique phenomenon, different from any other artistic phenomenon of the time. Dogmatism and tradition were combined with modern relevance in the new artistic consciousness and hence with keen interest from contemporaries. It was possible to personally discover and experience the aesthetic beauty and dogmatic depth of the icon, as Florensky showed in *The Pillar and Ground of Truth*.

We can also conclude that the philosophers of Europe almost simultaneously turned to medieval art and its aesthetic in their philosophical-theological inquiry (Jacques Maritain, Erwin Panofsky, Étienne Gilson, and others) but they actually served an entirely different purpose.

Bibliography

Bolkhovitinov, Evgenii. *Opisanie Kievosofiiskogo sobora i kievskoi ierarkhii*. Kiev: Tipografiya Kievopecherskoi Lavry, 1825.

Filimonov, Georgii. "Ocherki russkoi khristianskoi ikonografii: Sofiya Premudrost' Bozhiya." In *Vestnik Obshchestva drevnerusskogo iskusstva za 1874–1876 gg*, 1–20. Moscow: Universitetskaya tipografiya, 1876.

Florensky, Pavel. *The Pillar and Ground of the Truth: An Essay in Orthodox Theodicy in Twelve Letters*. Translated by Jakim Boris. Princeton: Princeton University Press, 1997.

Losev, Aleksei F. *Vladimir Soloviev i ego vremya*. Moscow: Progress, 1990.

---

17. For the first time Russian icon painting was presented to the public on February 28, 1913 at the Imperial Archeological Institute in Moscow at the exhibition of old Russian art to celebrate the three hundredth anniversary of the House of Romanov (for the most part, these were icons of Stroganov's painting from personal collections). The exhibition aroused great interest from different spectrums of society, unanimous glowing reviews and a series of repetitions. See Shevelenko, "'Otkrytie,'" 259–81.

Meyendorf, Dzhon. "Tema 'Premudrosti' v vostochnoevropeiskoi srednevekovoi kul'ture." In *Literatura i iskusstvo v sisteme kul'tury*, edited Boris B. Piotrovsky, 244–52. Moscow: Nauka, 1988.

Pokrovsky, Nikolai. *The Gospel in the Monuments of Iconography, Mostly Byzantine and Russian*. St. Petersburg: Appanage, 1892.

Shevelenko, Irina. "'Otkrytie' drevnerusskoi ikonopisi v esteticheskoi refleksii 1910-kh godov." In *Studia Russica Helsingiensia et Tartuensia X: "Vek nyneshniy i vek minuvshiy": kul'turnaya refleksiya proshedshei epokhi*. Part 2: 259–81. Tartu: Tartu Ulikooli Kirjastus, 2006.

Soloviev, Vladimir. "The Idea of Humanity in Auguste Comte." In *Divine Sophia: The Wisdom Writings of Vladimir Soloviev*, edited and translated by Judith Deutsch Kornblatt, 211–29. Ithaca: Cornell University Press, 2009.

Trubetskoi, Evgenii. "Svet Favorskii i preobrazhenie uma. Po povodu knigi svyashchennika P. A. Florenskogo 'Stolp i utverzhdenie Istiny'. Izd. Knigoizdatel'stva Put'. Moskva, 1914." In *P. A. Florenskii: pro et contra*, edited by Konstantin G. Isupov, 285–316. St. Petersburg: Izdatel'stvo Russkogo Khristianskogo Gumanitarnogo Instituta, 1996.

———. "A World View in Painting." In *Icons: Theology in Color*, translated by Gertrude Vakar, 13–39. New York: St. Vladimir's Seminary Press, 1973.

11

Structural-Semiotic Analysis as a Method to Reveal the Invisible World

Fr. Pavel Florensky's "Iconostasis"

ELENA TVERDISLOVA

In Russia, philosophers did not accept the Revolution, neither those who were brought to the West on the ship of "wise men" ("the philosophers' steamer") nor those who remained. In this environment, one of the most dramatic figures was Evgenii Trubetskoi (1863–1920), who fairly quickly understood the essence of the catastrophe and its irreversibility, and who, not coincidentally, died young (in Novorossiisk, from cholera), not living long enough to see his country perish. Educated as a lawyer, according to the spirit of the law rather than the letter, he recognized the reasons for the Russian tragedy in the underdeveloped legal consciousness of the people. He did not even pose the question of social responsibility. Trubetskoi's analysis of Afanasyev's *Skazki* (*Tales*), the heroes of which, according to his keen observations, were idlers, thieves, and swindlers, is telling. The radical nature of his critical position also had an impact on his philosophical insights—for example, on his polemics with Vladimir Soloviev, although he considered himself one of his followers.

Other philosophers took a less tragic view of the chaos. Some had confidence that the revolutionary events would be temporary, and believed they would one day return to their *own* Russia (Sergei Bulgakov, Nikolai Berdyaev, Semen Frank), while others banked on faith, believing that the end was coming.

In his 1922 work *Ikonostas* (*Iconostasis*), Pavel Florensky approaches the confirmation of the invisible world as the sole genuine proof of the existence of God, using iconostasis as a system for knowledge about the two worlds: the heavenly and the earthly.[1] Two aspects of his approach are unique. First, to uphold the invisible world, he applied a formalistic methodology: a structural-semiotic analysis as a means to reveal tacit structures. Second, his method was similar to the science of structuralism itself, which took shape throughout the first half of the twentieth century and took its final form as a method by the end of the 1940s, having incorporated the manifold avenues of Ferdinand de Saussure's Geneva School of linguistics, Russian formalism, Prague structuralism, the American school of semiotics, and more.[2]

I have never encountered research that considers *Iconostasis* as the subject of structuralism, though its interpretation of icon painting suggests certain parallels with analysis of the structure of language. I believe that, in many respects, this has caused an aberration in the reception of this text. Florensky's work never presented itself either as an artistic study or, even less so, a guide to the techniques of icon painting, although many have taken it as such, provoking understandable criticism from Berdyaev and others.[3]

In a certain form, *Iconostasis* is a study of the author himself, a confirmation of his own sense of the world and spirit—purely subjective, like a conversation with himself. This is reflected in a reconstruction of activity addressed simultaneously at both worlds, the visible and invisible: for Florensky, they are not identical and do not merge into one whole, in contrast to the well-known saying that an icon is the visible image of the invisible, which saying has been attributed to John of Damascus but more likely belongs to Dionysius the Areopagite.[4] Clearly, Florensky was not governed by the idea of the iconostasis as such, or by the practice of icon painting, but by the possibility of showing that the other world—celestial, heavenly, Godly—in fact exists. Consequently, the sort of icon (ancient or modern) made no difference. The icon itself was the proof of the invisible world.

Florensky nowhere expresses a desire to identify and describe the schools and trends in icon painting or to conduct a systematic overview, nor does he point out the specific features of icons in the Byzantine, Balkan, and Eastern Christian styles. He does not pursue the goal of classifying them into a hierarchy or contrasting them with each other. He does not look at the icon

---

1. See Florensky, *Iconostasis*, 43–44.
2. See Il'in, "Strukturalizm," 1042–43.
3. See Berdyaev, "Stylized Orthodoxy."
4. More precisely, Dionysius said, "Truly visible things are manifest images of invisible things." John of Damascus, quoting those words, formulates it this way: "Every *image* is a *revelation* and *representation of something hidden*." See Vysheslavtsev, *Etika*, 117.

as a genotypical (or one could say universal) concept, for the icon is only as universal as it is individual. Sensing a need to break free of the fetters of time, Florensky uses the most modern philosophical ideas, which were at the time only just beginning to develop and were largely theoretical. His audacity lies not just in the fact that he applied the newest scholarly innovations, including linguistics, but also in that he approached the icon as a resplendent image of the heavenly world, even though it was made on Earth. What makes the icon so distinctive is its ability to connect both worlds.

It is odd that such scholarly innovation escaped the notice of his contemporaries. According to Berdyaev, "one can find no traces in Father Florensky of that authentic new consciousness, of the consciousness that the world is now entering an epoch of anthropological revelation . . . that divine revelation is passing into man and continuing through him."[5] Imagine speaking of anthropological revelation and not seeing it in Florensky! After all, in Russia, he put his ideas on the line in opposition to the whole scholarly establishment, declaring that a modern-day proof of God's existence required a modern-day approach. I will not attempt to explain Berdyaev; it is all too common that people cannot see the innovations of which they speak in practice. More telling is something else: Florensky, in laying the groundwork for new theories, did not himself so much create as apply, ready-made, what was already present in his premonitions, and he used innovative methods and techniques as already existing systems. He sees the invisible world through the prism of formalism, and using it, he penetrates past the boundaries of mysticism and esotericism.

I first read Florensky's *Iconostasis* in Polish in 1981, in the apartment of some Polish friends who were living in Vilnius. My host was a fan of Józef Piłsudski, and I slept under his sword, which hung over a carpet on the wall by my bed. This fan of Piłsudski, a self-taught historian and a Catholic, immediately started asking me about Florensky and his *Iconostasis*, with which he had just become familiar. When he discovered that I had only heard about the work second-hand, he did not conceal his astonishment, and he offered me the recently published Polish translation. He was eager to discuss it. I spent several days reading it. The work left me with the strange impression that it had been written not long ago. Upon my return to Moscow, I asked a colleague at the Institute for Scientific Information for the Social Sciences of the Soviet Academy of Sciences—Ilya Ilyin, referenced above, an expert on structuralism and literary theory—whether the *Iconostasis* could be subjected to a structural-semiotic analysis, given that it was written in the early twentieth century. "Absolutely," he answered. It was Florensky who

---

5. Berdyaev, "Stylized Orthodoxy," 189.

pointed out the peculiarities of the structural-semiotic method, and who reinforced not just semiotics, but also structural linguistics with its focus on the poetics of literature and language, using as examples the language of the icon, the names of people and objects, and the connection between a work's composition and structure. He spoke about the spatial differences in individual types of art and, finally, about time as a "fourth dimension"[6] and photography as a "momentary image."[7]

Florensky's *Iconostasis* can be called the first structural-semiotic study of religious imagery. But its most striking aspect is its use not only of trends and concepts in metaphysics, but also of the new dialogical philosophy. From here we have his understanding of the icon as an integral structure. "The iconostasis is vision," Florensky emphasizes, specifying that the icon is "a line circumscribing vision" and that icon painting is "the metaphysics of existence."[8] As such, the icon is brought into the world of prototypical, celestial, "sacred beings."[9] The point of creating an icon lies in its being "visually manifest."[10] Florensky examines this as a model for the process of perception described in our own day by the existential phenomenology of Maurice Merleau-Ponty: "Perception is not knowledge about the world; it is not even an act, not a well-thought-through taking of a position. Perception is a foundation upon which our acts play out and it is suggested by them."[11]

All the methods Florensky uses in his icon research are also used by him, in one way or another, in his other work. In particular, in his article "Time in the momentary image: Photography," he uses the visual specificity of photography and the specificity of time to reveal the following: "One must speak about the further densification of time, when various moments in the process are posed within the limits of a single image, and are joined visibly with the very visibility of this image."[12] In his *Iconostasis*, Florensky makes the concept of time imprinted in an icon, with its linear perspective, and the concept of space, with its reversible perspective, more specific. These are all big themes, and in examining them, Florensky draws on a new philosophy and a new science already infused with the theory of

---

6. Florensky, "Vremia kak chetvertoe izmerenie," 190.

7. Florensky, "Vremia v momental'nom obraze," 226.

8. Florensky, *Iconostasis*, 62, 64, 113.

9. Florensky, *Iconostasis*, 114.

10. Florensky, *Iconostasis*, 115.

11. Merleau-Ponty, *Phénoménologie*, x. Citations from all non-English works referenced in this article are translated for this article by Shelley Fairweather-Vega.

12. Florensky, "Vremia v momental'nom obraze," 233.

relativity. He propounds ideas which had only just appeared in the world. In Tatiana Shteler's opinion,

> Florensky's and Merleau-Ponty's texts make it obvious that examining perspectives is of philosophical and even specifically phenomenological interest. Whatever the case, it becomes possible to ground the importance of this theme within classical Husserlian phenomenology.[13]

At the same time, Florensky continuously insists on a sort of conditional presence of any fact concerning icon painting; for him, one's own experience is neither mandatory, nor categorical, nor final. One relies upon it, but is not governed by it. Could this be the source of Berdyaev's reproach about Florensky's "sickly dualism" and "ambivalence"?[14] The uniqueness of Florensky's text in terms of genre is revealing. Beginning with an analysis of a psychological (borderline mystical) state, the original experience of which is a dream, Florensky indicates, on the one hand, that a dream is

> our first and simplest (in the sense that we are fully habituated to it) entry into the invisible world. This entry is, more often than not, the lowest. Yet even the most chaotic and crude dream leads our soul into the invisible, giving even to the least sensitive of us the insight that there is something in us very different from what we uniquely call life.[15]

On the other hand, he indicates that sleep and dreams are "the images that separate the visible world from the invisible—and at the same time join them." But dreaming is also a symbol: "From the heavenly view, the dream symbolizes earth; from the earthly perspective, it symbolizes heaven."[16] He proposes that it is in this state that artistic works arise, and the goal of an icon is to "lead our consciousness out into the spiritual realm."[17] In doing so, Florensky essentially leads the reader to the heart of creativity as a spiritual act, connecting it with the invisible world and endowing it with universal

---

13. "The problem of perspective transforms phenomenology from the classical phenomenology of perception into a phenomenology which includes the existential and religious dimensions of experience. Husserl began to set this idea in motion in his 'Crisis,' and studies by Florensky and Merleau-Ponty, very valuably, continued it. What results is an integral picture of life in which art and science are interconnected dimensions resonating with historically evolving methods of seeing the world." See Shteler, "Obratnaia perspektiva," 328.
14. See Berdyaev, "Stylized Orthodoxy," 185.
15. Florensky, *Iconostasis*, 34.
16. Florensky, *Iconostasis*, 42, 43.
17. Florensky, *Iconostasis*, 66.

proportions, but he also issues a warning: "[a]n icon is not an artwork, a self-enclosed piece of art," for it "is a work of witness" employing art *as well as* many other things." It also demonstrates the "clarity of the collectively carried and transmitted truth."[18] Florensky does not counterpoise the subjective origin to the collective (nor to the objective), but rather he speaks about a certain addition that is necessary for the recognition of a unified creative energy. This reveals that which exists, like a river with two "shores of existence"[19] which one can walk into. And that which has to do with sleep, with its transition from the terrestrial world to the celestial world and back again, is also characteristic of any transition from one sphere to the other.[20]

The suddenly-arising dialogue between the author and himself, or with someone else, allows him, first, to demonstrate his own attitude toward the religious tendency in European painting, which must necessarily be compared with icon painting, while not in any way hiding the subjective nature of his view, and second, to reveal the specific nature of icon painting as an original spiritual phenomenon. The dialogicity of the original text also encompasses ways of examining an icon as an object of study at all levels: physical (comparing the icon with an organ; its resonance and its structure); artistic and psychological (choice of subject, preparation of the board and paints, connection of the icon with the life of the icon painter); semiotic (hierarchy of colors and lines; execution of both background and faces); historical (traditions and execution); existential ("I" and "not I"); and mathematical (geometry and the "ostensibility" of geometry).

The argument about the icon as a conversation with God is logically convincing.

The icon's semantic field is thoroughly dialogical, as evidenced by the "pairs" Florensky endlessly constructs: the board and the image; the image assumes the background and the drawing; light and gold, light and hues, and color and lines all conduct their own dialogues, as do the colors amongst themselves, but most of all black and white; and finally, when the icon is varnished, it enters into a dialogue with both the board and with the image on it. In describing the "external" structure of an icon's ontological existence, Florensky lists the artists who become co-authors of the finished icon: the engraver, and colorists who concentrate on either the face or covered figures and backgrounds. In one way or another, they are all connected both with each other and with icon painting as a dialogical

---

18. Florensky, *Iconostasis*, 134–35.
19. Florensky, *Iconostasis*, 43.
20. See Florensky, *Iconostasis*, 43.

structure, confirming the *sobornost'*, the collective nature, of icon creation.[21] The name of the work, *Iconostasis*, is no accident. It most frequently means not one icon, but a whole internally unified set, as a complete genre with its own experts, a type of community, a collective operation in which not just the icon painter but others equally participate.

With its internal and external composition, the icon is endowed on the one hand with completeness and on the other with an openness of structure which assumes a certain parabolicity. "Iconpainting is a purely coherent art, one wherein everything connects to everything: substance and surface; drawing style and subject matter; the meaning of the whole and the way we comprehend that meaning."[22] Florensky's approach to the icon, which he believes is characterized by "coherence" and "rich organic wholeness,"[23] with regard to the structural model as well, justifies the various methods of analysis he applies as he proceeds from his own most important criteria: "Science does not explain, but only describes."[24] He moves easily from the metaphysical to the phenomenological sphere (I do not know a single other philosopher contemporary to Florensky who felt so at home in phenomenology), and from there the path was open to the problems of existentialism, of natural philosophy, and finally, of visual technique. In its own way, the icon is a visual formula for communing with God. With the help of that formula, it approaches verbal language, first and foremost because the icon is called something: it has a name (he wrote several essays on the "philosophy of the name"), continuing the tradition of onomatodoxy. But this does not exclude imagery, symbolism, and, ultimately, semiotics as the meaning of the image, which he considers in the chapter "Science as a Symbolic Description" (this was included in "Thought and Language," part of his powerful work *At the Watersheds of Thought*).[25]

The icon is a religious sacrament, and as a sacrament, it "connects the celestial and terrestrial, earthly and heavenly, transcendental and immanent." But "in order for it to be such, it necessarily has a secular aspect; and because only the sacrament is palpable and visible, sensually it is indiscernible from other manifestations and things of the world."[26] Florensky sees the sacrament from two points of view. "While metaphysically the sacrament

---

21. See Florensky, *Iconostasis*, 134–35.
22. Florensky, *Iconostasis*, 146.
23. Florensky, *Iconostasis*, 146–47.
24. Florensky, "Ob'ektivnaya znachimost' imen," 196.
25. Florensky, "Ob'ektivnaya znachimost' imen," 104–18.
26. Florensky, "Nauka," 191.

is above the world, phenomenologically, it is a product of the world."[27] This location on the boundary between two different scholarly fields dictates his own approach. He characterizes the icon as a metaphysical event, as part of "the metaphysics of light, for this is the primary characteristic of all iconpainting."[28] At the same time, he notes that "iconpainting considers light . . . the transcendental origin of things,"[29] considering individual aspects of icon painting phenomenologically, which, in the end, gives Florensky a justification for interpreting the icon as something whole, laying the groundwork for a diversity of scholarly approaches. Further, he interprets it as semiotically polysemantic, because to him every image is an idea, and as an idea, the icon represents prayer, contemplation, a conversation with God. All this means the laws of icon creation, revealed by Florensky, are not rules, which people often confuse with the path to communion with God. This is precisely why the icon acts as a "window" to the universal world, "because a region of light opens out beyond it; hence, the window . . . is that very light itself, in its ontological self-identity, that very light which, undivided-in-itself and thus inseparable from the sun, is streaming down from the heavens."[30] At the same time, the heavens are connected with the space inside and vice versa.

Florensky considers light to be the main construct of icon painting in various categories (such as the study of art and of spirituality and religion),[31] which provides him a basis for describing the icon along realist lines, according to the worldview of a man of faith. By this principle, the work takes on a demetaphorizing aspect (or, on the contrary, a cleansing from "the spirit of allegory"[32]) and assumes the status of an idea, tossing aside artistry and becoming a realistic incarnation of a semiotic sign. Florensky's argument coincides with his own assessment of the inverted perspective in space: "The iconpainter moves from shadow into light, from darkness into illumination," and for him there is no other reality. According to Florensky, for the icon painter, a shadow is not color, but rather a distortion at the root of ontology, or more precisely, the existential category of "absence" or a "void."[33] Twenty

---

27. Florensky, "Nauka," 187.
28. Florensky, *Iconostasis*, 153.
29. Florensky, *Iconostasis*, 150.
30. Florensky, *Iconostasis*, 65.
31. "Iconpainting depicts objects as forms created by light rather than as things lit by a light-source." Florensky, *Iconostasis*, 149.
32. Florensky, *Iconostasis*, 85.
33. Florensky, *Iconostasis*, 144–45.

years later, Sartre provided a philosophical basis for this using consciousness and thought as a starting point.[34]

There could very well be a source much closer to Florensky in its presentation of the reality of the invisible world and the luminescence of the spiritual life recorded in the icon. Here I mean the internal and even terminological connection between Florensky's *Iconostasis* and the well-known Kabbalistic teachings of Rabbi Shimon bar Yohai in the Zohar, translated as "radiance." The author of the Zohar was born forty years after the destruction of the second Temple, and it is believed that the book was written in the fourth century, but it was not discovered until the thirteenth,[35] giving rise to assumptions that it may be a hoax. Florensky's interest in Kabbalistic studies, and in this book, can be seen in his treatment of how man becomes acquainted with the work of creation, which, according to Kabbalistic teachings, is "*ur*-light-delight."[36]

> The Creator is the source of light-delight. People who come near to Him sense Him as such. . . . In order to create a human being at a distance from Himself, so that man could recognize his insignificance and take it upon himself to rise up, the Creator made all of creation in the form of a staircase descending down from Him. The light of the Creator traveled down along it and created, at the very lowest step, our world and, inside it, the human being. Recognizing his insignificance, and wanting to rise up to the Creator, man, to the extent of his desire, moves closer to the Creator, rising up along the staircase that was the scene of the descent.[37]

Remember that Florensky defines sleep as a first *step* into the invisible world.[38] Overall, the formal side of this teaching and its multifaceted scheme for orienting mankind, as he becomes acquainted with the light, as well as with the other reality—esoterics and mysticism, as they combine with earthly reality—probably attracted him more.[39]

---

34. Sartre, *L'être et le néant*.
35. See "Rabbi Shimon," 15.
36. Laitman, *Zoar*, 29.
37. Laitman, *Zoar*, 192–93.
38. See Florensky, *Iconostasis*, 34. While this English translation uses the word "entry," the original Russian uses the word *stupen'*, "step"—Trans.
39. In Pankin, "ARKTOGEYA," the author writes: "The most formidable religious thinker of the New Era, Pavel Florensky, wrote about Kabbalah: 'Kabbalah (literally, a legend handed down) is the collective name for the mystical teachings of Judaism, at the center of which stands a view of the Bible as a movable cosmos of symbolic meanings. In the narrow sense, the term is usually applied only to medieval Jewish

Florensky locates the origins of the icon in Egypt, constructing a logical differentiation: face/likeness, mask/countenance. He argues that the Egyptian sarcophagus (with a mummy placed inside) is "the progenitor of the icon."[40] That same mask also was an important step on the path to symbolism, absorbing, in particular, the Hellenistic portrait, which "was plainly a kind of icon of the deceased." For that reason, in the cult of the dead, the mask "was truly the *appearance* of the deceased, a heavenly appearance full of greatness and divine grandeur"; consequently, the icon was then no longer a *depiction*, but a witness.[41] The countenance is a witness of the divine world, Florensky concludes.

The anthropology of icon painting, starting with the painter and his co-authors, signals the chief value of the icon, namely, its concentration on the face. Florensky understands this figuratively and semiotically, more broadly than a simple image, although he writes about that as well: "In Genesis, *the image of God* is differentiated from *the likeness of God*."[42] The face is what connects a man in the visible world with the invisible world, in which sense the face can be compared to a manifestation, and thus "the countenance of a thing manifests its ontological reality."[43] The face on an icon, Florensky affirms, records forever both the Image of Man and the sacred. The contenance is what marks the differences between a painting and an icon. The icon is the path which a person can follow to discover the countenance. Florensky believes that ordinary painting begins with the personal, that is to say with the countenance, while "iconpainting finishes with it."[44]

The pattern Florensky notes—face/likeness, mask, countenance—foretells the *epiphany of the face*, as described by the French Jewish philosopher Emmanuel Levinas (1906–1995), who wrote on the topic in 1983: "In the phenomenon of the face there is included a kind of testament, like an instruction given to me by a teacher."[45] In analyzing the concept of the face in Levinas, the Polish philosopher Józef Tischner (1931–2000) was one of the

---

mysticism, culminating in the Book of Zohar ('Book of Brilliance'), written in Castilla after 1275. [Here Florensky confirms that the Zohar was created at the time when Kabbalah was discovered in Muslim Spain—E. T.] The concept of Kabbalah also includes much earlier attainments in symbolic exegesis (allegorical interpretation), which are described in relation to the Jewish religious seekers in Egypt as early as Philo of Alexandria (Philo Judaeus).'"

40. Florensky, *Iconostasis*, 160.
41. Florensky, *Iconostasis*, 163, 164.
42. Florensky, *Iconostasis*, 51.
43. Florensky, *Iconostasis*, 51.
44. Florensky, *Iconostasis*, 140.
45. Lévinas, "Éthique," 89.

first to develop and disseminate his ideas,[46] proposing that the face is given to us as a gift or a spirit—an epiphany in which *the other* reveals his truth. That is why he is our teacher. The French word *visage*, writes Tischner, tells us that as a matter of principle a face is visible. Does this mean we should assume, following Plato, the priority of sight? No, the opposite is true: the face is what allows him to hear more than see. One of the many commentators on Levinas, Ronald Paul Blum, proposed that for the French philosopher "the point is to see in the other, that is, in an individual not like me, he who is outside the relationship, who refracts all the closedness into the whole."[47]

Tischner believed that Levinas, in his analysis of the face from the point of view of its *openness*, was following the example of the German Jewish thinker Franz Rosenzweig (1886–1929), who interpreted the face as the star of redemption:[48]

> The eternal became the *gestalt* when it joined itself with the truth. And the truth is nothing other than the face of this *gestalt*. . . . The truth is not an image freely floating of its own accord, but only the resplendent face of God.[49]

According to Rosenzweig, the very structure of the face symbolically repeats the shape of a star made of two triangles: the first is the forehead and two cheeks (or the nose and two ears), and the second is formed by the eyes and mouth, laid on top of the first.[50] Here it is quite simple to discern the Star of David. (Furthermore, this design contains a persistent meaning: The triangle with its peak up is the symbol of the Jewish people, descending from God. The triangle with its peak down is the symbol of God, coming to meet those who seek him.) This gave rise to a "new theory of knowledge" allowing us to "learn everything."[51] The theory was laid out in his treatise, *Star of Redemption*, published in 1921.

Rosenzweig was among the first European philosophers to express the dialogical form of being, which is possible when a person encounters God. His ideas were later developed by Martin Buber (1878–1965), the Jewish

---

46. See Tischner, "Emmanuel Lévinas," 166–80.
47. Blum, "La percepcion d'Autrui," 73–79.
48. See Rosenzweig, *Der Stern der Erlösung*, 471.
49. Rosenzweig, *Der Stern der Erlösung*, 465.
50. See Rosenzweig, *Der Stern der Erlösung*, 470–71. Cf. the Kabbalistic teachings about the *sefirot*, the ten emanations of Ein Sof (the infinite or absolute), or the ten illuminations or manifestations of God's infinite light as revealed in creation. It can be imagined, perhaps, that some of the *sefirot* form patterns resembling the 'triangle' of the face. See Laitman, *Zoar*, 197–98.
51. Rosenzweig, *Der Stern der Erlösung*, 3.

philosopher and proponent of Hasidism, as a unique type of *tzadik*. "Any genuine life is an encounter," he wrote.[52] "God embraces but is not the universe; God embraces but is not the Self. On account of this which is unspeakable I can say in my language, as all can say in theirs, Thou. On account of this there is I and Thou, there is dialogue, there is speech, there is spirit (speech is, after all, the prime act of the spirit), and in eternity there is the Word."[53] The idea of the encounter receives further development in Buber's works: the encounter with the "eternal Thou" is an encounter with fate.

Florensky designates as the "encounter" the time between the "making" of the board and the completion of the icon, when its "visibility" first appears, in the combination of the earthly and heavenly, the visible and invisible worlds. This multistep process is complex in several ways, including in terms of form, for the icon acts simultaneously in different capacities: as part of an iconostasis, as a work of visual art, as a religious image of the spiritual world and, through this, as a component of the structure of the world, both terrestrial and celestial. Florensky believes the icon is "the factual certainty of divine reality,"[54] and that it records a perception of the other world. But in historical development the icon painter's spiritual experience is subjected to a decoupling and icons are sorted into four categories: biblical icons, portrait icons, icons painted according to "Holy Tradition," and finally those made according to personal spiritual experience ("revealed" icons).[55]

The icon also achieves its structural integrity due to the fact that it speaks with a special, self-sufficient language of symbols and images. This language corresponds with the language of the author, who elevates images to the level of ideas, but does not permit them to remain merely abstract concepts. In their visuality, he builds a dialogical hierarchy of all with all, emphasizing the dualism of being and interdependence.

The *Iconostasis* is shot through with dialogicity, inside and out, top to bottom, looking both up to Heaven and down from it, in a constant dialogue. And this dialogue is not just with God, but also with the whole bygone world. In Florensky, after all, the countenance always indicates something departed, and therefore sacred: the countenance is the likeness of God made manifest in the face. But this is also a dialogue of time—of the present and the future, or the present and the past. While the mask is a manifestation of the dead and gone (present tense), the countenance represents one who has

---

52. Buber, *Ich und Du*, 12.
53. Buber, *Zwei Glaubenswesen*, 69.
54. Florensky, *Iconostasis*, 73.
55. See Florensky, *Iconostasis*, 75.

already been resurrected and presented to God (future tense). The "division of the icon's content into the processes of *lichnoe* [the face] and *dolichnoe* [everything else]," along the lines of inward and outward, is a "profoundly meaningful division," Florensky notes. It "corresponds to . . . 'I' and 'not-I,' whereby the face expresses inward life while everything not the face serves to manifest the whole word created for humanity."[56] In this division, Florensky argues, "we can plainly see the Greek patristic understanding of existence being divided into *man* and *nature*; a division wherein each is at once distinct and inseparable from the other . . . a division expressing the primordial paradisical harmony of inwardness and outwardness."[57] Here his reasoning about the icon as a coherent type of art is at its most perfect.[58] This entire artistic complex does not exist in and of itself; its component parts are in motion. The originality of Florensky's approach lies first and foremost in that he regards the icon not as an established concept, but rather as a process. The icon is located first in the making of it, but the finished icon is located in dialogic action; otherwise there is no departing for God's world.

Bibliography

Berdyaev, Nikolai. "Stylized Orthodoxy: On Father Pavel Florensky." In *The Brightest Lights of the Silver Age*, translated by Boris Jakim, 175–95. Kettering, OH: Semantron, 2015.
Blum, Roland Paul. "La percepcion d'Autrui." In *La Communication. Actes du XV-e Congrès de l'Association des Sociétés de Philosophie de Langue Française*, 73–79. Montréal: Université de Montréal, 1973.
Buber, Martin. *Ich und Du (11 durchgesehene Auflage)*. Heidelberg: Lambert Schneider, 1983.
———. *Zwei Glaubenswesen*. Zürich: Manesse Verlag, 1950.
Florensky, Pavel. *Iconostasis*. Translated by Donald Sheehan and Olga Andrejev. Crestwood, NY: St. Vladimir's Seminary Press, 1996.
———. "Nauka kak simvolicheskoe opisanie." In *Sobranie sochinenii v 4 tomakh*, 104–18. Vol. 3(1). Moscow: Mysl', 2000.
———. "Ob'ektivnaya znachimost' imen." In *Sobranie sochinenii v 4 tomakh*, 195–97. Vol. 3(2). Moscow: Mysl', 1999.
———. "Vremia kak chetvertoe izmerenie. Osnovy vremiaponimaniia (gnoseologicheskie aspekty)." In *Sobranie sochinenii. Stat'i i issledovaniia po istorii i filosofii iskusstva i arkheologii*, 190–203. Moscow: Mysl', 2000.
———. "Vremia v momental'nom obraze: fotografiia." In *Sobranie sochinenii. Stat'i i issledovaniia po istorii i filosofii iskusstva i arkheologii*, 226–32. Moscow: Mysl', 2000.

56. Florensky, *Iconostasis*, 135.
57. Florensky, *Iconostasis*, 136.
58. See Florensky, *Iconostasis*, 146.

Il'in, Il'ia. "Strukturalizm." In *Literaturnaia entsiklopediia terminov i poniatii*, edited by Aleksandr Nikoliukin, 1042–44. Moscow: NPK Intelvak, 2001.

Laitman, Michael. *Zoar (Kaballa. Tainoe uchenie)*. Moscow: NPF Drevo zhizni, 2002.

Lévinas, Emmanuel. "Éthique et Infini." *Dialogues avec Philippe Nemo*. Paris: La procure, 1983.

Merleau-Ponty, Maurice. *Phénoménologie de la perception*. Paris: Librairie Gallimard, 1945.

Pankin, Sergei. "ARKTOGEYA." http://arcto.ru/article/1508.

"Rabbi Shimon." In *Fragmenty iz traktata "Zogar,"* translated by Mikhail Kravtsov, 14–30. Moscow: Gnozis, 1994.

Rosenzweig, Franz. *Der Stern der Erlösung*. Frankfurt am Main: Kauffmann, 1921.

Sartre, Jean-Paul. *L'être et le néant. Essay d'ontologie phénoménologique*. Paris: Callimard, 1943.

Shteler, Tatiana. "Obratnaia perspektiva: Pavel Florenskii i Moris Merlo-Ponti o prostranstve i lineinoi perspektive v iskusstve Renessansa." In *Istoriko-filosofskii ezhegodnik 2006*, edited by Nelli Motroshilova, 320–29. Moscow: Nauka, 2006.

Tischner, Józef. "Emmanuel Lévinas." In Józef Tischner. *Myślenie według wartości*, 166–80. Kraków: Znak, 2000.

Vysheslavtsev, Boris. *Etika preobrazhennogo erosa*. Paris: YMCA, 1931.

12

Finding Meaning

Sergei Bulgakov and a Sophiology of the Icon

WALTER SISTO

In his masterpiece *The Idiot*, Fyodor Dostoevsky wrote, "beauty will save the world." His statement inspired numerous Russian thinkers, including Father Sergei Bulgakov (b. June 16, 1871, Livny, Russia—d. July 12, 1944, Paris, France). Although Bulgakov never published a theological aesthetic based exclusively on Dostoevsky's thought, Dostoevsky's insight certainly influenced him. It was a phrase that Bulgakov continually iterated throughout his academic career, from his earliest major theological work, *Unfading Light: Contemplations and Speculations* (1917)[1] to his major study on pneumatology, *The Comforter* (1936).[2] Dostoevsky's influence on Bulgakov was undoubtedly related to the fact that Dostoevsky had succinctly captured in prose not only the importance of aesthetics for theology but also the transformative dimension of the modality for conveying beauty, art. Art was an important topic for Bulgakov and one which he wrote about throughout his career. The *raison d'être* of art is that it conveys beauty or uncovers "the wisdom-directed depths of the world."[3] Art is not a hobby, but a sacerdotal activity, or, as Aidan Nichols correctly observes, for Bulgakov, God reveals himself not only "in rational discourse but also to human vision in art."[4] The importance of art is that it is an intrinsically human activity. For Bulgakov,

1. Bulgakov, *Unfading Light*, 400.
2. See for instance Bulgakov, *Comforter*, loc. 4195 of 6301.
3. Cf. Treanor et al., *Being-In-Creation*.
4. Nichols, *Wisdom*, 298.

art is a creative attempt of a human being to make a divine idea concrete. Since humankind is made in the image of God, it has a peculiar capacity for artistic creation: to extract an idea from a divine prototype, and visually represent that idea.[5] This is the fundamental process of icon writing. For this reason, all art is in some sense iconic insofar as it depicts the primal idea or proto-image within the pan-organism of ideas, God's nature or divine Sophia. The experience of beauty as well as the creativity of the artistic endeavor is "a feeling after God."[6] Nevertheless, for Bulgakov, not all art is equal. The highest form of art is religious art, and iconography serves as the purest and most beautiful form of religious art.[7]

This essay endeavors to explore Bulgakov's iconology. Bulgakov proffers a fascinating perspective on icons that has received little relatively attention thus far by scholars. For him, because Sophia is the heavenly world and immanent to the material world, all of creation in some manner participates in the beauty of heaven or noetic beauty (cf. Pss 8 and 19). However, icons have a particular importance because they participate directly in the antinomy of unportrayability/portrayability in a way that is analogous to the antinomy involved in the dogma of the incarnation. The upshot is that Bulgakov develops his theology of the icon beyond the Church Fathers (e.g., St. John of Damascus, St. Nicephorus, and Theodore the Studite) and his contemporaries, because he was keenly aware that the theology of the icon is a question to be explored within Sophiology, not exclusively Christology. Thus, iconography serves Bulgakov's sophiological project to demonstrate the correlation between God and humankind, but results in a fascinating theological aesthetics, one that I argue reveals an "anticipated eschatology" for icons. Moreover, Bulgakov's iconology provides an important insight into the eschatological significance of the icon for human meaning.

For reasons of clarity, this paper is divided into three parts. Part one will briefly explain Bulgakov's assessment of the iconoclast controversy. Part two examines his response to the controversy based on his understanding of sophiological antinomy. After examining his response, part three looks more closely at his theology of iconography and the eschatological significance of the icon for human existence and church life.

---

5. Holland, "Icon," 16–17.
6. Bulgakov, "Religion and Art," 181.
7. Cf. Bulgakov, *Icons*, 99.

Part One: The Controversy

For Sergei Bulgakov, the icon was an important subject for theological investigation for at least two reasons. First, theology of the icon has been grossly underdeveloped. Apart from the Second Council of Nicaea (787) and, for Catholics, the Council of Trent (1575), the Church had not offered an official theology of the icon beyond the recognition that the creation and veneration of icons comport with Sacred Scripture and Tradition. Moreover, the great iconodules, such as St. John Damascus and St. Theodore the Studite, offer polemical responses to the iconoclasts, but in Bulgakov's estimation, fail to convincingly defeat the iconoclast's argument that while Christ's humanity is portrayable, divinity is not. Thus, the icons of Christ, who is the image of the invisible God and the icon of all icons, result in Christological error. Depictions of Christ exclusively portray Jesus's human nature, which in effect divides the human and divine natures in Christ, casually supporting a form of Nestorianism. Moreover, within religious traditions that accept the conciliar teaching on icons, such as the Catholic Church, icons are relegated to little more than "sacred images." Most Christians misunderstand what an icon is, and for Orthodox Christians, in Bulgakov's estimation, there was no persuasive iconology that addressed why icons are vital to the life and liturgy of Orthodoxy. The result is a missed opportunity for ecumenism with Orthodox Christians to articulate why icons are important to Orthodox life and worship, but also to human meaning and existence.[8]

Moreover, in Bulgakov's interpretation of the development of the doctrine of the iconology, the theology of the icon after the Seventh Ecumenical Council was eclipsed by a variety of socio-political factors including the aggression and the endemic threat of Islam as well as theological polemics between the Catholics and Orthodox that led to the schism in 1054 CE. Most importantly, however, Bulgakov argues that the Orthodox Church was unable to respond persuasively to the iconoclasts and develop a theology of the icon in a satisfactory manner because it contextualized

---

8. Bulgakov's claim in 1930 was accurate. There was very little written on iconography as opposed to other aspects of theology that were a subject of the great ecumenical councils, for example, Christology. However, since 1930 and particularly in the Western Churches there have been a myriad of articles, books, and courses at theological institutes on iconography. However, the Catholic Magisterium does not propound a specific theology of the icon. In contexts where one would expect the Catholic Church to clarify its teaching on icons such as the *Catechism of the Catholic Church* (2003), icons and iconography are subsumed under the heading "sacred images." The teaching simply reiterates the teachings of the Second Ecumenical Council of Nicaea that icons are acceptable subjects of veneration.

the icon debate within Christology rather than within the anthropology and cosmology that is contained in Sophiology.

This leads us to Bulgakov's second response; the icon served an important purpose for his Sophiology in as much as the veneration of icons affirmed the "union of the divine and creaturely worlds."[9] Icon veneration is an Orthodox devotional practice that confirmed Bulgakov's sophiological project.[10] Sophiology becomes the basis for responding to the iconoclasts as well as developing an iconology.

In his article "The Icon and Its Veneration" (1930), Bulgakov takes up the task of definitively rebuking the iconoclasts as well as advancing the theology of icons. He ingeniously reframes what he believes to be the most pressing iconoclastic argument that the Church Fathers were unable to definitively defeat.

The iconoclasts correctly observed that the Church teaches that God is unportrayable and imagelessness on the one hand, and yet Christ's human nature is portrayable on the other.[11] They set up an antinomy: God is unportrayable, God in Christ is portrayable. It is impossible to depict Christ in an icon without doing a disservice to this antinomy. Their argument is straightforward: icons of Christ depict Christ's human nature to the exclusion of his divine nature. The result is Christological heresy; icons of Christ subtly support a form of Nestorianism, dividing the unity of Jesus's divine and human natures. If the image of God cannot be depicted, then what basis is there to depict iconographically the images of the image of God (e.g., the saints)? They argue that there is no basis to do so.

Bulgakov perceptively notes that the iconoclast's argument rests on the antinomy that God is unportrayable, while God in Christ is portrayable. To make matters worse, the iconodules engage the iconoclasts in debate on the grounds of this antinomy. Yet this is where the Fathers' arguments fall apart; they grant too much to the iconoclasts and in Bulgakov's estimation are never able to overcome the iconoclast argument.[12] But in his negative evaluation of the iconodules, he recognizes that the entire argument about icons rested on a false antinomy. According to Bulgakov, an antinomy "attests to the equivalence of the contradictory propositions, as well as to their inseparability, unity, and identity."[13] The opposite of the unportrayability of God's

---

9. Bulgakov, *Icons*, 114.

10. His publications during his theological period (1925–1936) were inspired by icons. His minor trilogy is an extended reflection on the Deesis Icon.

11. Bulgakov, *Icons*, 36.

12. Nichols, *Wisdom*, 296.

13. Bulgakov, *Icons*, 32.

divinity is the portrayability of God's divinity. While the "the unportrayability and imagelessness of God" belongs to theology proper, "the portrayability of Christ's human nature" belongs to Sophiology. He finds fault with the Fathers for granting too much to the iconoclasts (e.g., engaging their false dialectic and thereby allowing them to control the conversation).

Thus, the theological debate on this point was misguided, and, in fact, the unportrayability of divinity and the portrayability of divinity occupy what Bulgakov calls the theological antinomy. But the theological antinomy in Bulgakov's estimation is concerned with the basic question about how to go about doing theology. The theological antinomy is a technical term for the two movements in theology proper: kataphatism and apophatism. In the life of Orthodoxy, both of these movements are not only acceptable but complement one another. They exist in an antinomic relationship that prevents theology from erring on the side of over rationalizing (i.e., kataphatism to the exclusion of apophatism) or under theologizing to the point where God is unknowable, so that theology is not possible (i.e., apophatism to the exclusion of kataphatism). In other words, God is both the Absolute God, who is beyond all knowledge and portrayability, yet God is the creator and revealer. Thus, apophatism and kataphatism are not only in the same conceptual series but they are opposites. The antithesis of the unportrayability of God is the portrayability of God, not the portrayability of the incarnate Word. Nevertheless, the hallmark of heresy is one-sidedness: stressing apophatism to the exclusion of kataphatism, which denies revelation, or vice versa, to stress the knowability of God to the point that God is not eternal and limited to God's revelation, are both heresies. Orthodox theology recognizes that God is both unknown, "the absolute NO of Divinity,"[14] but also known, the supra-eternal person, the Blessed Trinity.

For my purpose, the theological antinomy does not properly concern the possibility of portraying Christ artistically, because the theological antinomy does not involve creation or human nature. The portrayability of Christ's human nature is not the opposite of his unportrayable divine nature.

Part Two: Bulgakov's Response

In other words, the debate between the iconodules and iconoclasts should have been a debate centered on the antinomy of the Incarnation: that Jesus Christ has both a noncreaturely nature or divine nature but also a creaturely nature. We can rephrase this: The question of whether or not we can paint images of Christ rests on a more basic question of how the

14. Bulgakov, *Icons*, 29.

incarnation is possible (i.e., the invisible God becoming visible in Christ). Bulgakov's rationale is that the Incarnation presumes some sort of interrelation between the divine and human nature that not only allows for the Son of God to be incarnate, but also will allow for the prototypes within the noncreaturely nature to be depicted in creaturely nature. More precisely, Bulgakov subsumes the antinomy of the Incarnation and iconography under the "sophiological antinomy": God is the Revealer, who exists in Godself as the Trinity that reveals itself in wisdom (noncreaturely Sophia), but also that God creates by God's wisdom and this wisdom is the foundation of creation (creaturely Sophia). It is important to note that this antinomy cannot be synthesized without doing a disservice to foundational theology, and thus Bulgakov will always grant that just as human beings will never be able to comprehend how God became man, we cannot fully understand how the divine Sophia or divine nature sustains and subsists in created Sophia.[15] However, his point in reorienting the discussion of icons within an antinomic, sophiological context is to demonstrate that divinity as divine Sophia is portrayable through created Sophia. We cannot think of divine and human nature as totally unrelated spheres. Although there is an infinite distinction between the two, the divine Wisdom permeates and sustains the created Wisdom. Through this relationship, icons of Christ and the saints are justified. God as the Revealer orients Godself for Incarnation. God also constitutes creation in such a manner to be able to allow for the Incarnation without violating the constitution of created nature. Creation or the human nature of Christ can bear or take part in the hypostatic union because of its divine foundation. God seeks to be revealed in creation. By the same token, God seeks to be portrayed in Christ.

Nevertheless, Bulgakov anchors his sophiological antinomy in the unique role Sophia plays in Russian Orthodox liturgical life, in the Fathers, particularly Gregory Palamas, and also in the Sacred Scriptures. The wisdom literature in the Bible reifies wisdom: Wisdom was with God at the event of creation (Prov 8:22), God laid the world's foundation by God's Wisdom (Prov 3:19) and God preserves the world's foundation through God's Wisdom (Jer 10:12). Moreover, this Wisdom contains the forms or prototypes of all things, for the experiences we have here are, to use a phrase from Paul's epistle to the Hebrews, a "copy and shadow of the heavenly things" (Heb 8:5). Therefore, divine Sophia as God's nature or life is not simply an attribute, but the way in which God exists as God to creation. It is God's "pan-organism of ideas" that contain the original images

---

15. Christ is a unique hypostasis insofar as he has one divine image, but he possesses it doubly as a divine and human person. See Bulgakov, *Icons*, 62.

or prototypes of all things. The wisdom literature in the Bible reveals that God creates out of God's wisdom. The wisdom through which God creates creation is divine Sophia, or God's mind, God's living and eternal database that contains all the proto-types of creation. Creation is a "copy" of the divine Sophia, it is creaturely Sophia. More precisely, creaturely Sophia is divine Sophia mixed with nothing, or divine Sophia in a state of perpetual kenosis, releasing its divine prerogatives and relationship to the Blessed Trinity as "their" nature. Bulgakov interprets the doctrine of *creatio ex nihilo* anew. In creation, God does not simply turn nothing into something but rather divests the Godself of God's fullness so that *nothing* (not-God) gave way to *something* other than God. For my purposes, those prototypes in divine Sophia are seedlings in creaturely Sophia; they are an entelechy. They are the manner in which God's wisdom sustains the creaturely wisdom. Creaturely Sophia is human nature.

The anthropological implication of Bulgakov's Sophiology is significant. He follows closely the Orthodox tradition and the biblical witness that humankind is made in the image of the image of God, the Son. Bulgakov theologizes this point. He writes: "[m]an himself is an image of the Image, and he is characterized by imagedness of experience . . . he is an imaging being (*zoon eikonikon*), who not only thinks in images and receive images, but also creates images."[16] Similar to how the Son, the image of God made visible and the means "through whom God made all things" (John 1:3) or specifically copied the forms of the prototypes in his wisdom onto the canvas of creation, human beings are gifted with the ability of rational thought to be able to understand the prototypes in God's wisdom, but also to interpret and creatively give birth to images of these prototypes in creation. The process in which this can occur is art and thus Christ is the divine artist through whom all art is inspired. Bulgakov's anthropology makes axiomatic the biblical verse "You are gods" (Ps 82:6). In his theological anthropology, the human being's role in creaturely Sophia is analogous to the Son's role in divine Sophia. However, just as the human hypostasis will never unite with God, creaturely Sophia will never become divine Sophia, for what makes the creaturely Sophia different from God is precisely its createdness; but it nevertheless comports to divine Sophia. God not only continues to guide creaturely Sophia to become an image of the image within divine Sophia, but creaturely Sophia is a living nature, not an abstraction; it is the principle of human existence that compels humankind to recognize that there is beauty, but also to be unsatisfied with anything other than God.

---

16. Bulgakov, *Icons*, 144.

God's Sophia or divine life is filled with images that are for portrayal. This is for Bulgakov why the experience of beauty, particularly in art, is significant. The communication of beauty involves the communication of the prototype in God's divine Sophia, God's life, shining forth through the artwork. Beauty as an attribute of God is well-known and Scripture testifies to the "beauty of God" (cf. Ps 27:4; Isa 28:5). From the vantage of the subject, beauty itself is an experience that is beyond expression, but in Bulgakov's worldview it is nothing other than the glory of God's wisdom shining forth through creation; but this is all possible because of Sophia, which constitutes creation in such a way that the invisible can be made visible. Therefore, for Bulgakov, "[i]conology needs as its starting-point the sophiological principle by which God is figurable and the world configured in his image."[17]

The implications of Bulgakov's Sophiology for iconology are significant. Not only should human beings depict the image of God in icons, but by doing so they are in part realizing what it means to be made after God's image. Based on the relationship of humankind as an image of the image of God, the Son, art and icon creation analogically participate in the creative action of the Son of God to make visible the invisible prototype. The creation of an icon orients us towards the Son of God, who is the means through which access to the prototypes are possible. Bulgakov takes quite seriously the notion that regarding the image of God and the Logos, who is the means through which all things are made, no image can be created without and through Jesus Christ. But again, the portrayability of these prototypes is possible because the divine Sophia is portrayable through its creaturely counterpart. Nevertheless, no portrait of a prototype can ever fully encompass the prototype itself, for as St. Paul reminds us, we now only "see through a glass, darkly" (1 Cor 13:12). Thus, visible images are only a vestige of the way things will be.

Part Three: Sophiological and Eschatological Significance of Icons

Bulgakov's theology of the icon makes several fascinating claims about art and iconography. Art and icon writing are artistic endeavors to depict the prototype or some content within the divine mind. In other words, icon writing is a means through which humankind participates in the Word of God's creative action as revealing God's mind or will to the world. How the icon writer accesses the divine mind, so to speak, rests upon Sophiology, the interrelatedness between the human and divine mind. Creaturely Sophia is

---

17. Nichols, *Wisdom*, 301.

the world or microcosm of the divine Sophia; thereof it bears the imprint of the divine mind. Recall that the world is created Sophia or God's wisdom in a created form. It is imbued with the imprint or copies of the prototypes of the divine mind that humankind as made in the image of the image God has access to. The prototype shines forth through the representation in creaturely Sophia that humankind can represent in art. The key point is that Bulgakov interprets the mind holistically, as a repository of rational thought and aesthetics, beauty and images.[18] Art is what we denote as the means through which humankind accesses God's beauty. Or to put it another way, beauty and rationality are one reality for God. Bulgakov, in his other works such as *The Comforter*, argues that rationality and beauty in God are associated with the Second and Third divine hypostasis, the Son (the logos) and the Spirit (the Comforter) respectively. Thus, the experience of art, or the replication of the prototype and the evocation of beauty when that replication is created, are possible through the Son and the Holy Spirit. Accessing and representing the prototype involves the Son, but "beauty" that is experienced as a result of that representation involves the Holy Spirit.

However, religious art provides a special knowledge, not a new revelation, a means through which God can be encountered. What Bulgakov is getting at is that the artist, particularly the icon writer, is participating whether or not she is conscious of it in the very mission of the Holy Spirit, to realize the mission of the Son, to give life to it: to actively bring it about so "that God may be all in all" (1 Cor 15:28) or in the context of art to realize in creation God's prototypes. In so doing, the artists convey God's truth aesthetically. Expressions of art that transmit the aura of beauty is our perception of the "sophian idea shin[ing] forth in it."[19] This is not to say that every work of art is beautiful; Bulgakov is quite clear on this point that sin affects the relationship of humankind to God, and thus whereas the pinnacle of art is possible in the form of an icon, pseudo-beauty or the "lie of Sodom,"[20] a mirage of beauty that under inspection reveals nothing but death, is also a possibility for an artist.[21] Bulgakov has no shortage of vitriol for religious art that does not seek to be iconic. Raphael's Sistine Madonna is the recipient of his criticism.[22] In his Madonna, Raphael made no adequate attempt to communicate the living tradition of the Church, but

18. Cf. Nichols, *Wisdom*, 300.
19. Crum, "Doctrine," 44.
20. Bulgakov, *Comforter*, loc. 6194 of 6301.
21. Satanism is precisely the distortion of what is beauty.
22. He called Raphael's Madonna, an "artistic Arianism—a heretical overestimation of the human element in the divine incarnation." Cit. from Bershtein, "Notion," 225.

rather provides an image of the "historical Mary," revealing his puerile prejudice and arbitrariness.[23] Not every depiction of a saint is an icon, because icon writing is a distinctive churchly activity that requires the artist to work from within the Church's memory and life. The task of "art lies not in the real but in the ideal domain," Bulgakov writes.[24] True art must attempt "to [penetrate] into the world's heavenly fatherland"[25] and contain within itself "the rays of the truth of things, their *ideas*."[26] Raphael's Madonna may have a vestige of the ideal, but his attempt is overshadowed by his personality since Raphael lacked the guidance of the Church.

Bulgakov thinks of the Church in less hierarchical terms—although he by no means neglects the hierarchy—and more organically as the redeemed or human community that is most fully living out what it means to be made in the image of the Son of God. The Church must be involved, at least by means of blessing and naming in the process of religious art, for art to have significance beyond a creative expression of human subjectivity.[27] Icons are an aspect of churchly existence: icons are windows into the redeemed members of the Church's life, the Church triumphant.

Icon writing is only possible within the Church, for the Church provides the ecclesial vision necessary to attempt to portray the visible image of God. Artists acquire the vision of the Church through the use of the canon for icon writing. The canon is not an external rule but rather "the inner norm" that provides the guidelines for icon creation.[28] The canon helps to guarantee that the icon proceeds from a "treasury of the Church's living memory of the visions and representations."[29] However, the icon is not legitimized unless it has first been named and sanctified by the Church. Icons are sacramentals that closely relate to the sacraments. Just as the Eucharist cannot be consecrated without a validly ordained priest, since it would be a symbol of the Eucharist at best and not the glorified body and blood of Christ, the icon is not valid or does not communicate with that which it seeks to communicate without the Church's blessing. The Holy Spirit does not sanctify or activate

---

23. Note that that his mariological publication, *The Burning Bush*, is based on the icon of the Burning Bush that depicts the Mother of God in her glorification.

24. Bulgakov, *Icons*, 44.

25. Bulgakov, "Religion and Art," 180.

26. Bulgakov, "Religion and Art," 181.

27. Bulgakov argues that mirror-reflections of a person or a thing are not possible since art always involves the subjectivity of the artist. It is even impossible to depict images that we have seen with our own eyes objectively since "the natural image . . . is always a synthesis unconsciously performed for us." Bulgakov, *Icons*, 45.

28. Bulgakov, *Icons*, 75.

29. Quoted from Nichols, *Wisdom*, 303.

the icon without the Church. This is a crucial point: there is a true communication from prototype, the image itself, to the subject, to the representation in the icon. The consecration of the icon is the means through which the prototype shines through the icon. Thus, only after the religious artwork is sanctified by the Church is it properly an icon. It is transformed into a reflection of the prototype in material reality.

The upshot is that icons of Christ truly reveal the Image of the invisible God and thus they are windows into heaven. However, icons are radically different than the Eucharist: while Christ is substantially present in the bread and wine, in his icon it is only the image of Christ that is present. The materials used are not transmutated or transubstantiated. Icons remain paintings, but a painting in which Christ's presence shines forth. They are akin to personal encounters with the risen Christ, or heavenly visions in the concrete.[30] Similarly with non-Christological icons: they contain the prototype, the image of the saint, not the deified saint itself. Once sanctified, they are portals through which saints can communicate and encounter the believer. But it is the saint who is the primary cause of the encounter. Icons that have a reputation for being miraculous are simply those for which there is evidence that a saint has presented himself or herself through them. Non-Christological icons are of saintly or angelic persons who exist in heaven and who, as creatures, are circumscribed within creaturely Sophia and appear through the consecreated icon. Thus, the techniques of icon writing, which to the uninitiated might look like distorted pictures, are guidelines that help the painter represent the prototype of a person in order to facilitate an encounter with the subject of that depiction.

Nevertheless, the Church's involvement and established canon for icon writing should in no way be an impediment to the creativity of the icon artists. Bulgakov is adamant that icon writing must involve human ingenuity and creativity. In Bulgakov's theological anthropology, creativity means to hypostatize creaturely Sophia, or actively draw out from human nature or created Sophia the divine prototypes, and to do so within a distinct space, time, and culture. Within Orthodoxy, the existence of many schools of icon writing, together with new icons and icon styles, are evidence for Bulgakov of the ongoing creative process. According to George Kordis, a renowned icon writer and scholar based in Athens, icon writing is not the mere copying of an expression of Tradition, for tradition itself is creative: "[f]idelity to Tradition means creating on the ground of its stable values and principles."[31] Moreover, ecclesiastical icon writing is a liturgical experience that involves

30. Bulgakov, *Icons*, 106.
31. Justiniano, "Art."

prayer on the part of the artist; one cannot seek to hypostatize nature without pursuing holiness. In this aesthetics, beauty is one and the same with holiness. It is of no surprise that what is most beautiful is the content of the icon, depicting saints who have reached the pinnacle of holiness. The artist cannot communicate the spiritual beauty of the prototype, which for Bulgakov is also the beauty of holiness, without pursuing holiness. As "a god to the world" and the head of creaturely Sophia, humankind, whose goal is not only to evangelize but help bring about the kingdom of God on earth, must seek to incarnate God's beauty.

Moreover, Bulgakov's theology of icons highlights the eschatological significance of the icon. Icons are more than just windows into heaven. They depict reality as it is for the redeemed, that is, the reality to which all of us are oriented. Icons in the case of saints—saints experience theosis, but nevertheless are creatures, circumscribed by creaturely Sophia—depict the prototype with which the saint has self-identified. The icon portrays the saint's accomplishment: to be fully united with God's will before the Final Resurrection (cf. 1 Cor 2:9). What is beautiful about the icon is not simply God's presence but also its revelatory significance: the image of the image of God realized in an instance. God's beauty shines forth in an icon insofar as it is a realized eschatology. Iconic depiction of a saint, represented in the color scheme, large eyes, and small mouth, all points to the fact that the person has realized their sophianic potential. The saint is like a "God to the world" as he or she is actively deified by God's grace.

Since creation and corporeality are imbued with spiritual life, something which is evident by the fact that creation is God's wisdom and life-giving beauty, it is a materiality inherently open to spirituality. It is for this reason that religious experience, which is at the basis of any profession of faith, involves the senses. Yet, icons transcend the senses, and Bulgakov admits that for the materialist "the icon image turns out to be abstractly schematic, arid, dead."[32] However, icons evoke "a feeling after God."[33] They represent spiritual beauty that speaks to and evokes response from our spirit. This is why for devout believers icons are beloved, and icons are actively involved in the Orthodox liturgical celebration, for they open us to an encounter with God's beauty, which has deified the person depicted. What may be construed as an aesthetic weakness for a materialist or a non-initiate, is for Bulgakov the very strength of icons. Icons are not about depicting material reality, since they speak to a reality beyond the world as we know it. To fully grasp this requires work and, more precisely, prayer. This

---

32. Bulgakov, *Icons*, 76.
33. Bulgakov, "Religion and Art," 181.

prayer before an icon ultimately will reveal the reality of the icon, which we are all invited to join. The artistry, symbolism, rhythm, composition, and coloration are meant to make us aware of and help us communicate with the "ideal realism" of the icon. The icons of the Theotokos such as Our Lady of Czestochowa do not purport to depict Mariam of Nazareth who lived during the first decades of the Common Era, but rather the Mother of God who exists in heaven. As such, much like Jesus after his Ascension to the Father, Mary exists in a glorified state. Mary is unique among the saints for many reasons, including the fact that she experiences the grace of Resurrection before the Final Resurrection. My point is that what is depicted in the icon is a person in heaven, who is "dematerialized" but also deified by the grace of God. The importance of icons is that they remind us of our true heavenly home, as well as of our family in heaven who assist and encourage us to do the will of God. They point us towards the heavenly reality that awaits, putting our work, life and hopes into perspective; they also invite us to take part in this reality now and remind us of what awaits after death, and at the Final Resurrection.

Bulgakov's unique theology of icons has another important implication: icons are instances of the spiritual permeating the material world. Recall that in Bulgakov's cosmology, divine Sophia is God's pan-organism of ideas. In this sense, the divine Sophia contains the entelechy of all created images. Thus, when St. Paul speaks about God being all in all, for Bulgakov this means that the divine prototypes will be realized in creaturely Sophia at the end of time. Icons are instances where this has occurred. The creature has realized its sophic potential. Saint John the Baptist, for instance, has attained what God has called him to be; he realized his prototype in created Sophia. The icon becomes a means through which the saint can communicate with or interject in material reality. In an icon, we have an instantiation of the new world, of spiritual or heavenly beauty penetrating our world. Icons are more than symbols of what is to come, but a modality for encountering the grace of the general resurrection in the here and now. They communicate heavenly grace to our material reality.

For these reasons, Bulgakov's provides a unique sophiological theology of icons. To return to Dostoevsky, in *The Comforter* Bulgakov writes that "Beauty will save the world . . . but this will be the beauty of spiritual beauty."[34] For Bulgakov, icons are manifestations of this spiritual beauty in as much as they remind us that a beautiful end awaits those who love Christ. It is the beauty of salvation, or God's sophic life that shines forth in the icons. Icons in the life of the Church are a foretaste of what is to come. They are

---

34. Bulgakov, *Comforter*, loc. 4195 of 6301.

an anticipated eschatology, reminding us that the world is being and will be totally transformed with the second coming of Jesus Christ. The sophianic ideas will shine both in and through humankind, as they shine through the Church by means of the sanctified icon. Icons serve as reminders of what we human beings are called to become—saints!

Bibliography

Bershtein, Evgenii. "The Notion of Universal Bisexuality in Russian Religious Philosophy." In *Understanding Russianness*, edited by Risto Alapuro, 210–31. London: Routledge, 2012.

Bulgakov, Sergius. *The Comforter*. Translated by Boris Jakim. Grand Rapids: Eerdmans, 2004. Kindle ed.

———. *Icons and the Name of God*. Translated by Boris Jakim. Grand Rapids, MI: Eerdmans, 2012.

———. "Religion and Art." In *The Church of God: An Anglo-Russian Symposium by Members of the Fellowship of St. Albans and St. Sergius*, edited by Eric Lionel Mascall, 173–92. London: Society for Promoting Christian Knowledge, 1934.

———. *Unfading Light: Contemplations and Speculations*. Edited and translated by Thomas Allan Smith. Grand Rapids, MI: Eerdmans, 2012.

Crum, Winston Ferris. "The Doctrine of Sophia According to Sergius N. Bulgakov." PhD diss., Harvard University, 1965.

Holland, Ernest Beau David. "The Icon as Revelation: Sergius Bulgakov's Theoretical and Practical Understanding of the Icon." MA thesis, University of St. Michael's College, University of Toronto, 2013.

Justiniano, Fr. Silouan. "The Art of Icon Painting in a Postmodern World: Interview with George Kordis." *Orthodox Arts Journal*, June 25, 2014. https://www.orthodoxartsjournal.org/the-art-of-icon-painting-in-a-postmodern-world-interview-with-george-kordis/.

Nichols, Aidan. *Wisdom from Above: A Primer in the Theology of Sergei Bulgakov*. Leominster: Gracewing, 2005.

Treanor, Brian, et al. *Being-In-Creation: Human Responsibility in an Endangered World*. New York: Fordham University Press, 2015.

Index

ENT = Evgenii N. Trubetskoi

absolute/Absolute. *See also*
    God; knowledge of God
    (*Bogopoznanie*)
  as absolute consciousness and mind,
    10
  absolute principle, 68
  absolute thought, 70, 72, 74
  as All-one (*Vseedinoe*), 8, 10
  ENT criticizes Augustine for
    conflating the absolute with the
    natural world, 37–39
  ENT discovered through
    Schopenhauer, 3
  implied by human consciousness of
    ideals, 26, 30
  in Kabbalistic teachings, 191n50
  and knowledge of God through
    antinomies, 115–116
  role of faith and reason in
    knowledge of, 7, 13–14, 26n3
  Soloviev and ENT's philosophy of,
    7–11
academic freedom, 14–15
Academic Union, 14–15
Academy of Sciences, 15
Afanasyev, Nicholas, 173
Akhtyrka, 93
Alexander III (tsar), 105

Alimpy, 150
All-one (*Vseedinoe*), 8, 10
all-unity (*vseedinstvo*)
  as absolute consciousness, 10
  and Bogochelovechestvo, 31
  ENT's critique of Augustine, 37–38
  as goal of history, 72
  and human creativity, 74
  in thought of Soloviev and ENT,
    8–11
Alpatov, Mikhail, 137
Ambrose, 36n31, 83
anarchism, 46
Anisimov, Alexander, 128
Anthony of Sourozh, Metropolitan
  (Bloom), 135
anthropocentrism, 40–41
antinomy
  and Bulgakov's philosophy of
    language, 120–122
  ENT's criticism of Florensky, 117–
    120, 160
  Florensky on antinomic nature of
    truth, 112–114, 144n10, 160
  Kant on, 112–113, 115
  and portrayal of Christ in icons,
    144, 198–199
  and religious dogma, 112–119

antinomy *(continued)*
  "sophiological antinomy" of
    Bulgakov, 200
  as tragedy of fallen human reason
    for Bulgakov, 114–117
antiquity, 177–178
apophaticism, 115, 118, 199
architecture
  architectural quality of icons, 167
  of temples, 155, 173
Aristotle, 121n32
Arsen'ev, Nikolai, 17–18
art. *See also* creativity; icons
  eschatological role of, 133–134,
    206–208
  as giving concrete form to divine
    ideas, 196, 201–206
  image of God and human capacity
    for artistic creation, 196,
    201–202
  justified during iconoclasm/
    iconodulism debates, 142, 154
  theandric nature of all Eastern
    Christian art, 154–155
Art Nouveau, 178
asceticism, 37–38, 72, 150, 154
assist method, 165–166
Athanasius, 31, 114
Athos, Mount, 98, 100
Augustine
  in 19th-century Russian scholarship,
    80–81
  ENT's critique of, 33–39, 81–83
  on grace and human freedom, 31,
    35–37, 81–83
  on roles of church and state, 34–39
  version of all-unity, 37–38
autonomy of spheres of society
  and ENT's critique of free theocracy,
    42–43, 46
  foundational for ENT's liberalism,
    29

Balkans, 59, 61, 62
Balthasar, Hans Urs von, 139
Basil the Great, 152
beastmanhood (*zverchelovechestvo*), 48
beauty
  as absolute ideal, 10
  Balthasar on, 139
  Bulgakov associates with the Holy
    Spirit, 203
  as divine attribute, 202
  divine beauty revealed through
    human art via Sophia, 201–202
  Evdokimov on, 133–134
  holistic beauty, 139
  love of beauty (*philokalía*) and love
    of wisdom (*philosophía*), 151
  Plato on, 133
  spiritual beauty revealed in icons,
    133, 151, 206–208
  and theandric character of Eastern
    Christian art, 155
being
  Personal Being, 119
  triunity of, 120–122
Belinskii, Vissarion, 2
Belyi, Andrew, 94
Berdyaev, Nikolai
  on Christian culture, 73–74
  conversion to Christianity, 66
  on creativity, 69
  criticism of Florensky's iconography
    studies, 182, 183, 185
  eschatological view of
    Bogochelovechestvo, 90
  founder of *Put'*, 106
  negative view of discursive thought,
    75n36
  on Russian Messianism, 59, 69–70
  and traditional Orthodox doctrines,
    76
  view of Bolshevik Revolution, 173
Beschastni, Pavel (Brother), 136
Beseda circle, 14, 54
Blok, Alexander, 101
Bloom, Anthony, 135
Blum, Ronald Paul, 191
Bogochelovechestvo
  and Christ's incarnation, 35, 41, 74,
    90–91
  church as divine-human
    community, 3
  and consciousness, 8, 40
  contrasted with Augustine's
    theology, 31, 35–36
  and end of the world, 76

and ENT's liberal theology, 25–26
ENT's positive appraisal of Soloviev,
    39–42
foundational for ENT, 33
Godman (*Bogochelovek*)
    and Godmanhood
    (*Bogochelovechestvo*), 11
Harnack critical of, 81
and human dignity, 33
incompatible with free theocracy, 45
and meaning of life, 2, 31, 40
and extraterrestrial intelligence,
    40–41
and role of church and state, 89–91
role of human creativity, 69, 73–76
Soloviev's conception of, 2, 31–33,
    39–42
Bolkhovitinov, Evgenii, 172
Bolshevik Revolution, 48–49, 62, 75–76,
    173
Bryagin, Evgenii, 130
Buber, Martin, 191–192
Buckle, Henry Thomas, 2
Buddhism, 68, 72
Bulgakov, Afanasii, 80
Bulgakov, Sergei
    aesthetics influenced by Dostoevsky,
        195, 207
    on antinomy and portrayal of Christ
        in icons, 198–200
    on antinomy as tragedy of fallen
        human reason, 114–117
    on art and creativity, 151, 154, 195–
        196, 201–202
    assessment of and response to
        iconoclasm controversy,
        197–202
    founder of *Put'*, 106
    on icons, 132, 154, 179, 197–208
    idealist philosophy, 66, 67n6
    participation in ecumenical
        dialogue, 134
    philosophy of language, 120–122
    and reestablishment of Moscow
        patriarchate, 19
    religious experience while
        contemplating *Sistine Madonna*,
        153

religious worldview, 69
on Russian Messianism, 69–70
on Sophia, 199–206
and traditional Orthodox doctrines,
    76
view of Bolshevik Revolution, 173
Bunge, Gabriel, 136
Burning Bush icon, 204n23
Busalaev, Pavel, 136
Buslaev, Fedor, 128
Bychkov, Viktor, 146
Byzantium, 34, 44

caesaropapism, 6, 34, 44
Calvinism, 82n16
cataphatism, 115, 144, 199
Catholicism
    Catholic Church as independent
        spiritual power, 6, 34, 44
    considered one-sided and legalistic
        by ENT, 80, 85–89
    contrasted with mystical character
        of Orthodoxy, 43–44
    ENT's criticism of medieval
        theocracy and Soloviev's
        response, 85–89
    Slavophile criticism of, 82–83
    Soloviev's sympathetic view of, 80,
        85–89
    teaching on icons, 197n8
Cavour, Camillo Benso di, 42
Chicherin, Boris
    critique of free theocracy, 32–33
    on freedom of conscience, 28
    and Hegelian rationalism, 2
    on human dignity, 1, 12, 26
    on human freedom, 1, 12
    influence on Trubetskoi brothers,
        1–2, 4
    philosophy of law critiqued by ENT,
        12–14
    on reason and knowledge of the
        Absolute, 7, 13–14, 26n3
    on reunification of the churches,
        43n36
    shared ENT's idealist understanding
        of human nature, 27
Chirikov, Grygory, 130

Christ
  ascent to Christ embodied in
    vertical structure of icons, 167
  Bulgakov associates rationality with
    God the Son, 203
  Chalcedonian Christology, 11, 31,
    41, 144
  depicted in icons, 143, 145, 175–
    177, 197–202, 205
  Florensky excluded Christological
    interpretations of Sophia
    iconography, 175–176
  human nature of, 35
  as icon of the Father, 139
  as image of God, 201–202
  and papacy, 85–86
  portrayability of two natures,
    197–202
  as Proto-Icon, 146–148
  resurrection of, 117–118
  two natures and two actions/
    energies, 147
Christianity. *See also* Catholicism;
  church; Orthodoxy
  and idealist philosophy, 66, 68–70,
    71–75
  and meaning of life, 11, 71–75
  as synthesis of world religions, 72
church. *See also* Catholicism; church-
  state relations; Orthodoxy;
  Russian Orthodox Church
  and antiquity and tradition, 177
  as Divine-human
    (*Bogochelovecheskii*) community,
    3
  ENT's critique of Augustine, 36–39
  iconographer works within tradition
    of the Church, 148, 150,
    204–205
  independent spiritual power in
    Catholicism, 6, 34, 44
  as kingdom of ends, 32
  reunification of the Christian
    churches, 43–45, 53, 70
  role in consecrating and naming
    icons, 149n30, 204–205
church (building). *See* temple

Church Fathers. *See* Fathers of the
  Church
church-state relations. *See also* free
  theocracy
  and Bogochelovechestvo, 89–91
  caesaropapism, 6, 34, 44
  contrast between East and West, 34
  declarations of 1917-1918 Russian
    sobor, 110
  ENT's critique of Augustine, 38–39
  ENT's critique of free theocracy, 2,
    6, 33, 41–48, 70, 90, 103–104
  ENT's critique of medieval
    theocracy, 34, 38, 46, 85–89
  subordination of Russian Orthodox
    Church to tsarist regime, 6, 18,
    47, 48–49
Circle of Seekers of Christian
  Enlightenment, 17–18
City of God, 38–39
Clement, Olivier, 139
coercion, 12–13, 28, 29, 34, 37, 42–46
collectivism, 67
Comte, Auguste, 2, 172
Congar, Yves, 82
conscience. *See also* conscience,
  freedom of
  ENT's philosophy of, 8
  etymology, 8
  Pelagius on, 36
conscience, freedom of
  Augustine on, 35–37, 39
  ENT considered it the condition for
    all other freedoms, 18, 28
  foundational for ENT's liberalism,
    1, 28–29
  incompatible with theocracy, 6, 45
  inner and external, 28–29
  promised in October Manifesto, 47
  and revelation, 41
  and self-determination, 28
consciousness. *See also* knowledge
  (*soznanie*); knowledge of God
  (*Bogopoznanie*)
  absolute consciousness, 10, 71
  Bogochelovechestvo as highest
    expression of religious
    consciousness, 25–26, 40

collective, 71
content of, 70
ENT's philosophy of, 8
etymology, 71
and human creativity, 74
and human dignity, 26
in idealist philosophy, 67–68
and meaning of life, 70–71
Orthodox religious consciousness, 45
and right, 13
Constantine (emperor), 34
Constantine-Cyril, Saint, 178
Constantinople, 61–62
Constantinople IV, Council of (869-870), 146
constituent assembly, 15, 16
Constitutional-Democratic Party. *See* Kadet party
constitutional monarchy, 55, 62
Cornelius, 84
Councils, Ecumenical
    Constantinople IV (869-870), 146
    Nicaea II (787), 134, 146, 150, 152, 154, 197
countenance, 190, 192
creation
    as light in Kabbalistic teachings, 189
    role of Sophia, 115–116, 200–201
creativity
    and all-unity (*vseedinstvo*), 74
    Berdyaev on philosophy as a creative act, 69
    biblical foundations of, 133
    cultural creativity, 69
    and human role in Bogochelovechestvo, 69, 73–76
    icon painter gives witness to what already exists, rather than creating ex nihilo, 145, 147, 185–186
    icon painting as collaboration between divine energies and human creativity, 150–151
    image of God and human capacity for artistic creation, 69, 196, 201–202
    relationship to Church Tradition, 205
    role of Sophia, 201–202
culture, 69, 73–74

Dante, 168
Darwin, Charles, 2–3
December 1905 uprising, 16
Deesis Icon, 198n10
deification. *See also* Bogochelovechestvo
    as Bogochelovechestvo, 11, 25–26, 31–32
    definition, 2
    deified saints portrayed by icons, 205, 207
    ENT's modern twist on, 32
    and human creativity, 69, 73, 74
    as process involving self-determination, 25, 30, 32, 33
Demidov Juridical Lycée (Iaroslavl'), 4
Demina, Natalia, 137
democracy, 28, 55–56
Descartes, René, 26, 122
determinism, 29
Didache, 81
dignity, human
    Bogochelovechestvo as supreme manifestation of, 33
    ENT influenced by Chicherin, 1, 12, 26
    and ENT's Christian humanism, 29–31
    and ENT's liberal theology, 25–26, 28
    as foundation of democracy, 28, 55–56
    and freedom of conscience, 28
    as rational foundation for theism, 26–27, 30
Dionysius the Areopagite, 118, 182
divine humanity. *See* Bogochelovechestvo
divine principle
    as absolute principle, 68–69
    Augustine on, 37, 84
    and Bogochelovechestvo, 2, 3, 31, 47
    contrasting approaches of Orthodoxy and Catholicism, 43–44
    and free theocracy, 41–42

dogma
  and antinomy, 112–119, 144
  Christological controversies, 11, 31, 41, 144
  development reflected in iconography, 132, 133
  Florensky on lack of dogmatic presuppositions in early Russian Christianity, 178
  iconoclasm controversy, 134, 142, 152, 197–202
  relationship of Russian philosophers to traditional Orthodox doctrines, 76
Donatist schism, 83
Dostoevsky, Fyodor, 3, 153, 195, 207
dreams, 185–186
Duma, 15–17, 55, 57, 58

eclecticism, 116
Egypt, 190
Eighth Ecumenical Council (869-870), 146
Ein Sof, 191n50
Elijah, 166
empiricism, 66, 114
Epiphanius the Wise, 151
Ern, Vladimir, 59, 106, 108
esotericism, 183, 189
ethics
  and all-unity, 10, 69
  and deification, 69
  and idealism, 66
  and kingdom of ends, 32
  in worldview of Augustine, 81, 85
Eucharist, 148, 155, 204–205
Evdokimov, Pavel, 133–134
evil, 48
Evlampiev, Igor, 12n34, 34n28, 71, 82, 161
existence, 121
existentialism, 184, 187
extraterrestrial life, 40–41

face, 190–193
faith
  and consciousness of the Absolute, 7, 9, 13–14, 40
  in existence of external reality, 68
  freedom of conscience necessary for, 29n12
  and transcendent dimension of icons, 144
Fathers of the Church. *See also* Augustine
  on the Holy Spirit, 149
  on human nature, 30
  in icon research of Olga Popova, 134
  on icons and iconoclasm, 134, 145, 197–199
  on Sophia, 175, 200
  translations produced in 19th-century Russian academies, 80–81
Favorsky, Vladimir Andreevich, 169
Fellowship of Saint Alban and Saint Sergius, 134–135
femininity, eternal, 95, 102, 172
Fichte, Johann Gottlieb, 67
Filimonov, Georgy, 128, 175
Fischer, Kuno, 3
Florensky, Pavel
  on antiquity and tradition, 177
  Berdyaev's criticism of his iconography studies, 182, 183, 185
  on colors of icons, 146, 164–165, 176
  on colors of Sophia, 164n17, 176
  contrast with philosophy of ENT, 159–160
  cult philosophy, 130, 139
  dialogicity in *Iconostasis*, 186, 192–193
  on dreams and sleep, 185–186, 189
  on face and countenance in iconography, 143–144, 190–193
  on geometry, 162, 168
  on icon as ideal model of the visual arts, 162
  Iconostasis (book), 129, 161–162, 168–169, 173, 181–191
  on icons as boundaries between earthly and heavenly worlds (iconostasis), 162, 167–170, 181–182, 184–186, 188, 192

on icons as sacraments, 187–188
icon studies philosophical in nature rather than art history, 173–174, 183
interest in Kabbalah, 189
on lack of presuppositions in early Russian Christianity, 178
on light as boundary between earthly and heavenly spheres in iconography, 168–169, 188–198
member of restoration commission for Trinity Lavra of St. Sergius, 130, 161
philosophical interpretation of Sophia iconography, 174–179
The Pillar and Ground of the Truth, 113, 117, 122, 160, 174–179
reverse perspective, 129–130, 162, 174, 184, 189
on role of antinomies in faith and reason, 9, 112–114, 117–120, 144n10
structural-semiotic analysis of *Iconostasis,* 182–193
on symbols, 178–179
on the temple as "synthesis of arts," 154
on time and space, 184, 189, 192–193
on Trinity icon, 130, 155
Florovsky, Georges, 135
Florus and Laurus, 166–167
formalism, 182, 183
Frank, Semen, 66, 67n6, 173
freedom, human. *See also* conscience, freedom of; free will; self-determination
Bogochelovechestvo requires human autonomy, 33
Chicherin on, 1, 12
and divine friendship, 73
ENT's critique of Augustine, 35–36, 39, 81–83
Kant on human autonomy and self-determination, 27, 32
free theocracy
Chicherin's critique of, 32–33
definition, 6
ENT's critique and rejection of, 2, 6, 33, 41–48, 70, 90, 103–104
modeled on kingdom of ends, 32
free theosophy, 114
free will
as capacity for self-determination according to ideals, 7, 27, 30
Pelagius on, 35–36
Soloviev's positive appraisal of Augustine's view, 83–85
friendship with God, 73, 75
fundamentalism, 30

Gaidenko, Piama, 118
Geiden, Petr, 17
German idealism, 67, 70
Gessen, Vladimir, 54n5
Gilson, Étienne, 179
Gnosticism, 177
God. *See also* absolute/Absolute; knowledge of God (*Bogopoznanie*); Sophia; Trinity
essence-energies distinction, 119, 145–146, 147
friendship with, 73, 75
knowability of, 145, 147, 199
and nature of Sophia, 199–202
proofs of, 9, 26, 183
as Proto-Image of icons, 144–149, 152
Godmanhood. *See* Bogochelovechestvo
Goncharov, Ivan, 99
Goncharova, Natalia, 127
grace
ENT's critique of Augustine, 35–38, 81–83
as law, order, and unity for Augustine, 35–38
as precondition for deification, 73
and separation of church and state, 89
Soloviev's positive view of Augustine, 83–85
uncreated, 147
Greece, ancient, 68, 72
Gregory Palamas, 200
Gregory VII (pope), 85–89
Grot, Nikolai, 5, 67

Guchkov, Aleksandr, 56
Guseyev, Dmitrii, 81n8

Hagia Sophia, 61
Harnack, Adolf von, 81
Hart, David Bentley, 139
Hasidism, 191n50
Hegel
    logical monism, 120
    philosophy of history, 72, 114
    rationalism, 2, 38
    on world as creation of the mind, 67
Henry IV (emperor), 85, 88
Heraclites, 112
heresy, 34, 37, 199, 203n22. *See also* iconoclasm controversy
hierotopy, 131, 138–139
history, philosophy of
    and end of the world, 76
    ENT's critique of Augustine, 38–39
    Hegelian, 72, 114
    providentialist, 73
    and world religions, 72
holiness, 144, 151, 206
Holy Cross monastery (Lugano), 136
Holy Spirit
    Bulgakov associates with beauty, 203
    enables veneration of God in icons, 152
    inspiration necessary for icon painting, 149–151
    makes artistic creation possible, 203
    sanctifies icons through the Church, 204–205
Holy Synod, 6, 18
Hughes, Stuart, 66
human dignity. *See* dignity, human
human freedom. *See* freedom, human
humanism, Christian, 29–31
human nature. *See also* image of God
    and ENT's Christian humanism, 29–31
    ENT's critique of Augustine, 34–36, 38
    idealist conception of, 8, 27
    relationship to divine Sophia, 201
hymns, 113, 118

iconicity, 138
iconoclasm controversy, 134, 142, 152, 197–202. *See also* Councils, Ecumenical
iconostasis, 162, 167–170, 181–182, 184–186, 188, 192
icons. *See also* Trubetskoi, Evgenii, icon studies of
    CHURCH TRADITION
        canon for icon writing, 204–205
        criteria for considering a work of art an icon, 148, 149n30
        iconographer works within tradition of the Church, 148, 150
        role of Church in consecrating and naming icons, 149n30, 204–205
    CREATION
        absence of artist's name or signature, 149, 152
        ascetic practices by iconographer, 150
        "circumscribed" vs. "painted," 142n2
        divine-human aspects of, 148–151
        inscription of God's name, 149
        requires inspiration of Holy Spirit, 149–151, 203
        spiritual experience of iconographer, 149, 192
    FORMAL ELEMENTS AND TECHNIQUES
        allegoristic characteristics of late icon painting, 177
        assist, 165–166
        colors, 162–166, 176
        reverse perspective, 130–131, 162, 174, 184, 189
        semiotics, 137, 139, 155, 182, 183–188, 190
        vertical and horizontal characteristics, 166–170
    HISTORY
        1913 exhibition in Moscow, 128, 159, 179

antiquity of Sophia icon, 177
contemporary research,
 139–140
development of practice of
 sanctification by a priest,
 149n30
development of various styles,
 155
"discovery" at turn of twentieth
 century, 127–128, 159, 179
iconoclasm controversy, 134,
 142, 152, 197–202
improvement of restoration
 practices, 128
interest in postwar Europe,
 135–136
research constrained during
 Soviet era, 131, 137
research in post-Soviet Russia,
 137–139
research in Russian diaspora,
 132–135
sidelined during Petrine
 reforms, 127–128
studied by Anglicans and
 Catholics, 134, 135–136

SUBJECTS
 Christ, 143, 175–177, 197–202,
  205
 Elijah, 166
 Florus and Laurus, 166–167
 Mother of God, 204, 207
 saints, 143, 145–146, 200, 205,
  206–207
 Sophia, 163–164, 172–179
 Trinity, 20, 130, 136, 144, 145,
  147, 155

THEOLOGICAL-PHILOSOPHICAL
 CONCEPTS
 antinomies, 144, 198–200
 boundaries between earthly
  and heavenly worlds
  (iconostasis), 162, 167–
  170, 181–182, 184–186,
  188, 192
 Christ as Proto-Icon, 146–148
 communal character, 152, 186,
  187

contrasted with Western
 religious painting, 149, 153,
 162, 203–204
development of Church
 dogma, 132, 133
divine energies/names, 145–
 146, 147, 150–151
eschatological significance,
 133–134, 206–208
ENT as founder of "theology of
 the icon," 128–129, 173
hierotopy/spatial icon, 131,
 138–139
highest form of art, 162, 196
holiness, 144, 151, 206
imagery analagous to spoken
 language, 146, 187
light as boundary between
 earthly and heavenly
 spheres, 168–169, 188–198
liturgical significance and
 location within temple,
 132, 139, 152, 167, 170, 206
manifestation of Orthodox
 faith, 132, 136, 138
metaphysical and
 phenomenological aspects
 of icon painting, 188
no official Catholic teaching
 on, 197n8
refer to God as Proto-Image,
 144–145, 149, 152
reflect the spirit of the person
 depicted, 143–144
religious by definition, 153–
 154
reveal spiritual beauty, 133,
 151, 206–208
role of human creativity, 145,
 147, 185–186
significance of the face,
 190–193
signs and symbolism, 137, 139,
 146–147, 155, 176–177,
 182–188, 190
signs of contiguity between
 heaven and earth, 161–162,
 166

icons
   THEOLOGICAL-PHILOSOPHICAL
   CONCEPTS *(continued)*
      sophiology of Florensky
         and Bulgakov, 174–179,
         197–206
      structural-semiotic analysis
         of Florensky's *Iconostasis*,
         182–193
      time and space in Florensky's
         Iconostasis, 184, 189,
         192–193
   VENERATION
      act of viewing, 131, 151–152
      invitation to prayer, 144, 207
      John of Damascus on, 146
      made possible by Holy Spirit,
         152
      proskynesis vs. *latreia*, 152
      theandric character of, 151–
         154
"Icon" society, 131
idealist philosophy
   and Christianity, 68–70, 71–75
   and consciousness, 67–68
   of ENT and Soloviev, 7–11
   German idealism, 67, 70
   in late imperial Russia, 66–68
   and meaning of life, 70–77
   self-determination of human person
      according to ideals, 7, 14, 30
   and traditional Orthodox doctrines,
      76
   of young Trubetskoi brothers and
      Chicherin, 4
identity
   law of, 117, 121
   philosophy of, 69
Ilyin, Ilya, 183–184
Ilyin, Ivan, 109
image of God
   Christ as, 201–202
   and Christian humanism, 30
   differentiated from likeness of God
      in Florensky's iconography
      studies, 190, 192
   and ENT on human dignity, 28, 56
   and human capacity for artistic
      creation, 196, 201–202
   and immortality, 26n4
immanentism, 46
immortality, 26n4, 30, 102
incarnation
   as antinomy for Bulgakov, 199–200
   and Bogochelovechestvo, 35, 41, 74,
      90–91
India, 72
integral knowledge, 2, 4, 114
intellectual contemplation, 69
intuition, 71, 72
investiture controversy, 88–89
Ioanna, Sister (Reitlinger), 132
Islam, 61, 197

Janssen, Johannes, 81
Jesuits, 83–84
Jesus Christ. *See* Christ
Jews. *See* Judaism
John of Damascus, 144, 146, 182, 196,
   197
John Paul II (pope), 90
John the Baptist, 207
Judaism
   Kabbalah, 189, 191n50
   rights of Jews, 60
   Star of David, 191
   and synthesis of world religions in
      Christianity, 68, 72
judgment, 120–121
Juliania, Sister (Maria Sokolova), 138
jurisprudence, 7n15, 10
jurisprudence of ENT, 7
justice, 13

Kabbalah, 189, 191n50
Kadet party, 16–17, 19, 55–62, 105
kalokagathia, 151
Kaluga gymnasium, 2–3
Kant, Immanuel
   anti-metaphysical trends in neo-
      Kantianism, 9
   on antinomy, 112–113, 115
   definition of right, 12, 54
   and ENT's boyhood philosophy
      studies, 3

ENT's critique in *Metaphysical Premises of Knowledge*, 9, 109
on human dignity and autonomy, 27, 28
kingdom of ends, 25, 32, 47
on mind and consciousness, 67, 68
kataphatism. *See* cataphatism
Kazan Theological Academy, 80
Keidan, Vladimir, 110
Kern, Cyprian, 80
Khomiakov, Alexei, 1–4, 53
Kiev Theological Academy, 80
kingdom of ends, 25, 32, 47
kingdom of God
　and all-unity, 11
　as culmination of human progress, 29
　ENT's critique of Augustine, 38–39
　as goal of Bogochelovechestvo, 11, 25
　requires human cooperation, 32
　and role of state, 42–43, 45
　transcendence of, 38–39, 45–46
Kireevskii, Ivan, 1–2, 4, 82–83
Kirikov, Vasily, 138
knowledge (*soznanie*). *See also* knowledge of God (*Bogopoznanie*)
　communal character of, 71
　as divine intention for consciousness, 74
　integral knowledge, 2, 4, 114
　Soloviev's description of the three levels of, 114
knowledge of God (*Bogopoznanie*)
　and antinomies, 115–116
　made possible through church, 3
　and Morozova's defense of her love for ENT, 102
　relationship of faith and reason, 7, 13–14, 26n3
　role of philosophy, 4
Kondakov, Nikodim, 128, 131
Kondakov Archeological Institute, 131
Kordis, George, 205
Korkunov, Nikolai, 54
Kornblatt, Judith Deutsch, 48n40
Kotliarevskii, Sergei, 55

Kotrelev, Nikolai, 81
Kremlin, 19
Krug, Grigory, 133
Kruglov, Alexey, 109n58

language
　Bulgakov's philosophy of, 120–122
　of the icon in Florensky's *Iconostasis*, 182, 184, 187, 192
　in S. Trubetskoi's idealist philosophy, 67
latreia, 152
law. *See also* coercion
　Augustine on, 36
　Catholicism considered legalistic by ENT, 80, 85–89
　Chicherin's philosophy of law, 12–14
　ENT on underdeveloped legal consciousness of the Russian people, 173
　in ENT's critique of free theocracy, 46–47
　ENT's jurisprudence, 7, 7n15, 10
　ENT's legal theory, 10, 12–14
　ENT's philosophy of law, 53–54
　legal positivism, 13, 29, 54
　natural law, 12, 13, 29, 53–54
　positive law, 53–54
　rule of law foundational for ENT's liberalism, 29
Lazarev, Vladimir, 137
Lepakhin, Valery, 138
Levinas, Emmanuel, 190–191
liberalism, 1, 12, 25–29
Lidov, Alexei, 131, 138–139
Lieven, Dominic, 59
light
　Florensky on, 168–169, 188–189
　in Kabbalistic teachings, 189, 191n50
Likhachev, Nikolai, 128, 159
linguistics, 182–184
liturgy. *See also* temple
　and antinomy of mysteries of religion, 113, 118
　liturgical significance of icons, 132, 139, 152, 167, 170, 206
　relationship to sacred art, 154–155

Lopatin, Lev, 5, 67, 79
Lopatin, Mikhail Nikolaevich, 5
Losev, Alexei, 147, 172
Lossky, Vladimir, 118
  on divine essence and energies, 145n15
  on icons, 132
  on relationship of liturgy and sacred art, 154–155
  subject of Rowan Williams's dissertation, 135
Lot-Borodine, Myrhha, 82
love
  as absolute ideal, 10
  ENT's doctrine of, 104
  Soloviev's philosophy of male-female love, 101–105
Lubac, Henri de, 89n44

Makovets, 130
Malevich, Kazimir, 127
Manicheanism, 83
Marion, Jean-Luc, 139, 144–145
Maritain, Jacques, 179
Marxism, 66
masks, 190, 193
materialism, 66
Matisse, Henry, 127
Maximus the Confessor, 147
meaning of life
  and all-unity, 11
  and Bogochelovechestvo, 2, 31, 40
  and catastrophic circumstances of 1917-1918, 75–76
  and Christianity, 11, 71–75
  ENT's definition of meaning, 70–71
  in idealist philosophy, 70–77
Mechev, Alexii, 138
Mechev, Sergii, 138
Mendeleyeva, Liubov, 101
Merleau-Ponty, Maurice, 184–185
Messianism, Russian, 1, 6, 69–70, 108–109
Meyendorff, John, 173–174
Middle Ages, 85–89
Milbank, John, 89n44
Miliukov, Pavel, 54, 61n35, 99
Mill, John Stuart, 2

mind
  Absolute as, 9–10
  Bulgakov's "immanent intellect," 115
  Christian culture as work of, 69
  interrelatedness between divine and human mind in Sophia, 202–203
  transfiguration of, 117
  world as creation of, 67, 72
Mohyla, Petro (metropolitan), 149n30
Molina, Luis de, 83–84
monism, 119, 120
Morozov, Mikhail, 94
Morozova, Margarita
  ENT's misgivings about relationship, 97–101, 107
  financing of Constitutional Democratic Party, 105
  financing of *Moskovskii ezhenedel'nik*, 18, 56, 105–107
  financing of *Put'*, 18, 105–108, 160
  financing of religious-philosophical societies, 18, 105, 160
  justification of love for ENT, 101–103
  passionate relationship with ENT, 96–97
  role in Silver Age society, 94–95, 106
  Soloviev's ideas in her correspondence with ENT, 94–96
  on Soloviev's philosophy of eros, 103–105
  support of ENT's political activity, 105–108
Moscow Conservatory, 52
Moscow Institute of Historical and Artistic Research and Museology, 161
Moscow Judicial Chamber, 5
Moscow Psychological Society, 5, 17, 18, 58, 67
Moscow State University, 137
Moscow Theological Academy, 80, 113, 138
Moscow University
  both Trubetskoi brothers studied at, 4

elected ENT to State Council, 16
ENT's career at, 7
S. Trubetskoi as first elected rector, 2, 15, 54, 94
S. Trubetskoi's career at, 5
Moskovskaia nedelia, 55
Moskovskii ezhenedel'nik, 17, 55–58, 105–107
Mother of God
   depicted in icons, 204, 207
   and iconography of Sophia, 173, 175–178
   status in medieval Catholicism, 86
Muslims, 61, 197
mysticism
   characteristic of Orthodoxy, 43–44
   and Florensky's iconography studies, 183, 189
   and historical development of philosophy, 114

name
   divine names, 145–146
   of icons, 187
   inscription of God's name on icons, 149
naturalism, 26, 27, 29, 38
natural law, 12, 13, 29, 53–54
natural rights, 28
Neoslavism, 59–62
Nestorianism, 197
Nicaea II, Council of (787), 134, 146, 150, 152, 154, 197
Nicephorus, Saint, 196
Nicephorus I (patriarch), 145, 151
Nicholas II (tsar), 18, 55
Nichols, Aidan, 195
nihilism, 2–4
Nikolaevich, Petr, 52n1
non-resistance to evil, 48n40
Nosov, Alexander, 103
Novgorod
   church architecture in, 173
   icon of Sophia, 175–179
Novgorodtsev, Pavel, 27, 29, 104
Nowosielski, Jerzy, 148

October Manifesto, 47, 99
Octobrist Party, 17, 56–58, 60, 62
onomatodoxy, 187
order, 36–38
Orlov-Denissov, Liubov, 52n1
Orthodoxy. *See also* church; Russian Orthodox Church
   on antiquity and tradition, 177
   attitude to icons compared with other Christian traditions, 197
   conversions prompted by icon studies, 135
   icons as manifestation of Orthodox faith, 132, 136, 138
   mystical character contrasted with Catholicism, 43–44
   personal Orthodox faith of ENT, 1, 17, 26, 44, 76
   role in formation of Russian national identity, 178
Ostroukhov, Ilya, 127, 128, 159
Ouspensky, Léonid, 132–133, 144, 146
Ovchinnikov, Adolf, 136

Palamas, Gregory, 200
Palmieri, Aurelius, 82
Panofsky, Erwin, 179
papacy, 6, 43–44, 85–89
Parmenides, 113n5
patriarchate of Moscow, 6, 48
patriotism, 59–62, 109–110
patristics. *See* Fathers of the Church
Pavel, Brother (Beschastni), 136
Peaceful Renewal Party, 17, 56–59, 62
Pelagius/Pelagianism, 35–36, 83, 84
perception, philosophy of, 184
perfectibility, 25, 29, 32, 36, 40, 73. *See also* progress, human
Personal Being, 119
personalism, 28
personhood, human, 4, 13, 28, 35, 38, 66
Peter (apostle), 85–86
Peter the Great, 6, 127
Petrov-Vodkin, Kuzma, 127
phenomenology, 184–185, 187

philosophy. *See also* idealist philosophy
  and fallen human reason, 116–117
  as instrument of knowledge of God, 4
  and love of beauty, 151
photography, 184
Pilsudski, Józef, 183
Plato
  on beauty, 133
  Christian Platonism and icon painting, 145
  and ENT's philosophy of meaning, 70, 75
  on law of identity, 121n32
  on priority of sight, 191
Pogodin, Aleksandr, 59, 61
Pokrovsky, Nikolai, 128, 175, 176
Poland, 60
Polyanskaya, Elena, 99
Poole, Randall, 59, 61, 65
pope, 6, 43–44, 85–89
Popova, Olga, 137
positivism
  antipositivist reaction, 66
  contrasted with divine self-revelation in icons, 147
  dominant in late nineteenth-century Russia, 4
  ENT's boyhood enthusiasm for, 3
  legal positivism, 13, 29, 54
predestination, 35, 36
progress, human
  Augustine considered impossible, 36, 37, 39
  essential to Christian humanism, 30–32
  and human creativity, 73
  human perfectibility foundational for ENT's liberalism, 25–26, 29
  perfectibility as essentially human attribute, 40
  and rule of law, 46–47
proskynesis, 152
Provisional Government, 61–62
Ptolemaic system, 168
Put' (publishing house), 18, 105–108, 160

Quenot, Michel, 136
quietism, 101

Radlov, Ernst, 84
Raphael Sanzio, 149, 203–204
rationalism
  Bulgakov and Florensky criticize Soloviev's sophiology for excessive rationalism, 113–114
  disintegrating consequences of, 4
Raushenbach, Boris, 131
reason. *See also* antinomy
  Bulgakov associates rationality with God the Son, 203
  Bulgakov on antinomies as tragedy of fallen human reason, 114–117
  and Bulgakov's philosophy of language, 120–122
  and consciousness of the Absolute, 7–10, 13–14
  Florensky on antinomic structure of reason and ENT's response, 9, 112–114, 117–120, 160
  human dignity as rational foundation for theism, 26–27, 30
  and human freedom, 27
  role of logical thought in ENT's religious worldview, 75, 76
Rech', 57
Reitlinger, Ioanna (Sister), 132
relation, 145
relativity, theory of, 185
religion. *See also* Christianity
  Christianity as synthesis of world religions, 72
  defined by ENT, 75
  defined by Soloviev, 68
Religious-Philosophical Society. *See* Vladimir Soloviev Religious-Philosophical Society
Renaissance
  humanism, 30
  religious painting, 149, 203–204
resurrection of Christ, 117–118
reunification of the churches, 43–45, 53, 70
revelation
  and antinomies, 116

INDEX

and church tradition, 178
complementarity of philosophical and religious, 75
philosophical, 71
reverse perspective, 130–131, 162, 174, 184, 189
reverse time, 168
revolution. *See* Russian Revolution
Revolution of 1905, 14, 55, 59, 106
Revolution of 1917. *See* Bolshevik Revolution
right
 ENT on, 12–13
 external, 32
 human rights and rule of law, 28–29
 Kant's definition of, 12, 54
Roerich, Nicholas, 148
Rojek, Paweł, 112
Rome, 43–44
Rosenzweig, Franz, 191
Rovinsky, Dmitry, 128
Rublev, Andrei, 130, 136, 149, 150. *See also* Trinity icon
Russia. *See also* Russian Revolution
 national identity of, 18, 55, 69–70, 178
 Russian Messianism, 1, 6, 69–70, 108–109
Russia Christiana, 136
Russian Civil War, 110
Russian Liberation Movement, 14
Russian Orthodox Church
 Congress of Clergy and Laity (1917), 18, 110
 ENT deplored its subordination to tsarist government, 18, 47, 48–49
 and formation of Russian national identity, 178
 liberated by collapse of tsarist regime, 48–49
 national sobor (1917-1918), 18–19, 48, 110
 as official religion of Russia, 19
 patriarchate of Moscow, 6, 48
 ruled through Holy Synod, 6, 18
Russian Revolution
 Revolution of 1905, 14, 55, 59, 106

Revolution of February 1917, 109
Provisional Government, 61–62
Bolshevik Revolution, 48–49, 62, 75–76, 173
Russkii vestnik, 3
Russo-Japanese War, 14
Ruthenia, 149n31
Ryabushinsky, Stepan, 128, 159
Ryabushinsky, Vladimir, 131

Sakharov, Afanasi (bishop), 138
Sakharov, Sophrony, 118–119
salvation. *See also* deification
 Augustine on, 31, 35–36
 as process involving self-determination, 25, 30, 32, 33
Samarin, Yuri, 53
sarcophagus, 190
Sartre, Jean-Paul, 189
Satanism, 203n21
Saussure, Ferdinand de, 182
Sazonov, Sergei, 61
Scalfi, Romano, 136
Schelling, F. W. J. von, 67, 69, 114
Schneider, Christoph, 119n28
Schönborn, Cristoph (cardinal), 134
Schopenhauer, Arthur, 3
scientism, 3
Second Coming, 76, 86–88, 208
secular, 77, 89–91, 153–154
sefirot, 191n50
self-determination
 and freedom of conscience, 28
 of human person according to ideals, 7, 14, 30
 role in Bogochelovechestvo/deification, 25, 30, 32–33, 36, 40–42
Seminarium Kondakovianum, 131
semiotics, 137, 139, 155, 182, 183–188, 190
Sendler, Igor (Egon), 135–136
Sergiev Posad, 20
Sergius of Radonezh, 20, 130n4
Seventh Ecumenical Council (787), 134, 146, 150, 152, 154, 197
Shimon bar Yohai (rabbi), 189
Shipov, Dmitry, 17

Shteler, Tatiana, 185
Signposts (*Vekhi*), 16, 58
Sistine Madonna (Raphael), 149, 153, 203–204
skepticism, 3
Skvortsov, Konstantin, 81n8
Slavic movement. *See* Neoslavism
Slavophilism. *See also* Neoslavism
 and ENT's criticism of Catholicism and the West, 82–83
 influence on ENT, 1–2, 4, 59
 on messianic role of Russia, 1, 6
 Soloviev's criticisms of, 82
sleep, 185–186, 189
Smirnova, Engelina, 137
sobornost, 4n8, 20n78, 187
Society of Slavic Culture, 59
Sokolova, Maria (Sister Juliania), 138
Soloviev, Sergei Mikhailovich, 81, 84
Soloviev, Vladimir
 on the Absolute, 7–11
 on all-unity, 7–11
 apocalyptic tone in late works, 88
 on Augustine's teachings on grace and free will, 83–85
 on Bogochelovechestvo, 2, 31–33, 39–42
 on church-state relations, 89–91 (*See also* free theocracy)
 Critique of Abstract Principles, 3, 4, 9, 32, 41–42, 68
 on cultural creativity, 69
 death at Trubetskoi estate, 94
 on deification, 25–26, 31–32
 ENT's critique in *Vladimir Soloviev's Worldview*, 39–48, 103–104, 106
 free theocracy (*See* free theocracy)
 on icons, 172–174, 179
 idealist philosophy, 68–69
 ideas influenced the correspondence of ENT and Morozova, 94–96, 103–105
 influenced by Catholic scholarship, 81
 influence on ENT, 1–2, 5–6, 79–80, 160
 interactions with ENT, 4–6, 53, 79, 94
 Justification of the Good, 32, 33, 46–47, 84, 88, 89–90
 Lectures on Divine Humanity, 68–69, 72, 90
 Philosophical Principles of Integral Knowledge, 9, 69, 114
 philosophy of male-female love, 101–105
 rationalism criticized by Bulgakov and Florensky, 113–114
 on religious freedom, 6
 response to ENT's criticism of medieval theocracy, 85–89
 on reunification of the Christian churches, 43–45, 53, 70
 on Russian Messianism, 69–70
 sophiology, 113–114, 172–173
 sympathetic view of Catholicism, 80, 85–89
 and traditional Orthodox doctrine, 76
 utopianism criticized by ENT, 41–43, 47–48, 70, 73, 103–105
Sophia
 associated with specific colors in iconography, 163–164
 as both divine and creaturely, 199–202
 enables human artistic creativity, 201–202
 ENT envisioned restoring Sophia to the world through conquest of Constantinople, 61
 and knowledge of God through antinomies, 115–116
 philosophical interpretations of Sophia in iconography, 163, 172–179
 and purpose of history, 73
 relationship to Christ's incarnation, 199
 reveals divine beauty, 201–202
 role in creation of the world, 200–201
 Soloviev on, 113–114, 172–173
 sophiology versus Christology as locus of theology of the icon, 196–199

Soviet School of Art Studies, 137
Soviet Union, 131, 137
spatial icon, 131, 138–139
Spencer, Herbert, 2–3
Špidlík, Tomáš, 154
Spinoza, Baruch, 122
Stakhovich, Mikhail, 17
Stankiewicz, Mikolaj, 154
Star of David, 191
state
    and coercion, 12–13, 28, 29, 34, 37, 42–46
    not part of kingdom of God, 42–43
State Council, 15–16, 58
St. Petersburg Theological Academy, 80
Strakhov, Nikolai, 3
Struve, Peter, 59, 61, 66
St. Sergius Orthodox Theological Institute, 133
St. Vladimir's University (Kiev), 7
Suarez, Francisco, 83–84
sublimity, 155
substance, 120–122
suffering
    and ENT's reflections on his love for Morozova, 101
    and meaning of life, 11, 70
Sugiura, Shuichi, 160
Suslov, Ivan, 130

Tataryn, Myroslaw, 80–81
Tavernier, Eugène, 83
Taylor, Charles, 76–77
temple
    church architecture in Novgorod, 173
    role of icons in, 167
    as spatial icon, 137
    as synthesis of all sacred arts, 154–155
    vertical structure of, 167, 170
theanthropy. *See* Bogochelovechestvo
theocracy. *See also* free theocracy
    ENT critical of all its historical forms, 6, 42
    and ENT's critique of Augustine, 33–39, 83

    and ENT's critique of medieval Catholicism, 34, 38, 46, 85–89
Theodor, Zinon (archimandrite), 136
Theodore the Studite, 196, 197
Theophanes the Greek, 149, 150, 151
theosis. *See* deification
theosophy, 114
theurgy, 154
Thomism, 120n30
thought. *See also* reason
    absolute thought, 70, 72, 74
    and antinomies, 115
    and meaning/truth, 70
    role of logical thought in ENT's religious worldview, 75, 76
Tischner, Józef, 190–191
Tolstoy, Leo, 48n40
transcendence
    of kingdom of God, 38–47
    of meaning/truth, 70
    transcendent being, 66
    transcendent ontological reality, 65
transcendental method, 9
Trent, Council of, 197
triangles, 191
Trinity. *See also* Christ; Holy Spirit; Sophia
    depicted in icons, 20, 144, 145, 147
    and knowledge of God through antinomies, 115–116
Trinity icon (Rublev), 130, 136, 155
Trinity Lavra of St. Sergius, 130, 138, 161
Trinity-Sergius monastery, 20
Trubetskaia, Olga, 14
Trubetskaia, Vera Aleksandrovna, 98, 107
Trubetskoi, Evgenii (ENT)
    LIFE
        academic career, 4–7, 12, 53, 94
        boyhood intellectual crisis, 2–4, 53
        death, 110, 173
        education, 2–4, 6
        family background, 2, 53
        financial situation, 52–53, 93–94

Trubetskoi, Evgenii (ENT)
LIFE *(continued)*
  interactions with Soloviev, 4–6,
    53, 79, 94
  Orthodox faith, 1, 17, 26, 44,
    76
  participation in 1917-1918
    sobor, 18–19, 110
  personality, 94, 99, 106
ICON STUDIES
  on colors of icons, 162–166
  connections with his religious
    philosophy, 1, 19–20
  on Florensky's philosophical
    art history, 174
  founder of "theology of the
    icon," 128–129, 173
  on icons as sign of contiguity
    between heaven and earth,
    161–162, 166
  on location of icon within
    temple, 167, 170
  perceived icon as a new
    phenomenon, 179
  on vertical spatial motion,
    166–167, 170
POLITICAL ACTIVITY
  affiliation with and criticism of
    political parties, 16–17, 54,
    56–62
  criticism of government, 58, 60
  editor of *Moskovskii
    ezhenedel'nik,* 18, 55–58,
    105–107
  elected to State Council, 16, 62
  involvement in student affairs,
    54
  nationalism and patriotism,
    59–62, 109–110
  not appointed Minister of
    Education, 99
  participation in academic
    unions, 14–16
  supported by Morozova,
    105–108
RELATIONSHIP WITH MARGARITA
MOROZOVA
  ENT's misgivings about,
    97–101, 107
  and ENT's political activity,
    105–108
  passion of, 96–97
  role of Soloviev's ideas in their
    correspondence, 94–96,
    103–105
THEMES
  Absolute, 3, 7–11, 13–14
  Bogochelovechestvo, 31–33,
    39–42
  contrast with philosophy of
    Florensky, 159–160
  criticism of Augustine, 33–39,
    81–83
  criticism of Catholicism, 6, 34,
    43–44, 80, 85–89
  criticism of free theocracy, 2, 6,
    33, 41–48, 70, 90, 103–104
  criticism of medieval
    theocracy, 34, 38, 46, 85–89
  critique of Augustine, 33–39,
    81–83
  human dignity, 29–31
  influenced by Protestant
    scholarship, 81
  influenced by Soloviev, 1–2,
    5–6, 79–80, 160
  jurisprudence, 7, 7n15, 10
  legal theory, 10, 12–14
  liberalism, 1, 12, 25–29
  meaning of life, 70–77
  philosophy of law, 53–54
  religious worldview, 66, 68–70,
    71–75
WORKS
  The Meaning of Life, 8, 11, 19,
    29n12, 65, 70–77, 91, 109,
    119
  memoirs (*Vospominaniia*), 2–4
  *Metaphysical Premises of
    Knowledge,* 9, 109
  Russia in Its Icons, 19, 128, 161
  St. Augustine's Worldview,
    33–39, 80–83
  Theology in Color, 19, 128–129

INDEX 227

Two Worlds in Old Russian Icon-Painting, 19, 128, 161, 162–163, 173
Vladimir Soloviev's Worldview, 7–11, 39–48, 103–104, 106, 160
A World View in Painting, 161, 173
Trubetskoi, Grigorii, 2, 46, 56–57, 59–61, 94
Trubetskoi, Nikolai Petrovich, 52
Trubetskoi, Petr, 52n1, 58
Trubetskoi, Sergei
  academic career, 5
  death, 2, 55, 94
  early life and boyhood intellectual crisis, 2–3, 5
  ENT's inaugural lecture at Moscow University dedicated to, 30n15
  family background, 2, 53
  financial situation, 52–53, 93–94
  first elected rector of Moscow University, 2, 15, 54, 94
  friendship with Harnack, 81
  idealist philosophy, 27, 67–68
  nationalism and patriotism, 59–62
  political activity, 14, 54–55
  on theistic implications of human dignity, 26
truth
  as absolute ideal, 9, 10
  Florensky on antinomic nature of, 112–114, 144n10
  freedom of conscience as condition for recognizing, 29
  and meaning of life, 70–71
tsar. *See* Nicholas II (tsar)
Tulin, Vasily, 130

Union of Liberation, 14, 54
Union of October 17, 17
Union of Unions, 15
Union of Zemstvo Constitutionalists, 14, 16, 54
universalism, Christian, 1
universities, autonomy of, 15–16
Uspenskii Cathedral, 19

Uspensky, Boris, 137, 146
utopianism
  ENT's critique of Soloviev, 41–43, 47–48, 70, 73, 103–105
  Morozova on, 104–105
Uzkoe, 94

Valliere, Paul, 31
violence, 37, 56, 62. *See also* coercion
virtue politics, 90
Vladimir Soloviev Religious-Philosophical Society, 18, 19n75, 105, 108, 159–160
Vladimir-Suzdal, 173n7
Vrubel, Mikhail, 148
Vyborg Manifesto, 17, 57

Ware, Kallistos (metropolitan), 82, 139
Weidlé, Vladimir, 144
Wenzler, Ludwig, 74
White Army, 110
wholeness (*tselost'*), 3–4
Willard Jones, Andrew, 89
Williams, Rowan (archbishop), 135
Wisdom, Divine, 69, 163, 200–201. *See also* Sophia
Witte, Sergei Iu., 17, 99
world
  Berdyaev contrasts with "cosmos," 69
  ENT criticizes Augustine for conflating eternal and natural world, 37–39
  sanctified through Bogochelovechestvo, 11
World War I, 59, 61–62, 108–109

Young Czech movement, 59

zemstvo, 14, 16, 54–55
Zenkovsky, Vasilii, 75, 143
Zeno, 113n5
Zernov, Nicholas, 66, 67n6, 135
Zhegin, Lev, 130–131, 139
Zinon (Theodor) (archimandrite), 136
Zohar, 189

www.ingramcontent.com/pod-product-compliance
Lightning Source LLC
Chambersburg PA
CBHW051642230426
43669CB00013B/2403